Dispatches from the Land of Erasure

POETS ON POETRY

Derek Pollard, Series Editor
Donald Hall, Founding Editor

TITLES IN THE SERIES

Wendy Xu, *Your Historical Loveliness Knows No Bounds*
Philip Metres, *Dispatches from the Land of Erasure*
Jason Schneiderman, *Nothingism*
Amy Catanzano, *The Imaginary Present*
Khadijah Queen, *Radical Poetics*
Nathaniel Perry, *Joy (or Something Darker, but Like It)*
Dan Beachy-Quick, *How to Draw a Circle*
Christina Pugh, *Ghosts and the Overplus*
Norman Finkelstein, *To Go Into the Words*
Major Jackson, *A Beat Beyond*, edited by Amor Kohli
Jane Miller, *From the Valley of Bronze Camels*
Tony Hoagland, *The Underground Poetry Metro Transportation System for Souls*
Philip Metres, *The Sound of Listening*
Julie Carr, *Someone Shot My Book*
Claudia Keelan, *Ecstatic Émigré*
Rigoberto Gonzalez, *Pivotal Voices, Era of Transition*
Garrett Hongo, *The Mirror Diary*
Marianne Boruch, *The Little Death of Self*

ALSO AVAILABLE, BOOKS BY

Elizabeth Alexander, Meena Alexander, Kazim Ali, A. R. Ammons, John Ashbery, David Baker, Robert Bly, Bruce Bond, Philip Booth, Marianne Boruch, Hayden Carruth, Amy Clampitt, Alfred Corn, Douglas Crase, Robert Creeley, Donald Davie, Thomas M. Disch, Ed Dorn, Martín Espada, Annie Finch, Tess Gallagher, Sandra M. Gilbert, Dana Gioia, Linda Gregerson, Allen Grossman, Thom Gunn, Marilyn Hacker, Rachel Hadas, John Haines, Donald Hall, Joy Harjo, Robert Hayden, Edward Hirsch, Daniel Hoffman, Jonathan Holden, John Hollander, Paul Hoover, Andrew Hudgins, T. R. Hummer, Laura (Riding) Jackson, Josephine Jacobsen, Mark Jarman, Lawrence Joseph, Galway Kinnell, Kenneth Koch, John Koethe, Yusef Komunyakaa, Marilyn Krysl, Maxine Kumin, Martin Lammon (editor), Philip Larkin, David Lehman, Philip Levine, Larry Levis, John Logan, William Logan, David Mason, William Matthews, Joyelle McSweeney, William Meredith, Jane Miller, David Mura, Carol Muske, Alice Notley, Geoffrey O'Brien, Gregory Orr, Alicia Suskin Ostriker, Ron Padgett, Marge Piercy, Grace Schulman, Anne Sexton, Karl Shapiro, Reginald Shepherd, Aaron Shurin, Charles Simic, William Stafford, Anne Stevenson, Cole Swenson, May Swenson, James Tate, Richard Tillinghast, C. K. Williams, Alan Williamson, David Wojahn, Charles Wright, James Wright, John Yau, and Stephen Yenser

For a complete list of titles, please see www.press.umich.edu

Dispatches from the Land of Erasure

Essays and Conversations

PHILIP METRES

University of Michigan Press
Ann Arbor

Published in the United States of America by the
University of Michigan Press
First published September 2025

A CIP catalog record for this book is available from the British Library.

Library of Congress Cataloging-in-Publication data has been applied for.

ISBN 978-0-472-03999-9 (paper : alk. paper)
ISBN 978-0-472-22229-2 (e-book)

Authorized Representative: Easy Access System Europe, Mustamäe tee 50, 10621 Tallinn, Estonia, gpsr.requests@easproject.com

Cover Image: Samia Halaby, *Our Beautiful Land of Palestine Stolen in the Night of History*, 2016. Courtesy of the artist.

Contents

Acknowledgments

Thanks to my ancestors, who brought me here, and to those who come after. May these words be a way station.

Thanks to these friends and co-conspirators (those who breathe together) whose conversation has lifted and challenged me, and whose words liven and leaven this book: Mosab Abu Toha, Zaina Alsous, Conor Bracken, Susan Briante, Hayan Charara, Safia Elhillo, Marwa Helal, Randa Jarrar, Sahar Khalifeh, Farid Matuk, Erika Meitner, Rachel Neve-Midbar, Naomi Shihab Nye, Craig Santos Perez, M. NourbeSe Philip, and Milena Williamson. I believe in the we that we make when we share words like bread.

Thanks to all the editors who helped clarify my writing and thinking, including Supriya Bhatnagar, Jen DeGregorio, Jonny Diamond, Ben Friedlander, Nathan Goldman, Rachel S. Harris, Stefania Heim, Ramen Omer-Sherman, Daniel Simon, Ron Slate, Keaton Studebaker, Naomi Toth, and Stephen Voyce. Thanks to Anthony Shoplik, for doing a super helpful close reading near the end of the process. Thanks to Kevin Oliver, for all your work on the footnotes; you have so much light and good in you, and ahead of you.

Thanks to the folks at the University of Michigan Press Poets on Poetry series, especially Derek Pollard (series editor), Danielle Coty-Fattal, Delilah McCrea, Haley Winkle, and Marcia LaBrenz, and copy editor John Raymond.

Thanks to the following literary magazines, scholarly journals, and anthologies for publishing original versions of these essays, under the following titles:

Boston Review: "Dispatches from the Land of Erasure."
College Literature: "Vexing Resistance, Complicating Occupation: A Contrapuntal Reading of Sahar Khalifeh's *Wild Thorns* and David Gross-

man's *The Smile of the Lamb*." Reprinted, with revision, in *Narratives of Dissent: War in Contemporary Israeli Arts and Culture*.

Jewish Currents: "Revolution in the First Person Plural: Workshops for the Revolution."

Literary Hub: "Imagining Iraq"; "Same as It Ever Was"; "To Be the Poet of Troy: An Interview with Mosab Abu Toha"; "The Wall of Silence: On Trying to Talk About Palestine, Israel, and the US"; and "Dispatches from the Land of Erasure During a Genocide."

MLA Guide to Teaching Arabic Literature. "Teaching (Beyond) the Conflict: A Contrapuntal Reading." Reprinted in *Teaching the Arab Israeli Conflict*.

New Ohio Review: "Of Seeing, the Unseen, and the Unseeable: Technology, Poetry, and 'When It Rains in Gaza.'"

On the Seawall: Review of *Theory of Birds*.

Paideuma: "Never/Enough: Afterword on *Paideuma*'s Symposium on War and Literature."

Poets & Writers: "In This Time of War" (from the introduction).

Synthesis: "Poetics/Documents/Justice: A Roundtable."

World Literature Today: Interview with M. NourbeSe Philip.

Writer's Chronicle: "Black Lives Matter and the Poetics of Racial Justice"; "'Nothing Will Stop Me From Writing What I See': An Interview with Sahar Khalifeh."

WWrite Blog: "I Never Saw Him Drowning: Great-Uncle Charlie and the Great War." Reprinted in *Beyond Their Limits of Longing: Contemporary Writers & Veterans on the Lingering Stories of WWI*.

Permissions

Thank you to the following:

Fadhil al-Azzawi, "Toasts," reprinted by permission of Khaled Mattawa, translator.

Samih al-Qasim, "End of a Talk with a Jailer," reprinted by permission of Ibis Editions and Samih's son, Watan.

Zaina Alsous, poems reprinted by permission of the author.

Zeina Azzam, "Write My Name" first published on Vox Populi on October 30, 2023. Reprinted by permission of the author.

Dionne Brand, "Verso 34.1" and "Verso 34.2," in *The Blue Clerk*, 178–79. Copyright 2018, Dionne Brand. All rights reserved. Republished by permission of the copyright holder, and the publisher. www.dukeupress.edu

Jericho Brown, "Bullet Points" from *The Tradition*. Copyright © 2019 by Jericho Brown. Reprinted with the permission of The Permissions Company, LLC on behalf of Copper Canyon Press, coppercanyonpress.org.

Hayan Charara. Reprinted by permission of the author.

Lucille Clifton, "won't you celebrate with me," from *Book of Light*. Copyright © 1993 by Lucille Clifton. Reprinted by permission of Copper Canyon Press.

Toi Derricotte, "Why I Don't Write About George Floyd," reprinted by permission of the author. Originally published in Poem-a-Day on July 3, 2020 by the Academy of American Poets.

Ross Gay, "A Small Needful Fact," first published in Split This Rock's *The Quarry: A Social Justice Poetry Database*, https://www.splitthisrock.org/poetry-database/poem/a-small-needful-fact. Reprinted by permission of the author

Fady Joudah, "[. . . .]," reprinted by permission of the author.

Audre Lorde, "Power," Copyright @ 1978 by Audre Lorde, from *The Collected Poems of Audre Lorde*. Used by permission of W.W. Norton & Company, Inc.

Harryette Mullen, "Elliptical," first appearing in *Sleeping with the Dictionary*. Copyright @ 2002 by The Regents of the University of California. Published by the University of California Press. Reprinted by permission of the author.

Danez Smith, "summer, somewhere," from *Don't Call Us Dead*. Copyright © 2017 by Danez Smith. Reprinted with the permission of The Permissions Company, LLC on behalf of Graywolf Press, graywolfpress.org.

Introduction

Dispatch on Omelas

In his Vietnam War–era classic *Dispatches*, Michael Herr wrote that he went to Vietnam because he believed that he had to be able to witness it in person. But what he realized later was that "you were as responsible for everything you saw as you were for everything you did. The problem was that you didn't always know what you were seeing until later, maybe years later, that a lot of it never made it in at all, it just stayed stored there in your eyes."[1]

I'm thinking about this because last night, people on social media were circulating images of a baby in Gaza beheaded by an Israeli strike on Rafah. We are indeed responsible for what we see—literally and figuratively, given ongoing U.S. support for Israel's attack—and also for what we do and say in light of what we have seen, whether on handheld screens or live and in person. But writers try to translate what we have seen, and what we have done, since the hurtle of images does not slow. Tomorrow will bring its own horrors, and by the time you read this, at least a year from now, it will be a matter of history. This is the predicament of Walter Benjamin's Angel of History, facing the past, wanting "to stay, awaken the dead, and make whole what has been smashed," all the while being blown forward into the future by terrible winds (of "progress," as Benjamin sardonically reveals).[2]

The writer's job, in light of the bullet of information—and the actual bombs—is to slow down time, rewind, examine the image and the statement, and the structures of power that undergird them, rewinding again, to help the soul catch up. Reexamine. Place word next to word, trying to defeat the silencing while not violating the truth of silence. Meanwhile, demagogues, disinformation humanoids, venture capitalists, and social media influencers leap in, eager to sow the whirlwind, proclaiming and pronouncing and capitalizing. The challenge for the poet is to meet the moment in all our steady curiosity and ruminative confusion, our quicksilver compassion and ethical hesitancy, and our keen conscience. If we tarry too long or speak too quietly, we miss the chance to intervene in the public conversation. Not as pundits, weighing arguments by their potential impact on their audience, but as poets—keen eyewitnesses, close readers, modern prophets, unblinkered skeptics, and moral scourges. We must offer, amid the chaos of apocalypse, a vision of another world, one that is already taking shape in this one.

That was my task while writing many of these pieces: to respond with alacrity, precision, and compassion, and to offer a vision of the future mixed with a dose of history. These dispatches are not meant to be war journalism, but rather something like peace journalism. They are topical pieces, personal and scholarly investigations, literary analyses, interviews, and conversations with other writers that witness to and attempt to capture the way we face imperial violence through writing and action in the first quarter of the twenty-first century. The word "dispatch" comes from the early sixteenth century, either the Italian *dispacciare* or the Spanish *despachar*, meaning to expedite. A reversal (*dis/des*) of hindrances (*pacciare/pachar*). Something delivered quickly. Of course, people can also be dispatched—that is, sent on an errand, and problems can be dispatched, or dealt with. To dispatch someone can also mean to kill them. To erase them. It begins in the language, Joseph Brodsky once said to Marie Howe: "You think evil is going to come into your houses wearing big black boots. It doesn't come like that. Look at the language. It begins in the language."[3] But something else can begin in the language. We are not mere recorders of passing events, but makers and shapers of the future. As we articulate ourselves in the present, and articulate the present with all its erased pasts and peoples, we also can envision and inhabit, in language, a new present and heretofore unimaginable futures.

So, what is this Land of Erasure? It is not a place, exactly, but a metaphor for the imperial and settler colonial ideology that functions through erasure. An Arab American writer situated at the center of empire, I live in a country where its indigenous inhabitants have been—and continue to be—erased in the long genocide of colonial rule. It is the open secret that remains mostly unspoken, a silence that somehow requires further silencing by school boards, legislation, and disinformation media networks. It began with a group text of Arab American writers. Randa Jarrar suggested that we begin a "multi-voiced essay addressing our erasure," and Marwa Helal suggested a name: "dispatches from erasure." This is why you will find, while reading *Dispatches from the Land of Erasure*, many voices and perspectives, not just my own. This vision-work is not done alone. It happens in conversation, as a collective plural that comes to take shape as we gather ourselves.

So what can poets and writers do in times of genocidal war and violence? For those of us paying attention to U.S. foreign policy, we have seen, time and time again, a massive ongoing project of imperial erasure that begins in the language and has ended in brutality in Iraq, Afghanistan, and Palestine, and elsewhere in the Global South. The first section of *Dispatches*, "Erasing the Erasures: Writing While Arab," explores the politics of Arab American writing and writers, and the imperial and colonial erasures that are part of American life, particularly regarding the War on Terror, the Iraq War, and the ongoing genocide of Palestine.

When Hamas broke through the barbed wire and flew over the walls around Gaza on October 7, 2023, my twenty-five years of working on peace and justice initiatives for Palestine and Israel did not prepare me either for the initial shock—the attack killed about 1,200 Israelis, with 200 taken hostage—or the subsequent horrors of the Israeli destruction of Gaza. While the attack certainly brought up traumatic memories for Jews, what has followed has been the most traumatic period of a traumatic history for Palestinians. At the time of this writing, eighteen months into this epochal moment, at least 50,000 Palestinians have been killed and at least 113,000 injured. On July 5, 2024, *The Lancet* published an article that asserted "it is not implausible to estimate that up to 186 000 or even more deaths could be attributable to the current conflict in Gaza."[4] It remains unclear whether Israel's actions will end with a total ethnic cleansing of Gaza and the annihilation of its people.

This period has caused me to fear that I've been too temperate in my language around Palestine and Israel. For years, I've weighed each word, each sentence of my work for its impact on readers. I know enough of the trauma and pain of my Palestinian and Jewish friends to try to avoid worsening their hurt and fear. My sister married a Palestinian man over twenty years ago, and I'd made a promise to do what I could to educate myself, my students, and readers about the conflict between Israel and Palestine, particularly about what Palestinians have had to endure—the expulsions, the indefinite detentions, the checkpoints, the wall, the expropriation of land.

Since the mid-2000s, I've taught a course on Palestinian and Israeli literatures, founded on the idea that writers offer a prophetic witness to the depredation of war and oppression as well as a vision of a shared future, something that U.S. politicians and corporate media have failed to do. It has been, I've hoped, a way to invite students into seeing themselves as participants in movements for a just peace. After publishing *Shrapnel Maps* (2020), my book of poems on the Palestine-Israel predicament, I'd been disappointed by what I've called the "Wall of Silence"—the ongoing effort to demonize, ban, or chill speech that is deemed pro-Palestinian. Later, after yet another bombing of Gaza in 2021, I'd written "Remorse for Temperate Speech" (published in *Poetry* and later in *Fugitive/Refuge*), an apology to my friend Mosab Abu Toha, a Palestinian poet, for the times my words had been too measured about the unendurable realities for Palestinians, especially in Gaza. But my apology wasn't enough. In November 2023 Mosab's house in Gaza—along with his lovely library—was destroyed by a bomb. He and his family fled south and finally found shelter in Egypt, but not before Mosab was taken by Israeli soldiers and beaten. Only a massive political effort—online and backdoor—secured his release in December. As of this writing, he remains in exile.

The second section of *Dispatches*, "On Palestine," tracks the evolution of my thinking during twenty years of writing on the literature of Palestinians, Israelis, as well as my book of poems, *Shrapnel Maps*. My sister's initial visit to Palestine in the early 1990s invited me on a path of increasing commitment to the cause of a just peace for Palestinians and Israelis. My first public poetry readings in the late 1990s were celebrations of Palestinian poetry—part of our work for a Bloomington, Indiana, group called Committee for Peace in the Middle East. Back then, we held demonstrations to oppose Israel's policy of collective punishment through house demolitions of Palestinians, not imagining that twenty-five years later, a total destruction of Gaza would be underway. In this section, sometimes contrapuntally, I explore the work of Palestinian and Israeli writers as they confront the brutality of occupation and work of resistance.

"When the guns roar, the muses are silent." That's what a Russian poet once told me, when I lamented the silence around the slaughter perpetrated by the United States during the 1991 Persian Gulf War. It's hard to be human right now, knowing what humans can do. And it's hard to be a poet, knowing what words can't do. In the enormity of the unfolding horror since October 7, I've struggled to balance my life as a writer, academic, and activist. I began by organizing a few silent peace walks at John Carroll University in Cleveland, where I am an English professor, believing that if we, the campus community, could grieve together, we could live together. On the first outing, about thirty of us gathered—faculty, staff, and students—and walked silently around the main quad. The faculty chairs in Jewish studies and Islamic studies walked together; between them walked a Palestinian student wearing his keffiyeh draped over his shoulders, under his backpack. It was something, but it wasn't enough. Each walk had fewer participants; the autumn rains came, and the peace walks stopped altogether.

I thought back to 2020, when I'd brought a group of Jewish and Arab poets together as an experiment in dialogue across difference. We met first on Zoom, and then started to write email letters to one another, exploring how we were surviving both the isolation of the COVID-19 lockdown and the rise in racial hatreds in the U.S. But we had to talk about Palestine, about Israel, and about the future. In one beautiful moment, the American Israeli poet apologized for what her country had done to a Palestinian poet's country. (This conversation, under the title "Poetry, Precarity, and Israel/Palestine: A Pandemic Lockdown Dialogue," can be found in section four). Now, years later, our conversations seem to have taken place in another century. It was something, but it hadn't been enough.

As the bombs fell in October, I reached out to the Palestinian writers whom I've mentored through We Are Not Numbers, a nonprofit founded in 2015 to nurture young writers in Gaza: Ahmed Dremly, who'd written a story about his passion for horses and how the horses had endured the suffering of the four wars in Gaza that preceded this one; Lubna Abuhashem, who'd covered the poor medical treatment offered to Palestinians in detention; and Asmaa Kuheil, who'd written a poem in 2021 about a baby named Omar who was recovered in rubble after a bomb killed both of his parents. I asked if they had anything that I could pass along to the world outside. All of them thanked me, apologized for their short messages and dying devices—then went silent. Reaching out was doing something, but it wasn't enough.

In mid-November, after my failed attempts to get my fellow professors to commit to a teach-in, our university held an educational event called "My First Visit to Israel/Palestine." Colleagues and I shared our diverse experiences of visiting or living there. The conversation was respectful even when we disagreed about the root of the problem: Violent extremism or colonial violence—or both? Occupation or Zionism itself? I'd hoped we'd modeled a way to passionately, yet peacefully, hold different views. But the ongoing quiet on campus disheartened me. Perhaps we'd been too "balanced," too "complex." It wasn't enough.

A peacemaker cannot be silent during a genocide. In January, the International Court of Justice made a preliminary ruling that Israel was plausibly committing genocide, and called upon it to desist from killing. Israel has flagrantly defied that ruling. I've had to get over my own self-protective fear, my own intemperate temperance, to stand up unapologetically for and with Palestinians at this time. To call for a ceasefire was not difficult for me since, as the child of a war veteran, I deplore war. To call for a ceasefire also means caring about the Israeli hostages and their fates, and to condemn collective punishment as a war crime. But the harder work for someone who wants peace is to recognize that Hamas's attacks—as deplorable as they were to me—did not come out of nowhere. Moreover, they were the only thing that caught the world's attention about the plight of Palestinians. In fact, many have argued compellingly that Palestinians have the right to resist their own oppression and murder. But why is it that the U.S. responds only to Hamas's violence, and not the slow, dehumanizing grind of occupation and colonial dispossession?

We must consider the work of justice in order to find our way to peace. The third section of *Dispatches*, "The Poetics of Justice," explores the possibilities of poetry and poets to contribute to justice work. In conversation with poets like Susan Briante, Mark Nowak, Craig Santos Perez, and NourbeSe Philip—and the Black Lives Matter movement more broadly—*Dispatches* centers the work of poets who see their practice as part of social movements for liberation and justice.

As the catastrophe in Gaza has unfolded, a new generation of writers, journalists, and activists has arisen to document not only the onslaught of massacres, but the larger context, speaking out with an uncompromising moral fierceness on social media and in the halls of power, both on the ground in Gaza and throughout the world. In the U.S., Palestinian American poet Fady Joudah—after being devastated by the killing of more than fifty members of his extended family in Gaza—appeared on CNN and *Democracy Now*. In a fever of writing in the fall of 2023, Joudah wrote a whole book of poems called *[. . .]*, which appeared in March. One of those richly allusive poems explores the logic of colonial violence, blinkered by its own traumatic story:

> They did not mean to kill the children.
> They meant to.
> Too many kids got in the way
> of precisely imprecise
> one-ton bombs
> dropped a thousand and one times
> over the children's nights.
> They will not forgive the children this sin.
> They wanted to save them from future sins.
> Or send them wrapped lifetimes
> of reconstructive
> surgical hours pro bono,
> mental anguish to pass down
> to their offspring.
> Will the children have offspring?
> This is what the bomb-droppers
> did not know they wanted:
> to see if others will be like them
> after unquantifiable suffering.
> They wanted to lead
> their own study, but forgot
> that not all suffering worships power
> after survival. What childhood does
> a destroyed childhood beget?
> My parents showed me the way.[5]

A practicing physician, Joudah employs medical and scientific language to hauntingly allude to the way in which colonial practice relies on a scientific, subjectless subjectivity to rationalize its horrors, which amount to a form of sadistic experimentation—to see "if others will be like them / after unquantifiable suffering." Among other allusions, Joudah's poem lays bare the absurdism expressed by Israeli prime minister Golda Meir, when she said that though Israelis "will perhaps in time be able forgive the Arabs for killing our sons, but it will be harder for us to forgive them for having forced us to kill their sons."[6] In this statement is the repellent intimation that the colonial state cares more about the colonized children than the colonized people themselves. Yet if the poem ends bleakly—his parents, after all, had a destroyed childhood as well—it also contains, perhaps, a sense of the impossible resilience of Palestinians and all those who have been subject to genocide.

At this year's annual Association of Writers and Writing Programs conference in Kansas City, the board of the Radius of Arab American Writers made a creative intervention, sending every panel moderator an email inviting them to read a land acknowledgement statement that would also recognize "an active genocide taking place in Gaza" against Palestinians:

> The event organizers would like to acknowledge that we are gathering during an active genocide taking place in Gaza, and that the current violence in Palestine is the continuation of decades of colonial violence under Israeli apartheid. We stand in solidarity with victims of genocide in Sudan and Congo, and with the Indigenous peoples on whose ancestral homelands this conference is being held, including the Osage, Kaw, Missouria, Shawnee and Wyandot tribes. We stand firmly against anti-Blackness and recognize that police violence and all white supremacist violence must be named and opposed. These forms of violence, along with transphobic violence being legislated in Missouri and other states, endanger the lives of trans, queer, gender-nonconforming, and nonbinary people. Therefore, as we begin our event, we wish to underscore that none of us are free until all of us are free, and that all anti-racist, liberationist, and decolonial struggles are intertwined.

It was an email that launched a thousand conversations—perhaps the most consequential literary artifact of the conference. At both panels in which

I participated, and in every one I attended, the moderators read this statement. On the Friday of the conference, Tariq Luthun—who has family in Gaza—led a rousing protest through the book fair and on the streets.

Writers have also staged boycotts of literary organizations that have been neutral, silent, or outright hostile to Palestinian rights, including the 92nd Street Y, the Poetry Foundation, and PEN America. I'm also particularly in awe of the moral courage of Jewish Voice for Peace in standing in solidarity with Palestinians and engaging in acts of widespread civil disobedience. All of us who wish for peace and justice for Palestine, for liberation, have been constantly emailing and calling our congressional representatives, leaving voice messages with versions of the same message—a call for a ceasefire, for ending arms shipments, for increasing humanitarian aid, for freedom for Palestinians, for what must be a shared future between Israelis and Palestinians.

Closer to home, in Cleveland, I joined poet and cultural worker Naazneen Diwan and the group of people—Palestinian, Arab, Muslim, and Jew—she gathered for a poetry reading in support of Palestine. We called it "Sumud," an Arabic word that means "steadfastness," a characteristic of Palestinian endurance despite oppression. The violence in Palestine has been going on for a century. The British promise of a Jewish homeland, articulated in the Balfour Declaration in 1917, never acknowledged the political rights of Palestinians, including their right to self-determination. About 80 percent of Palestinians in Gaza are refugees, or the descendants of refugees, turned out of their homes during the 1948 violence that established the state of Israel, an event of ethnic cleansing referred to by Palestinians as the Nakba, the catastrophe.

Seventy people gathered in Vessel City, an art studio on Cleveland's West Side, to listen to the poetry of Sumud. Kicking it off was Shereen Naser, a Palestinian American who has been leading a weekly demonstration during Cleveland City Council meetings calling for a ceasefire. As Naser read her own poems, her young daughter crawled around her mother's leg and into her arms, offering her own words lisped into the mic: Free Palestine! Robin Beth Schaer, active in the Cleveland chapter of Jewish Voice for Peace, proclaimed that "as a Jew, I care about Palestinian liberation because we are kin, because I carry expulsion & genocide in my bones & cannot bear expulsion & genocide committed in my name, and because I want to see a free Palestine in our lifetimes." She shared her friend Nathalie Handal's poetry, including her words that poetry "has always played a fundamental role in freedom and democracy. It leads us to pose necessary questions, not steeped in rhetoric but in instinct and invocation. Poetry is inquest and rumination—it's the narratives of our transformations."

I read, among other poems, "End of a Talk with a Jailer" by Palestinian poet Samih al-Qasim, in a translation by Nazih Kassis:

> From the narrow window of my small cell,
> I see trees that are smiling at me
> and rooftops crowded with my family.
> And widows weeping and praying for me.
> From the narrow window of my small cell—
> I can see your big cell![7]

Al-Qasim's poem situates itself on the margins—literally, in prison—and prophetically observes how the entire society that imprisons him is also imprisoned. Imprisoned in its own ideology. Yet the visionary nature of this poem is hard won. Al-Qasim was jailed multiple times for his writing and his resistance to Israeli rule. Thousands of Palestinians languish in Israeli detention now, and two million in Gaza have endured prison-like conditions for two decades. It occurred to me suddenly, having reread Ursula LeGuin's story "The Ones Who Walk Away from Omelas," that Gaza itself was like that basement in Omelas. In that story, LeGuin depicts a prosperous, orderly society that has a dark secret. Everyone in the society knows—but turns away from the fact that—there is a child held against its will in deplorable conditions, and that their society depends on that child's torture for its own prosperity.

I can't help but be awestruck by how Palestinians in Gaza, in their situation of utter precarity, confinement, and outright imprisonment, have seemed freer than our handwringing politicians, who can't seem to say what should be plain: we must do everything in our power to stop the massacres of civilians, no matter their authors. And understand that this genocidal campaign is part of a long-standing effort to erase Palestinians entirely. In their relentless energy to document the vicious attacks on them and to try to change global policy, Gazans have shown us what hope against hope looks like. When the bombs roar, they will not accept their murder quietly. They dig with their bare hands to excavate their people from the rubble, and they will not allow us to look away. They expose the truth that empires try to bury.

The Sumud event concluded with journalist Samer Badawi. First he read "Write My Name" by Palestinian American poet Zeina Azzam, which she wrote after learning that parents in Gaza were writing their children's names on their legs in case they needed to be identified after being killed:

Write my name on my leg, Mama
Use the black permanent marker
with the ink that doesn't bleed
if it gets wet, the one that doesn't melt
if it's exposed to heat

Write my name on my leg, Mama
Make the lines thick and clear
Add your special flourishes
so I can take comfort in seeing
my mama's handwriting when I go to sleep

Write my name on my leg, Mama
and on the legs of my sisters and brothers
This way we will belong together
This way we will be known
as your children

Write my name on my leg, Mama
and please write your name
and Baba's name on your legs, too
so we will be remembered
as a family

Write my name on my leg, Mama
Don't add any numbers

like when I was born or the address of our home
I don't want the world to list me as a number
I have a name and I am not a number

Write my name on my leg, Mama
When the bomb hits our house
When the walls crush our skulls and bones
our legs will tell our story, how
there was nowhere for us to run

Badawi then shared that when he was covering Gaza after the 2014 war, he and a stringer reporter he was working with went to visit a recently bombed house. Inside, two teenage boys picked through the remains of their former home. When their guests arrived, they pointed to a wall, saying, "The couch was there." They weren't recounting the floor plan but lamenting that they had nowhere to offer their guests a place to rest. From the rubble they somehow extracted a Fanta and two cups, pouring them for Samer and his stringer. These two boys' parents may have been dead, but they wanted their guests to feel at home. That's the Palestine that I've known.

Some people, of course, as LeGuin's title suggests, decide to walk away from Omelas. They cannot bear the fact of this moral compromise. Most of us just stay, trying to forget. The days grind on; the war continues, and nothing seems to stop it. Ceasefire offers float up, first rejected by the U.S., then by Israel, and then by Hamas, as each tries to lay the blame at the feet of the others. In February 2024 I printed out the names of Israeli hostages and a list of Gaza's dead children to try to bring the devastation closer. To say their names. The list of dead Palestinian children, published by Al Jazeera, came to one hundred full pages of names, beginning with children under the age of one. At the end of the list, it read: "These are the names of only half of the children killed." Around fifteen thousand of them have been massacred in all, as of this writing. The numbers addle the mind and assault the heart. Even one death is too many.

This mass death reminds me of the maxim about the silence of the muses, the one shared with me by the Russian poet all those years ago, and how it echoes Cicero's adage "Inter arma enim silent leges" (In times of war, the law falls silent.) The killing continues, with full U.S. backing and weaponry. The wildness of this violence, and the silence of the powerful—particularly the U.S. government, which could stop this almost instantly—is almost too much to bear.

But something happened—first at Columbia University in mid-April, and then throughout the country. College students rose up, occupied space at universities, and called for an end to U.S. and institutional complicity with genocide. In early May, I got the chance to visit Case Western Reserve University's encampment and was struck with such force by the sheer marvel of it. They occupied a grassy pedestrian circle in front of the library, as generations have done before, and made it into a new community, surrounding the fencing with signs that declared their values. They called it the "People's University for Palestine," as one sign proclaimed. Another sign, "Students for a Free Palestine," called for amnesty for students and faculty punished for activism, along with the demand to disclose, divest, and boycott, and of course for a permanent ceasefire and an end to the occupation. Other signs proclaimed: "Israel destroyed every Gaza university! Why does our education matter more than theirs?"

That this generation has gathered to oppose mass death and militarism and advocate for the Palestinian people—brought me such hope. To hear and see the speakers—a young Black activist, a Black songwriter, a group of Jews celebrating a social justice Seder—was to have a window into a transnational solidarity come alive. For erased peoples who continue to refuse their erasure. To see an ethic of mutual aid emerge, where people fed and sheltered each other, was to witness to a vision of a better world. One of the poems, painted on diamond shapes like a kite, was the Gazan poet Refaat al-Areer's "If I Must Die." On multiple kites, the heart of the poem unfolded:

> so that a child, somewhere in Gaza
> while looking heaven in the eye
> awaiting his dad who left in a blaze—
> and bid no one farewell
> not even to his flesh
> not even to himself—

sees the kite, my kite you made, flying up above
and thinks for a moment an angel is there
bringing back love[8]

Yes, it's true, the encampments were all retaken by the universities, with students punished and sometimes even expelled. It's true that some people (provocateurs?) have sowed chaos by deploying antisemitic tropes and made it harder to see that the struggle for liberation is one in which Jews have played a key role. And it's true that I have faced scrutiny and I've been harassed and reported for bias because of what I've said, even in the temperate ways that I have said it. Other teachers have been fired or forced to resign for speaking out, including Samer Badawi's wife. Both of my daughters, at their institutions of learning, faced censure and silencing for engaging in this work (see "Dispatches in the Land of Erasure During a Genocide"). But youth like them have not walked away from Omelas. Instead, they have occupied it, shining a light in the basement. This is the love that Cornel West once called "justice made public."

The final section of *Dispatches*, "The Poetics of Peacebuilding," begins with the aforementioned conversation of Arab and Jewish poets during the early pandemic years, as everyone wrestled with a new shared precarity. The only future, the only liberated future, is a shared one. I began this work because of a deep conviction that war is always a crime against humanity, and that we are called to be peacemakers. In the final essays of the book, I explore my own work with the Peace Show in Cleveland, which was an alternative to the militaristic Air Show that would buzz the skies every Labor Day. Many years ago, I learned that my great-uncle Charlie, who was said to have died during World War I, actually survived. But because he came back utterly destroyed by his time in the army—he would spend the rest of his life in a sanatorium—his sister (my grandmother) was never told he was alive. The secret is that war so often destroys not only its immediate victims but also its perpetrators. Telling these stories is a way of refusing to hide the truth.

Poetry alone was never enough to end war. "In order for me to write poetry that isn't political," Palestinian poet Marwan Makhoul writes, "I must listen to the birds / and in order to hear the birds / the warplanes must be silent." Who knows what will be enough to end not only this war, but the slow-moving devastation of Palestine—not to mention the many other countries and peoples brutalized by the machinery of empire.

At the end of the day, those of us who know have knocked and knocked, when even hope fails inside this obdurate empire, this Land of Erasure, this Omelas. By putting words on the page, by calling the powerful to account, by demonstrating, by gathering together over words, by advocating for boycotts of war criminals and divestment from arms dealers, by occupying spaces and refusing to be erased; the knocking is not just a demand for a door to be opened, but for a wall to come down, until the house that war built cannot stand, and so that a child chained in darkness will walk once again into the light.

June 2025

I.

Erasing the Erasures: Writing While Arab

CHAPTER ONE

Same as It Ever Was

On Edward Said, *Orientalism*, and the Depiction of Arabs in America

"Why do they have to show that? That—that—*violence*," I said to my mom hours later, burying my face in my pillow, unable to sleep, my little body convulsing with this strange grief.

In the packed dark of our local theater, eleven years old, I'd been reeling, gripping the armrests in terror as *Raiders of the Lost Ark* flashed across the huge screen. The swashbuckling Indiana Jones had somehow escaped a trap-filled temple in Peru with the golden idol in hand, but his local guide hadn't. The image of a wide-eyed, brown-faced man with a spike piercing his forehead had seared itself in my mind, but now they were somehow in Cairo, and Indiana, having escaped a chase in the casbah, found himself face-to-face with a black-cloaked, scimitar-wielding Arab. Smiling, laughing even, the man flung and swung the comically large sword from hand to hand. World-weary, Indiana pulled out his pistol and blew him away. The crowd around me erupted in cheers. Was I supposed to laugh? Before I could react, we were off again, with our American hero, between local "savages" and Nazis, until in the fury of the opened ark, the bad guys' faces literally melted off. Walking out of the theater, I did everything I could to hold back sobs.

Growing up Arab American in the 1980s, I couldn't escape these depictions of Arabs as vile, cruel terrorists. I was confused why so many movies I watched featured a bloodthirsty Arab vanquished by white American heroes. It wasn't just *Raiders*, of course, it was also the weird creatures of the Tatooine desert in *Star Wars*, the vicious Sand People, who seemed more than a little familiar. And later, *The Black Stallion Returns* (1983), and not too long after that, the runaway time-traveling hit, *Back to the Future* (1985). What were Libyans doing in Hill Valley, California, and why did they have plutonium? It was such a non sequitur that we never asked what they were doing there. Of course, the movie wanted us to say, those wretched Libyans! And like the Egyptian sword-wielder in *Raiders* who was really a white stuntman, a whole parade of terrorists played by actors in "arabface" were trotted out in movie after movie produced by the Israeli-led Cannon Films.

Later, when I read the work of Edward Said and Jack Shaheen, I learned that my experience—and these films—are not the exception. Shaheen's *Reel Bad Arabs: How Hollywood Vilifies a People* (2001) looked at nearly 1,000 films and found only a dozen that depicted Arabs in a complex or positive way.[1] Watching television, it was more of the same. I secretly loved the wrestler "The Iron Sheik," who wore a keffiyeh, robe, neat mustache, and played the heel. He was Iranian, actually, but he was as good as Arab to me (shout-out to the Iranians). When he palled around with the Russian Nikolai Volkoff, I thought of the Russians as odd comrades. Of course, The Iron Sheik played the heel. Whenever the crowd began to jeer him—or anyone—I felt something churn in me. Some kind of fire ignited in my head. I was drawn to the one who was hated. Whether the person was Black or Brown or queer or just different, I wanted to stand beside them.

Occasionally, hanging out with my dad watching TV, he'd proudly point his finger at a visage or a voice and reveal their secret identity: "Casey Kasem: he's one of the brothers!" "Ralph Nader: good Lebanese boy!" "Helen Thomas: one of the sisters!" I would feel invited into a secret world, where some people passing as normal were secretly Arab. Like us. Apparently, even my pants had some secret Arab origins: "It's pronounced Hajjar, not Haggar!" (Marwa Helal reminds me that the Egyptian dialect would say otherwise; there isn't Arabic, but Arabics!)

The negative representations confused and vexed me, since the Arabs in our father's family—mostly congregating around 290 Hicks Street in Brooklyn Heights—were ridiculously hospitable and overwhelmingly demonstrative. By the end of any visit, I was so stuffed with food and love and hugs that I could barely move from the couch after meals. Which was fine, since every Lebanese goodbye, as we came to call them, would take at least an hour and involve kissing and hugging and saying goodbye in at least three rooms (kitchen, living room, at the door) and one last time outside. Of course, life in an Arab household meant more than that; the attendant squabbles, judgments, and drama of every family were very much present. But the warp and weft of the fabric of human life has been so entirely absent from the depictions of Arabs in America that every representation feels instantly political and freighted with sinister meanings. The political, Gilles Deleuze and Félix Guattari once wrote, stains every utterance.[2] That's unfortunate for all concerned—both Arabs and non-Arabs alike.

I can see now how the film and television and media industries were not merely reflecting popular sentiment but also promulgating an imperial narrative—as if they'd received the message from on high. In some strange way, they had. Related to our white supremacy problem, Orientalism involves a way of seeing the other (the Arab) that justifies an ongoing system of domination. Edward Said's landmark analysis of the problem, *Orientalism* (1978), is now forty years old, and yet the phenomenon it describes feels as entrenched and normalized as it was when he wrote it. Orientalism, for Said, is the Western practice of projecting upon the East "a system of representations framed by a whole set of forces that brought the Orient into Western learning, Western consciousness, and later, Western empire."[3] In other words, applying a bit of psychoanalysis to Said's treatment, Orientalism is a fantasy projection upon the people of the East of that which the West has repressed about itself, a projection and project that motivates and justifies colonial rule and imperial force. Every accusation, it's popular to say now, is a confession. For Said, "The limitations of Orientalism are . . . the limitations that follow upon disregarding, essentializing, denuding the humanity of another culture, people, or geographical region."[4]

That's precisely what I'd been feeling, as a teenager, as I watched the same television and movies as everyone else in my white-bread Midwest neighborhood. Instead of complex Arabs, we were treated to the repertory of Orientalist projections: images of predatory, conniving, deceitful men (sheikhs, despots, and terrorists) and passive women needing saving (belly dancers in harems with plenty of veils). The Oriental is deceitful and only understands the language of force. The Orient is a place of blank and brutal deserts, without history or civilization, and it's hiding our oil.

It's been a century since the Orient emerged as a powerful fictive presence in the American imagination, since the end of World War I and the carving up of the Middle East into European spheres of influence (principally the British and the French). I say "carving up" because, quite literally, during the war, the secret agreement known as Sykes-Picot promised to split the spoils of war among the victors. After the war, in which Arabs fought on the side of Western forces against the Ottoman Empire, European powers drew maps, created countries, and installed Western-friendly rulers. Though the maps did acknowledge some natural geopolitical realities on the ground, others (for example, the Kurds and Palestinians) were entirely erased. Many argue that the present-day Middle East (the ongoing dispossession of Palestinians, the civil wars in Iraq and Syria, and the rise of ISIS) are the legacy of that map-carving. American foreign policy, inheriting the British role, has mostly been about oil and Israel.

Forty years later, in 2018, Edward Said's work hasn't been forgotten, but it's not known well enough either; despite forty years of exegesis and new thinking around postcolonial theory and empire studies, it's as if the machinery of empire continues to cripple our thinking about ourselves as Americans. Nearly every time I speak to fellow Americans, I need to presume that they've heard none of this, that they've been indoctrinated in the same ways that I was, though it could only colonize me halfway.

At the same time, much has changed. Al Jazeera exists. Social media platforms enable everyday Arabs to share their stories and voices in a hundred ways. Arab Americans have wider prominence in the culture: not just Tony Shalhoub, but Mo Amer and the Hadid Sisters; not just Diane Rehm and Steve Jobs, but also Linda Sarsour and Zainab Salbi. And lesser-known but more important to me, writers like Naomi Shihab Nye and Lawrence Joseph and Etel Adnan, not to mention the Arab American writers in the past decade who have finally become irrefutably visible.

Yet, despite the widening of the general frame, Orientalism still reigns; though it's not as brazen, its subtle forms are everywhere. Consider the opening chapter of Adam Valen Levinson's *The Abu Dhabi Bar Mitzvah*, entitled "The Fine Art of Learning to Say Nothing in Arabic," published in *Literary Hub*.[5] The book is part travelogue and part exploration of Arabic language, written by a Jewish American. That fact in itself is fascinating, and though the first chapter doesn't really make much of it, I imagine that an American Jew who comes to study Arabic is a rather interesting person. Either he aspired to understand the other or spy on him, or both; either way, he's taken a risk and I want to know more.

I see myself in him. During the Cold War, I decided to study Russian because I simply could not believe that all Russians were evil, despite President Reagan's famous statement about the Soviet Union being "the evil empire." I wanted to learn about these demonized people and culture, only half aware of my own othering. I ended up, like Levinson, traveling to that land, wanting to see it for myself, and to come to my own understanding of these people.

The opening chapter, however, is so replete with Orientalisms that it halts me in my tracks, making me not want to follow this narrator. He, too, seemed interested in learning more about these people after the 9/11 attacks, but not necessarily as a peace mission: "The attack had made us all forcefully self-conscious. We perceived them, assumed their perceptions of us, and then canceled all the flights to Beirut. But by learning the primary language of this region, some of us thought, we might be able to figure out what they were really thinking."[6] It's hard not to read this as a subtle version of the question that the media promulgated after the September 11, 2001 attacks: "Why do they hate us?" "We perceived them" and saw them as terrifying, since we canceled our flights. "What were they thinking?" is the operative idea, in both senses of the phrase—*What are they thinking about, and how could they have done this to us, and made us decide to skip seeing the Paris of the Middle East?*

I would have loved to hear how he personally—and not this strange white "we"—decided to make this journey into language and land, because we learn later that his cousin in the Israeli army bluntly asks him why he's decided not to study Hebrew. All he can come up with is that everyone in Israel speaks English already. It seems too coy, since I've heard Jewish Israelis often report hearing Arabic as a threatening language.

When learning about the root word for carrot, Levinson makes a joke about the strangeness of seemingly related words: "Of course, it was total coincidence in that place where linguistic bloodlines run tangled back into ancient history, but as we headed toward Jazirat al-'Arab, I couldn't help but imagine our destination like a great carrot on the map."[7] And later, the coup de grace of the piece, "And we descended and the triangle of Abu Dhabi stuck out into the water like a slice of baklava."[8] On the one hand, the tone here is humorous, even silly. It led to a hilarious parody on Twitter written by Laura Haugen, called "The Fine Art of Learning to Bullshit in America," which ends: "The plane arcs toward New York, and the concrete buildings stab the sky like a handful of French fries stretching toward ketchup."[9] It's preposterous, when you translate it.

In the comment stream beneath the book excerpt on *Lit Hub*, Fatima Khansahib's note on the baklava was equally amusing: "GREEK Baklava is triangle-shaped. Everyone knows baklava in the Middle East is either rolled or DIAMOND shaped. . . . But only a true orientalist would want to come to the Middle East with so much enthusiasm and would have the arrogance not to understand the complexities of what is an incredibly important cultural pastry."[10] Plus, we don't call it baklava, but *ba'lawa*.

To Arabs, whose experience of imperialism and colonialism is brutal and direct, talking about their land as delectable bits of food, sweets to be consumed, can feel like more than mere caricature. It's the way that the West has perceived the lands of the Middle East—something for our consumption. "It's *our* oil, after all. It's our Holy Land, after all."

Learning any foreign language is always full of mystery, and so I'm willing to grant Levinson the natural fascination and eros that accompanies this relationship. Yet, Orientalist metaphors stain his description: "I was hooked long before I felt the language let fall the first of its veils, revealing morphology as finely calibrated as the engine of a race car." And, of course, the veil. What would the Orient be without those diaphanously erotic (or repressively suffocating) veils?

It gets more unfortunate when it comes to the Arabic language as a metaphor. Levinson: "'To live in Arabic is to live in a labyrinth of false turns and double meanings,' Jonathan Raban wrote in *Arabia Through the Looking Glass*. 'No sentence means quite what it says. Every word is potentially a talisman, conjuring the ghosts of the entire family of words from which it comes.' Its trademark haziness can only be cleared, as far as it will ever be cleared, by knowing as many members of that family as possible."[11] Raban has a history of explaining the Oriental mind, but my dispute is with how he's summoned here to describe the slipperiness of Arabic language. Language itself is the slippery thing, as Derrida and any five year old will demonstrate. It's not the Arab mind. But it's blamed on

Arabic because that's what Orientalism does: disavows our own uncertainty and unconscious and projects it onto the other.

I hope that Levinson's journey in his book complicates this Orientalist opening, though I don't want to read further. I write this not out of the desire to bash a fellow writer who made an intrepid journey into Arabic language and the Middle East. But how is it possible that no one—himself, his agent, his editor, anyone at Norton—could have questioned this depiction?

Most importantly, and here I want to say that this is more important than the matter of the baklava or the language, this first chapter about Arabic language and culture and places is, astonishingly, *remarkably free of Arabs*. There are no Arabs at all in it, as far as I can tell—only a love interest with the Slavic name of Masha. Perhaps the "pretty attendant" on the plane is Arab.

In the process, what have we Americans missed? Who are Arabs, and what are they like? Denise Levertov had a prophetic poem about the Vietnamese, written during the height of what Vietnamese term the American War, called "What Were They Like"? There was the sense among activists that we were perpetrating a genocide of the Vietnamese. Think about it: even our lauded and beautiful memorial to the American dead of that war does not mourn the Vietnamese casualties, which outnumbered our dead at least twenty-fold. Maybe the question should be: *What are we like?*

As crazy as it sounds, this is how you destroy cultures and nations, how you kill them softly. The sad fact is that we (I include myself in this, as an American) have been destroying Arab countries for a long time. I became politicized during the first Iraq War (1991). After that censored war, in which so-called smart bombs were heralded as the first heroes of a "surgical" war, we learned how the U.S. and allied bombers targeted civilian infrastructure such as water filtration facilities and the electrical grid. According to UN humanitarian reports, the consequences of bombing and sanctions led to the deaths of hundreds of thousands of people, often by preventable disease, due to a lack of sanitary water and medicine.

But almost no Americans knew or seemed to care about what our little war had wrought, other than kicking the Vietnam syndrome and kicking Saddam's ass. We were still cheering our Indiana Joneses and our superior weaponry, while the local fanatics fell ridiculously on their swords. In 1996, on *60 Minutes*, Lesley Stahl asked U.S. ambassador to the United Nations Madeleine Albright whether the death of half a million Iraqi children (from sanctions in Iraq) was a price worth paying, Albright replied: "This is a very hard choice . . . but we think the price is worth it."[12] Can you imagine someone saying this about American children?

By the time the second Iraq War happened, in the midst of the larger War on Terror, I was ready to write about it myself. In *Sand Opera*, a book of poems, I investigated the traces of that war as it appeared in documents such as the Standard Operating Procedure manual of the Guantanamo Bay Prison, the testimonies of tortured Abu Ghraib prisoners, the drawings of a man captured and rendered in secret Black sites. These explorations, alongside my own reflections as a young father on the home front, listening to the war unfold on the radio with our daughters, helped me make sense of what the imperial and Orientalist narratives constantly tried to efface.

I think as well about what continues to happen in Palestine, where the dull dehumanizing grind of colonialism and slow-motion dispossession that has carried on since 1948 is now backlit by Trump's 2017 declaration that the U.S. would move its embassy to Jerusalem and call it Israel's capital. This act was, of course, in contravention of fifty years of U.S. and international policy to keep the status of Jerusalem as a part of the so-called peace process.

I actually want to encourage more American writers and citizens to do this work. But, as an Arab American writer, I expect the best from our brothers and sisters of the pen, of writing, and literature, to be attentive to this epistemological violence, this cutting out by caricature, by accident, or by conscious intent. I expect attention to this great blind spot of our empire, that we stop erasing Arabs. That we listen to Arabs. That we publish Arabs and Arab Americans, rather than those who report on those "natives" over there and their wily language. That we listen to everyone—not Arabs only, of course—who is being silenced.

I am well aware that I have my own blind spots; I've had them pointed out to me more times than I care to admit—around class, gender, sexuality, race, or ability. I struggle with the same issues when representing others; working on a memoir about living in Russia makes me aware of how easy it is to exoticize the other. The larger question I want to ask here is not merely about representation, but about the power structure of American literary publishing. Why does our literary establishment rhyme so easily with the imperial project? How can we challenge and change it, and trace the distance, for example, between Ferguson and Palestine?

In addition to reading the classics like Edward Said and Jack Shaheen, I recommend exploring contemporary Arab and Arab American writers and scholars. There is no shortage of them, of us. For one place to start, check out the list of Arab American Book Award winners. In terms of scholarship, Evelyn Alsultany's *Arabs and Muslims in the Media: Race and Representation After 9/11* (2012) updates Said to explore how contemporary media often deploy a "good Arab" to create the illusion of complex representation, what she calls a "simplified complex representation."[13] In terms of literature, Khaled Mattawa's lyrical poems and translations have brought into English so much beauty and wisdom. Likewise the work of the indefatigable Marilyn Hacker, in her poems and translations. Marcia Lynx Qualey's blog called Arabic Literature in English provides a constant reading list. Interlink Books deserves special mention, and there are at least three literary magazines devoted to Arab literature: *Mizna*, *Banipal*, and *Sukoon*. For me, the existence of RAWI (the Radius of Arab American Writers) has made me feel a little more at home in the world, and at home in myself. RAWI is home to many prominent Arab American writers, including a core group with whom I regularly group text: Hayan Charara, Marwa Helal, Randa Jarrar, Fady Joudah, Farid Matuk, and Deema Shehabi.

In poetry, Hayan Charara is the master of dread, whose poems tip the earth beneath us, sliding into the unspeakable; on text, he shares goofy photos of his kids, usually dressed up in hilarious outfits. In poetry, Marwa Helal invented a new kind of poem, the arabic, which reads right to left; on text, she's the one who hearts us most, and keeps us hip to slang and people like DJ Khaled, whose embrace of the good life is equal parts hip hop and Arab. In her essays, stories, and Tweets, Jarrar is drawn to the funny and provocative; one troll called her novel "a handbook on masturbation." In group text, she alternates between hilarity and sweetness. Fady Joudah's just another award-winning poet and translator, whose surprising response to the Levinson affair and other grotesqueries, "Say It: I'm Arab and Beautiful," ought to be read by everyone, vibrating as it is with the birth pangs of something new. Farid Matuk's baby girl pops up in group text, as she does in his new and highly experimental poems, when he's not going high theory in voluminous and impeccable texts. Deema Shehabi's two boys, and her kindness, radiating always, rhymes with her jasmine-scented and fierce poems. What does it mean to know her grandfather was once the mayor of Gaza?

That's our little group text, rife with photos of ourselves and our families, and notes about everything—from the theoretical and political to the mundane. They aren't the only Arabs you should be reading, but they're among my closest friends. If any of us is wielding a scimitar, it's as a joke. We're working on a collective essay called "Dispatches from the Land of Erasure"—stay tuned for that. We don't always agree, but we listen to each other, and don't have to explain everything from the beginning. Every few days, they remind me that I'm human, and that I'm not alone. We're human, each little text proclaims, and we are Arab, and we are not alone.

2018

CHAPTER TWO

Dispatches from the Land of Erasure

(with Philip Metres, Marwa Helal, and Farid Matuk)

A Prologue by Philip Metres

On April 17, 2018, Arab American writer Randa Jarrar responded to the lavish praise by Bill Clinton (among others) of Barbara Bush by tweeting that the former first lady was "a generous and smart and an amazing racist who, along with her husband, raised a war criminal." The subsequent tweetstorm between her and an outraged crowd of Bush defenders led to her public vilification, calls for her to lose her tenured job at Fresno State University, and thousands of racist invectives and death threats. Among other since-deleted messages that she shared with friends on Facebook, Jarrar—a celebrated writer whose stories meld a provocatively comic sensibility with a keenly empathic imagination—is called a "third world dune coon cunt," a "sand n—," a "rag head piece of shit," and "a hideous waste of human flesh." One writer says that his brother stationed in Afghanistan has assured him that because of what she said, "TODAY, he will search out and KILL 3 Muslims. Shalom!"

No fewer than eight free speech organizations and the Radius of Arab American Writers came out publicly in support of Jarrar. Yet lost in the defense of Jarrar's freedom of speech is what underlay her anger at the effusive encomia of Barbara Bush in the first place: the elite's erasure of Bush's callous words about Black people who fled the devastation of Hurricane Katrina or about the mass death caused by the Iraq War, not to mention her part in raising the president who botched the rescue operation in New Orleans and began the war that led to the deaths of over a million people in Iraq. Why is a devastating and criminal war not considered an outrage, but calling someone a racist is?

Writers of color have led the way in articulating such questions. Laila Lalami tweeted that "in calling Barbara Bush 'a racist,' [Jarrar] said bluntly what newspaper obituaries disguised when they wrote that Mrs. Bush was 'never shy about expressing her views,' or that, in the aftermath of Hurricane Katrina, her 'candor got her into trouble.'" Jericho Brown shared on Twitter that "I stand by @randajarrar and I completely understand that she and others can very well and with reason feel joy when very powerful people die, especially if those are people to whom we can trace the unnecessary murder of millions."

The year 2018 marks the fifteenth anniversary of the Iraq War, the seventieth anniversary of the Nakba, the catastrophe of Palestinian dispossession, and the hundredth anniversary of the end of World War I, when European remapping of the territories of the Ottoman Empire sowed the seeds for the conflicts in the Arab world today. And yet these cataclysms barely register on the Richter scale of American consciousness. With few exceptions, the mass media representations of the fifteenth anniversary of "Operation Iraqi Freedom" minimized the criminality of the war and the botched postwar plan, and focused instead on the divided public opinion about the necessity of that war. In May, we can expect some celebration for Israel and perhaps only some parenthetical mention of the plight of Palestinians. Very little will be said about the erasure of over 400 Palestinian villages and the dispossession and expulsion of 750,000 Palestinians in 1948–49—despite the many Palestinian voices insisting on their narrative.

In other words, if you're Arab or Arab American, you'll be affixed inside the mute margins of empire. While the Palestinian narrative is indelibly marked by exile and loss, it is also one of persistence and insistence. Emerging from his Palestinian family's dispossession, Edward Said's foundational critique of Western projections upon the Middle East, *Orientalism* (1978), has become one of the pillars of postcolonial studies and a rallying cry for Arab American writers to reclaim their stories and voices against imperial erasure. Like other marginalized and oppressed people in the United States, Arab Americans have struggled to make their voices heard over the din of empire, to become visible as fully human in a culture eager to use them as voiceless props in its imperial drama.

Over the past year, a group of Arab American writers—Hayan Charara, Marwa Helal, Randa Jarrar, Fady Joudah, Farid Matuk, Deema K. Shehabi, and I—began a group text, sharing stories about our own lives and the predicament of being Arab in America. This group text often touched on matters regarding the state of literary arts, though it was equally a space full of photos of our kids and lives. We had the sense of wanting to archive these conversations for future Arab American writers, and somewhere along the line the idea of a group essay emerged. I proposed that it would catalog the erasures we'd witnessed or experienced, but that it also would celebrate the liberatory work happening in our community, the poems and stories and art that hold us together and raise us up. In that group text we were after an asylum, a safe space, where we could explore and share inchoate thoughts, half dreams, and the rough edges of our feelings.

These dispatches emerge from the inspiration of that space, though they lack the rough and informal improvisatory quality of a community talking with itself. Three other recent essays are also points of departure for these "Dispatches"—all of which were informed by the group text. Fady Joudah's "Say It: I'm Arab and Beautiful," Randa Jarrar's "Ask Auntie Randa" pieces, and my "Same as It Ever Was" confront the poison of white supremacy and Orientalism in American politics, literature, and culture, while offering antidotes. reclaiming beauty, liberation, and community. This dossier of essays addresses these dynamics and attempts to propel the conversation forward—beyond the bounds of Arab American experience and into the broader discussion about how to join in solidarity with other marginalized communities, embracing intersectionality, and writing our spaces against empire and all forms of domination. The dispatches—including ones by George Abraham, Randa Jarrar, and Lena Khalaf Tuffaha—were published by the *Iowa Review*. A second conversation, "Beyond the Land of Erasure," was also published by the *Boston Review*. They can be read online.

Dispatch from the Land of Erasure (I)

[Philip Metres]

At a progressive prep school in Greater Cleveland, my daughter Adele recently told a classmate that she is Arab American. He responded, "You know that song, 'Killing an Arab?'" "Really?" she said, "that's the first thing that comes to your mind?" When a friend leapt to her defense, she laughed it off as one kid's stupidity. Still, it's astonishing that the first thing that came to this kid's mind was an obscure Cure song from 1980. About killing an Arab.

It reminded me that a couple of months back, I got a text from Fady Joudah: a screenshot of a tweet, now deleted, in which a prominent American poet wrote that the Iraq War "was terrible, but Bush was pretty good on ceremonial, symbolic inclusiveness." The current president, she asserted, is not. In her justifiable anger at our current president and predicament, she had forgotten.

Though she later erased the tweet, it still burns in my mind. Not only what she said, but the fact that she had minimized how George Bush and company pushed our country into the Iraq War as a result of false claims, conducted the occupation in a haphazard fashion, and bungled its nation building so badly that the country has never recovered. So badly that the very idea of Iraq as a viable modern state is in doubt. That between 250,000 and 500,000 Iraqis have died. These numbers are mind-numbingly large; one wants to say they are "staggering," but we don't stagger when we hear them. After all, the deaths are happening so far away and our own suffering is a tinnitus that drowns out farther sounds. Perhaps, scrolling through our phones, our hearts quail at the sight of a dead child on the seashore, unable to flee the war. But usually, we just lower the gates of our hearts. It's just easier that way. Meanwhile, more Iraq War veterans have died by suicide than in battle. The war, whether we like it or not, slips between the bars and into our keep.

"Ceremonial, symbolic inclusiveness." Why this book of forgetting? Who is included in the ceremony of innocence? Who is being drowned?

Perhaps, in the mathematics of our age, our privilege plus empire equals imperial dementia. We have forgotten too much. Of course, it's not just one prominent American poet. I, too, happily forget the mess that my country has left in Iraq. I often think of Ilya Kaminsky's poem

"We Lived Happily During the War," which ends: "in the street of money in the city of money in the country of money, / our great country of money, we (forgive us) / lived happily during the war."[1] It is partly a defense mechanism, to forget, to bracket out not simply what we cannot see, but what we cannot control. It is a way to survive.

Yet, every time I face a new audience, having been asked to read poems from *Sand Opera* or talk about my work, I'm reminded I can't just let the work speak for itself. We "awaken in the wake of a sentence half-written, / the missing past tense / cordoned by comma."[2] As Arab American writers, we have to rehearse the history that brought us here, the history that we carry in our spines and lines. As if we had to start by unwriting the history that had written us there. In order to appear.

Whose child washes ashore, played by the waves? Not playing in the waves.

The MapQuest of empire: What is the distance between Operation Enduring Freedom and the 2017 truck terrorist in Manhattan? Our leaders believed we knew what was best for the Iraqi people though their decisions would kill hundreds of thousands and cause a power vacuum from which the Islamic State would arise.

Erasure. From the Latin, "erase" is related to "rasen": scratch, scrape, slash, and raze.

What is the distance between the language at home and razed homes beyond borders, the cries outside our hearing?

I haven't even mentioned Syria, the land my grandfather called his country of origin when he crossed the Laredo border into the U.S. a century ago. What to say about a country that for seven years has been turned inside out? A country in which the vultures of empire pick over the carcass of a once-proud people? It rends the heart and paralyzes the mind.

And yet, amid the cruelty and ruins, something stirs. In a 2015 photograph, Palestinian father Salem Saoody leans over a tub, gathering water into his palms as his child and niece frolic, their faces delighting and gleaming in the brisk water—the sense of being clean, of your whole self rinsed. Around the tub, the walls are open to the outside, just a couple of stone columns hold the roof up. Beyond this scene of domestic bliss, the buildings in Gaza have been reduced to concrete skeletons, as if the whole landscape has been turned into rubble. The tub was the only thing to have outlasted the bombing from Operation Protective Edge. And yet, at the center of the photograph: laughter and water and a father's smile.

At a 2008 town hall meeting with presidential candidate John McCain, a woman said, "I can't trust Obama. I have read about him and he's not, he's not uh—he's an Arab. He's not—." McCain interjected, shaking his head: "No, ma'am. He's a decent family man [and] citizen that I just happen to have disagreements with. He's not [an Arab?]."[3]

When news broke that McCain was suffering from brain cancer, someone tweeted the video exchange of McCain talking to a voter who wondered if Obama was "an Arab." McCain shakes his head and says, "no he's not, he's a decent family man." The video was shared presumably as a way to illustrate his nobility, his goodness. I replied that though McCain ran a mostly honorable campaign, "this Arab thinks he failed." Another tweeter explained (whitesplained) to me that "he was dispelling the myth that O[bama] was not American." But Arabs can be American, I wrote back. "I don't disagree that what McCain was doing, but can people just stop erasing us?!"

"Racen": to "pull or knock down."

This Orientalism (the globalization of racism at home) is deeply embedded in American culture. It takes vigilance to recognize it and courage to dismantle it. My interlocutor replied to my tweet about erasure with something that touched me deeply: "I'm sorry for the prejudice. It's borne of fear, like that old white lady. I work with talented folks of all color[s] and am better for it."

I think of Hayan Charara's poem "The Problem with Me (Beginning with Abu Ghraib) Is the Problem with You (Ending Where the Earth's Surface Appears to Meet the Sky)":

> what makes me frightening—terror in her heart, her mind—
>
> is invisible, capable of being identified or anticipated
> only by those in the know. She has big brown eyes and I believe
>
> that she believes at my mercy she will thrive or perish.
> I reduce myself to clichés: talk about the weather.
>
> When she says nothing at all, I think she is like everyone else,
> myself included—an expert of sorts:

everyone knows something about someone.
And the wise are interpreters for those who cannot read the signs:

turbulence ahead, trouble to come, and on every horizon,
a disappearance.[4]

But I think, as well, of these lines by Deema K. Shehabi, from "Ghazal 1," that celebrate the opening that can happen in us when we don't have to expend our energies fending off attacks or attending only to our wounds:

Pain dominates, says your father, but your smile bargains with that devil,
and lightens loads for dreams when the balcony opens.[5]

My humanity does not depend on the recognition of strangers. But it thrives when it is recognized. Once, I talked about poems to students of color at University of Chicago College Prep—a high school with almost no white students. They were a sea of nods, of recognizing brown eyes. They knew in their bones what I was talking about, *even more than I knew*, and when they lined up to thank me and shake my hand afterward, I wanted to thank them. There is no other way to put this: it is a fucking relief to be heard, to be seen.

Meanwhile, in another state of the Land of Erasure, the comment stream of my essay "Same as It Ever Was: *Orientalism* Forty Years Later," is composed equally of honey and bile. For every troll proclaiming the essay is "yet another self-pitying whine about Islamophobia," there is someone who writes, "as a white American woman, I am particularly struck by your challenge: 'I actually want to encourage more American writers and citizens to do this work,' i.e., to ask the questions 'what are we like?' I think most of us in white America are quite blind to 'us.' I appreciate how you carefully and respectfully draw this out in your essay."

This isn't easy work—to explore our own contradictions and blind spots, privilege and wounds—for any of us, myself included. Because white supremacy is so stitched into American thinking and being, the unstitching can be quite painful. So many white people are riven by capitalism, alienation, oppression, violence, and other real suffering—why would they give up the one thing that makes them feel special?

Still, I've learned more in group texts from Marwa and Randa and Hayan and Farid and Deema and Fady than I ever learned in school. We see each other, reverse erasure, and hold each other up—whatever our background—not only when we challenge each other and speak out for each other, but also when we own our vulnerability, our complicity, our limits. To ask ourselves: Who's not here? Whose voice am I not hearing right now?

Our silence has been the soundtrack to disappearances—not only our own.

For a recent poetry project, I began reading and redacting Mark Twain's *Innocents Abroad* (1869), a travelogue that features his noxious impressions of the Middle East. Needless to say, the book has not aged well. "Why should anyone care about this," a fellow poet asked me, "given that the book is nearly 150 years old?" Why pillory Twain?

The reason is simple: I learned about this text while researching right-wing Zionist narratives online. Over and over, the same quotations from Twain's text were recycled as evidence that the so-called Holy Land was a desolate backwater, full of wastelands and diseased humans. "A land without a people," Israel Zangwill's Zionist slogan once proclaimed, "for a people without a land."[6]

These quotes were taken from Joan Peters's *From Time Immemorial: The Origins of the Arab-Jewish Conflict Over Palestine* (1984), a text Norman Finkelstein publicly lambasted for being riddled with errors, but which nonetheless remains a bulwark against criticisms of Israel. The same quotes were again summoned—with the same ellipses that sometimes elide numerous pages—by yet another book, *A Durable Peace: Israel and Its Place Among the Nations* (2000), by Benjamin Netanyahu, the current prime minister of Israel. In those ellipses, in the land of erasure, Palestinians have disappeared. To read this text is to make visible the settler colonial roots of our own white supremacy, to suture the distance between Deir Yassin and Wounded Knee, between Palestine and Flint.

Yet, as I cross out the lines of Twain's text, something else begins to appear:

I can see easily
I must

unlearn a great many things
concerning Palestine. I must begin a system
of reduction.

In an interview, Palestinian poet Ghassan Zaqtan calls people to a deeper sense of belonging, one that requires us to "accept that we are the conclusion of all of these histories" of this ancient land, with its many names and stories. The problem is, in his words:

> Some start history with the Battle of Ajnadayn, when the Muslims invaded Palestine 1,300 years ago, as if there is no history before that. This ignores 10,000 years. The Israelis start with the Hebrews' journey to Palestine. . . . This narrow perspective results in settlements and what we have now, because they have to ignore the land and its past, they have to ignore the villages that were here. They just see the last 70 years and they see God's promise. Okay, we have another promise from the same God. . . . If you want to belong to this place, you have to belong to all of its history and respect 10,000 years of several civilizations.[7]

Zaqtan invokes a wider memory way of belonging, one in which no one is erased by another's dream of a place.

"Let's put our heads together," Michael Stipe of REM sings in "Cuyahoga," "and start a new country up. / Our father's father's father's tribe / erased the parts he didn't like. / Let's try to fill it in."[8]

Now living in Cuyahoga County, home of the crooked river that once burned and burned from chemical sewage and capitalism's disregard, I walk to work every day, looking at the land around me. I wonder what has been erased, both far away, where my ancestors lived in the "Middle East," and close by, in this Indian-erased Midwest, and even closer, in my own heart and home.

What countries could we see, and what countries could we make, if we erased the erasures?

[Marwa Helal]

On October 10, 2002 I submitted the following as part of a required essay for my undergraduate journalism course in Media Ethics, following a presentation by an alum, Byron Pitts, who had returned to his alma mater to speak about his coverage of Iraq and Afghanistan for CBS News:

> Pitts proudly announced that seventy-five people worked on the production of this piece on Islam. My question is who these seventy five people are, and how many of them were Muslims?

I gave a copy of that essay to Mr. Pitts along with my résumé and got my first job at CBS News in Washington, D.C., in 2003. I quit in 2004.

It is 2018, and I find myself still asking the same question as the one in that undergraduate essay. I find myself still clarifying that not all Arabs are Muslim and not all Muslims are Arab.

Poetry is my journalism.

PART ONE: The Translator Is Not an Ally or It Goes Down in the DMs

The archive speaks for itself:

1.09.2016

After reading an interview with a translator working from a language she cannot read, write, or speak, I ask her, via direct message, the obvious: How can you translate if you don't speak the language? I also inquire about other factual errors cited in the interview: "Iran is not part of the Arab world, why mention the Arab Spring in this context when their revolution happened a couple of decades ago?" I add, "Also, Persian is not a language. That is like saying I speak Mexican."

Her response is cordial. She explains that she co-translates with a native speaker. "As for the Arab Spring, I know Iran was not one of the countries but the writer refers in his poems to unrest in the region." As to the poems being written "in Persian," she writes that her co-translator "is Iranian and I defer to his judgment," though she admits that she also found the terminology odd.

To review: this co-translator has no knowledge of the language or culture she is working from. The editors trust her answers and do not fact check them. The editors do not ask follow-up questions that would add nuance or place the co-translator's answers in the appropriate context. Someone chose the Western co-translator alone for the interview, most likely because she is seen as more accessible. The result: readers walk away believing they have learned something about a culture and region. They have actually read the inaccurate half-account of a nonnative co-translator.

END 1

3.23.2017
A prominent white Arabic translator jokes about how she wishes the TSA [Transportation Security Administration] would "flourish [her] with Arabic in [her] next encounter" with them. This comment is left on my own post about the audacity of a TSA agent wishing me safe travels in Arabic during a time when many Arab and Muslim passengers are being removed from flights for using Arabic phrases. I ask this translator via direct message if she is Arab. This person has so successfully co-opted our language and culture that most Arabs assume she is Arab or, maybe, mixed. When she confirms that she is in fact non-Arab and white, I make myself clear: "That's fine. No problem that you aren't Arab but it is a problem when you make as if your experiences or interactions with TSA, border guards, and customs have the same political, cultural, and racial ramifications as mine do."

END 2

I am interested in how such conversations can be a starting point for defining the nuances and complexities of our shared (and not shared) interests as writers, editors, translators, and consumers of translated works. Where do the boundaries of cultural ownership for translators begin and end? On different occasions I have contacted emerging women poets with interest in translating their work and have been thanked for my interest and then told that *GASP* they are already being translated by a white person. Translation isn't just about choosing the "correct" words, it is also about achieving sentiment and conveying experience. What troubles me are the systems that enable these nonnative translators to be the spokespeople of our languages.

The entire Arab region has been colonized by English. Is it really possible that there isn't a fluent Arabic-English speaker that might be our foremost translator? I want to interrogate the systems that allow for the proliferation of foreign educational institutions in our homelands but keep us from managing our own voices and experiences; that allow the nonnative and usually white translator to continue a legacy of colonization. How do we unmath that lazy arithmetic that keeps us the immigrants and them the expats? An arithmetic, I will remind you, that extends into every facet of the system that consistently puts our bodies, our language, our culture, our children at risk.

In a recent *Guardian* interview the Libyan-British writer Hisham Matar says, "International literature remains hugely underrated and, as a side effect, English books are often overrated. About 1.5% of books published in the UK and 3% of those published in the USA are works in translation. And the sales are often dismally modest. This impoverishes culture and nourishes narcissism. Put very simply, it is boring and dangerous."[9] Narcissism here can also be read as imperialism.

Just as we are overtaking the canon in the colonizers' language, we must also take control of our translations and their dissemination. This critique cannot end without a note also about the prominent Arab male translators who routinely translate works that center the patriarchy and partake in the objectification and exotification of Arab women.

Move out the way. Onwards.

PART TWO: Post-West, Postbeauty

When I first read Fady Joudah's essay "Say It: I Am Arab and Beautiful"—a response published on the blog of *the Los Angeles Review of Books* to the incredibly Orientalist Adam Valen Levinson essay "The Fine Art of Learning to Say Nothing in Arabic"—it reminded me of a vital question Camonghne Felix prompted during a conversation with Cathy Park

Hong at Poets House: "How do we do the work of intersectionality without relying on the Black body to do the work, the labor?" I think about this question daily.

In his response, Joudah missed an important opportunity to connect with other marginalized groups; instead he appeared to dismiss Western literature's erasure and misrepresentation of these communities. In addition to the title, which read as cultural appropriation, he wrote: "I cannot imagine any class of editors at *Lit Hub* publishing a piece like Levinson's about the English language . . . , or about Chinese or Hebrew in 2017. No editor at *Lit Hub* would publish such an insensitive piece of travel memoir into Blackness."[10] It is precisely in this conflation of experiences that Joudah's piece panders to the white liberal gaze. It is a gaze I have no interest in engaging, unless of course it is to gouge it (right to left), or hold a mirror to its ugliness, its limitations, its superiority complex.

If I were to ever teach Joudah's essay, it would be to challenge my students. The assignment: Rewrite this piece 1. without appropriating the language of Black liberation—that language Black people have died creating; 2. without mentioning or relying on comparisons to other marginalized groups; 3. without naming any poets who have been mistaken as Arab; 4. using only source quotes from published pieces about or by Arabs, of which there is a long history of intersectional writing that demonstrates how we share pain and learn from each other. One of my favorites to cite: Suheir Hammad's *Born Palestinian, Born Black.*

This is the work. It requires nuance. And everything is only a starting point. Even this.

I am interested in showing how even an Arab can sometimes fail to see another Arab. How deeply unrepresented I felt by Joudah's piece—and how in some way, even in writing this, I may be guilty of the same erasures or misrepresentations. Arab identities are complex, vast, multiple; as are other races and ethnicities.

The Arab body is the unlisted and unconsidered body: a choice missing from most forms, absent from the U.S. Census. The Arab body is the mistaken body: mistaken for an endless list of other bodies, always Other, even when passing or presenting as white. It is the colonized body. The fleeing body. Fleeing the aftermath of revolution, of occupation, of wars perpetrated by imperial lies. The fleeing body becomes migrating body. And as the body migrates it is subjected to constructs of the land it has migrated to.

In this country it is as if one only *has* a body if it exists on a form, and the Arab body seems always to be writing itself in. We are still writing ourselves in. And often when the Arab body is written in—and my years studying and practicing in the field of journalism confirm this—it is as a brief headline. Our bodies are left uncounted, unnamed. Our genocide is an accepted norm. No news cycle exists without it.

I am interested in writing truthfully in a way that helps us see each other. I am interested in burning down invented hierarchies so that we can run with easy breath toward a more just way of living together.

The trap of identity only remains a trap if the structures we work within support it.

Which brings me to the establishment: All of those "editors," most of them ill-equipped to judge our work, who readily and easily give space to poetry celebrities, often men, who have been, already, widely published. I do not mean to diminish some of the great work celebrity poets have made, but here it goes beyond tokenization—a phenomenon that has been well documented—the unfortunately prevalent idea that there are limited "minority spots" available in the industry. This is where the intersection of identity politics and capitalism hurts us all, as it commodifies our bodies, our identities, our rich and diverse histories. I have stopped reading the publications that partake in this commodification, but now I am looking at them with a shotgun pointed between their virtual eyes.

When I wrote about the nonprofit organization Radius of Arab American Writers, Inc. for *Poets & Writers* and asked the Poetry Foundation's blog to share it, I was ignored twice. I asked again and was met with a dismissive, "Oh, I missed this the last time, will let you know if we have space." When I reviewed Hayan Charara's must-read *Something Sinister* and again asked for space to share the review, his work, with the establishment, you guessed it: I never heard back. We all have these stories. They are part of our industry's culture. But that doesn't mean we have to accept it. And just as I ask that we interrogate the systems that give white translators ownership over our work and, thereby, our cultures, I ask the establishment: Why do you so readily see us when we are implying our

I. "poem for brad who wants me to write about the pyramids" by Marwa Helal.

he says the substance is lacking a center [sic]; a traditional plot / says [i] miss where [im] from and [i] set flashbacks while [i] walk around san francisco / he wants to know what makes [my] story so much more interesting and provocative than others? / says egypt is a wonderfully exciting place ([he is] told by others) / [he does] not like my scenes of policemen and sunflower seeds / says [he has] heard the pyramids are very interesting wants to see more of egypt in my writing ////// this is where the poets will interject / they will say: show, dont tell / but that

assumes most people	can see and i bet
most of you thought	brad was white but
brad is not but brad	is hot so the class
lets him get away	with being dull but i
understand that what	brad means is he
wants to see camels	and more of his own

ideas of egypt in my work and this is how this poem becomes its own genius annotation: see what brad missed is that i didnt give up my spot in med school for this / and if brad had read / he wouldnt have missed the generous foreshadowing / would have seen i was saying my country has become a POLICE state / and when i say my country / i mean both / of them / the poets will say this poem is trash / but i dont care my mother says if you want to know what the future of the world looks like then look to egypt and let every poem i write be a response to the cumulus cloud of aggression that follows me and let every word work to reverse the effect of the slow meting out of system[at] ic violence let every letter represent a human standing in protest

"Some days past I have found a curious confirmation of the fact that what is truly native can and often does dispense with local color; I found this confirmation in Gibbon's Decline and Fall of the Roman Empire. Gibbon observes that in the Arabian book par excellence, in the Koran, there are no camels; I believe if there were any doubt as to the authenticity of the Koran, this absence of camels would be sufficient to prove it is an Arabian work. It was written by Mohammed, and Mohammed, as an Arab, had no reason to know that camels were especially Arabian; for him they were a part of reality, he had no reason to emphasize them; on the other hand, the first thing a falsifier, a tourist, an Arab nationalist would do is have a surfeit of camels, caravans of camels, on every page; but Mohammed, as an Arab, was unconcerned: he knew he could be an Arab without camels. I think we Argentines can emulate Mohammed, can believe in the possibility of being Argentine without abounding in local color." —*Borges, The Argentine Writer and Tradition* ugliness (as in Joudah's title), but not *actually celebrating our beauty*, as we do in the pieces I pitched to the Poetry Foundation blog? This isn't merely rejection or erasure. It is selective seeing: seeing us, Arabs and people of color, when it benefits the status quo. The establishment knows the celebrity poet is going to get that web traffic, those ad sales. The celebrity poet makes the publication look good to the white liberal gaze. That gaze that is still learning to see, to read.

It is just a matter of time. The days of the establishment as we know it are numbered. We keep making our own spaces, spaces that love and celebrate us for *us*. And because I am loved, I will lower the shotgun now. And bring my own canon everywhere I go.

Thank you to my community. Critique like this doesn't happen without the prerequisites of trust and safety.

[Farid Matuk]
In September of 2013, U.N. inspectors concluded that Assad's regime used chemical weapons on its own people near the Ghouta area of Damascus, killing roughly 300. This, reported through liberal U.S. media outlets such as NPR, finally brought the civil war that had been developing since 2011 in the land of my mother's people to my liberal U.S. awareness. It was during this time that white U.S. writer friends, on learning I was working on a new manuscript of poems, started asking, "Are you writing about Syria?"

The most generous take on the question I can imagine still renders it ridiculous since, at least for those sincerely interested in artistic experiences of conflict, positioning really should matter. Given a choice between my book and, say, *Adrenaline* by Ghayath Almadhoun, it is absolutely Almadhoun we should be reading—since he is a Palestinian refugee born and raised in Syria whose positioning has situated his imagination in relation to particular acts of witness; since he is the one who has, by his own account, lost some 200 friends and acquaintances since 2011 to Assad's regime; since it is he, now living in Sweden, who hears bombs in the background when he can get through by mobile phone to his mother who is still in Damascus.[11]

The less generous take on my friends' curiosity about my writing is that they were asking with a mixture of compassion and disgust. I assume compassion because otherwise every interaction would be reduced to the pursuit of advantage. But I believe that behind my friends' question there was also some measure of disgust. I couldn't help hearing this friendly question as a more intimate version of the exchanges I've had with some white U.S. writers who felt they could ask me to account for what they saw as the increased market value of writers "of color" in the wake of the intense attention cultural commentators, critics, and readers gave to Claudia Rankine's *Citizen*. The arched civility of these exchanges barely concealed the implication that white reading series curators, prize judges, hiring committees, editors, and publishers were failing in their responsibility as gatekeepers of distinction out of fear of being called out, usually on social media, for more or less passively maintaining a white supremacist order.

These exchanges were particularly painful when they touched on the multiplicity or imprecision of my own heritage, blending as it does my father's Andean mestizaje with my mother's line of migrating Syrians. When my writing was included in *Poetry* magazine as part of a folio from a Latinx anthology, a white poet and editor who knew that my work had previously been awarded an honorable mention in the Arab-American Book Award asked, "Are you going to use every identity to get published?" Such "microaggressions," at least among my network of writers of color, are a fairly banal part of our professional and artistic lives. Just as routinely we assure ourselves that white U.S. writers have to dismiss our work as a function of some current frenzy of political correctness because they cannot imagine that their own success may have ever been the outcome of lazy reading practices conditioned by long-standing racialized habits of assessing value. The "haters," we say, suffer from imaginations so impoverished that they cannot account for one or another form of "excellence" or "magic" honed through the very act of surviving generations of such "haters."

Is it solipsism or codependence that these self-affirming formulations betray? In any case, most days I believe them. But it's also true that our very inclusion into this or that journal, this or that list of finalists, this or that reading series can sometimes be a kind of erasure. Take, for example, this introduction to three contemporary Syrian poets—Akram Al-Katreb, Osama Esber, and Firas Sulaiman—each writing about their country's civil war:

> Their poems have in common the voice of the suffering in the ancient lands of the Middle East and the longing of the exiled poet. We loved these fiery new works, their live language, and the love the poets show for their native war-torn country. We hope you'll like them, too.[12]

I don't mean to trash the good work of a venue such as National Translation Month (nationaltranslationmonth.org) where this introduction appeared. We're starved for literary translation outlets, and I'm grateful to learn about more contemporary Syrian poets. Still, the breezy way this passage "appreciates" art born of trauma should feel, well, off. The way this language associates contemporary suffering with "ancient lands" risks naturalizing that suffering by coding it ahistoric and inevitable.

If white U.S. writers can't see how their educations, career paths, and their very concerns are racialized, that doesn't mean U.S. writers of color should insist on pretending our success or inclusion is in every instance natural and self-evidently earned. When a culture's excellence, such as Syria's today, is included into the U.S. literary conversation in simplifying terms, it seems we are in fact caught up in some cold market calculation, executed however unwittingly, that trades in reductive identities instead of in art or in the questions from which art is born.

I'm not interested in prescribing anything for anyone, particularly in regard to how we identify or how we show up publicly and in our work. Writers and artists who tend to their ancestors and who find their work nurtured by ancestral wisdom fascinate me. Cautiously, and on the recommendation of writer Raquel Gutierrez, I'm reading Gloria Anzaldua's posthumous *Light in the Dark/Luz en lo Oscuro*, in which Anzaldua develops her ideas about how preconquest indigenous knowledge can inform her artistic, spiritual, and political practices. I approach this work with caution because unlike many of my friends, or many of the writers with whom I'm happily grouped, I recognize more degrees of displacement between my life and the traditions observed by the generations that precede me. As far back as I can see I come from opportunists and immigrants who were ready to leave whatever they had so they could keep moving and who were ready to weaponize what privileges and resources they carried with them to get over in each new context. I reserve the right to explore all traditions through which my ancestors articulated their lives, but I offer preferential treatment to their acts of resistance, such as these were, not to their avowals of racial identities that were never, in any damn way, devised for our benefit.

I am interested, for myself, in both taking advantage of moments of inclusion and in troubling them. I'm proud to be included as an Arab American, or as Latinx, or queer, but know that I'm writing as a real American. What could that mean? One of my favorite writers, Brandon Shimoda, recently sent me this excerpt from Alexis de Tocqueville's *Democracy in America*: "Not only does democracy make each man forget his ancestors, it hides his descendants from him, and divides him from his contemporaries; it continually turns him back into himself, and threatens, at least, to enclose him entirely in the solitude of his own heart."[13]

Of course de Tocqueville was wrong. American democracy, such as it is in 2018, could not more tightly bind me to my ancestors, descendants, and contemporaries. The binding is made of bodies, their muscle and sinew that hold the memory of tensing in anticipation of and against forced displacement, tensing in anticipation of and against local racial and sexual terrorism, tensing in anticipation of and against exploitation in corporatized farm, factory, and university, tensing in anticipation of and against anticipatory criminalization. If I'm a real American I'm not alone, I've got all my victims with me.

I won't illustrate the point by inserting here the ubiquitous posters and memes that remind us that the only good Arab is a dead Arab. I will say that maybe the only good American is a suicidal American. I am reading and studying about it, growing and getting better every day. I've learned enough to know that American suicide of the kind I'm imagining could not be material. When the white U.S. citizen Rachel Corrie knelt her body between the home of a Palestinian pharmacist and an Israeli Defense Forces armored bulldozer, she was killed, and her death generated no policy, legal, or diplomatic consequence.[14] I guess I'm talking about killing the idea of America in ourselves. Haven't you heard of the bell makers of medieval Europe who, once they realized warmongers found their molds to be close enough approximations of the shapes of early cannons, destroyed their molds rather than letting them be used for war, and so destroyed the capital that generated their livelihoods and their identities? Haven't you heard of the Vietnam War veterans honored as heroes who presented themselves before the White House en masse to throw their medals over the fence and unpin themselves from the state? Haven't you heard of the hundreds of thousands of Americans who in 2018 marched to the border with Mexico and threw their passports over the fence and into the dirt? Would you like to?

My friend, the Palestinian American poet Fady Joudah, says that's just stupid. He says only someone with a passport's sure purchase on a powerful state would dream such a theoretical suicide. Months earlier it was my turn. I ended whatever long and winding conversation we were having over the phone by raising my voice to say that everybody chooses their own comfort and safety first unless they're pushed, irrevocably, into radical action. Maybe the realest American is not a type of person, maybe it's the act of oscillating between those two positions, between the dream of whole cloth undoing on the one hand, and of inclusion into some awful guarantee of safety on the other. And maybe by turns, with my victims and my friends, we're doing it together.

2018

CHAPTER THREE

Imagining Iraq

On the Fifteenth Anniversary of the Iraq War

Three years after the Persian Gulf War, I met Shakir Mustafa in the graduate student lounge at Indiana University. He looked like an uncle of mine, so I asked where he was from. He was the first Iraqi I'd ever talked to.

"What are you studying?," I asked.

"Irish literature," he said, in his gravelly voice.

"Really?!," I said. It seemed hilarious. After all, wasn't Iraq the birthplace of literature?

"Of course," he said, pursing his lips and smoothing his cool mustache, before smiling. "Irish history and Iraqi history are closer than you think. Remember, the British Empire."

Shakir, his wife Nawal, and their children had left Iraq for graduate school in the States a few years earlier. Though he was already a professor in Iraq with one scholarly book published, he now had to start over—as if his previous life hadn't existed at all.

Before that war, I was completely ignorant about Iraq. It's a paradox of modern imperial life: only when we bomb a country do we actually learn something about it. As we reach the fifteenth anniversary of the Iraq War, I cast back to when my fascination with Iraq began—in 1990, when Saddam's forces invaded Kuwait due to an oil dispute, and the U.S. threatened a military response.

What do I know of Iraq, I wondered then, where I'd heard our Lebanese ancestors had come from? Not enough. The land my junior high teacher called "Messy Mesopotamia," for no reason I could gather, except for an alliteration fetish and natural Orientalism. In 1990, the machinery of demonization was humming, as when the *New Republic* doctored a cover photo to make Saddam's mustache appear more like Hitler, and President George H. W. Bush pronounced his name "Sodom" and promised to kick his ass.

In college, hunting in the library stacks and talking with professors, I learned Saddam was a cruel dictator, but he also had been an American ally. Thanks to Ronald Reagan, during the Iran-Iraq War, Saddam was able to develop chemical weapons. I also heard Father Joe LaBran's stories about teaching young Iraqis at Baghdad College, a Jesuit high school, a generation before. He loved his pupils, their generous and warm families, and angrily waved his thick shillelagh at a college rally I'd organized as he castigated the president and media for their drum beats for war.

Despite protests in the U.S. to oppose the use of military force, the vote in Congress ended the argument. I watched on television, along with the whole nation, as the green tracers lit the sky over Baghdad. The first live TV war, of course, authorized by the Pentagon and cosigned by a journalistic class eager to prove its patriotism. The TV movie version of the Gulf War censored dissent and erased the dead. For Saudi financier Adnan Khasshoghi, the war was "like going to a movie: we paid our money, we went to the theater, we laughed, we cried, the movie ended, and an hour later we had forgotten about it."[1]

Our imperial dementia, this rapid forgetting, comes from not knowing the full extent of the war in the first place. So, the Persian Gulf War (1991) leads to a decade of brutal economic sanctions, to bombing in 1998, to the Iraq War (2003), like a drunk stumbling down unfamiliar stairs—and taking down the whole building with his fall.

The real war would not be televised. But could I find traces of it in the archive? In graduate school, I'd come to spend a whole semester researching everything that I couldn't see on TV or read in the papers. In Ramsey Clark's book *The Fire This Time: U.S. War Crimes in the Gulf* (1994), I'd learn about the massive U.S. bombing of Iraqi infrastructure: power stations, water filtration plants, railroads, and bridges—bringing a modern society to its knees. I'd read about the Highway of Death. The use of depleted uranium in weapons that contributed to spiking cancer rates and birth defects.[2] The 1991 Al Amiriyah bombing, in which 400 Iraqi civilians, mostly women and children, were killed in a bomb shelter. How Dima

Yassine was ten minutes from the bombing, and could smell the burned flesh for days afterward. What would it mean to remember Al Amiriyah as clearly as 9/11?

We have to unerase the disappeared war. Yet depicting the real war is not enough—whether we're speaking of the 1991 or 2003 iterations, or stretching back to Western imperialism's beginnings in Iraq after World War I, during the 1920 revolt, when British forces killed as many as 10,000 people and planned to drop chemical weapons with the Royal Air Force.

The answer to antiseptic coverage (Gulf War) or embedded coverage (Iraq War), however, is not merely to provide images of corpses and flag-draped coffins, better body counts and eviscerated flesh. We need to unmake our own imperial narrative, to dial down its noise. Part of that dialing down will require us to listen to Iraqis themselves, who will help us hear again, *to remember what we have never known*, so that we might not repeat the disasters of the past.

In *Baghdad Diaries* (1998), Nuha al-Radi also watched the war from home: "Christiane Amanpour on CNN says: 'The noise is so loud, can you hear me?' It's what never leaves me."[3] The noise of empire is the noise of war, but that noise begins with the ideological noise that shuts out voices like al-Radi's. The real war, as William James proposed in "The Moral Equivalent of War," is the ceaseless, permanent, and "intensely sharp preparation for war."[4]

Still, making the war visible in Iraq is not seeing Iraq. Even *Three Kings* (1999), the most provocative film about the Gulf War—with its stunning dialogue between an Iraqi and American soldier about race, "the problem with Michael Jackson," and the grief of war—slips into imperial heroism by the end.[5] It's a good idea to read the works of Americans and military veterans of the Iraq War—the subversive novel *War Porn* (2016) by Roy Scranton, the agonized memoir *Consequence* (2016) by Eric Fair, the poetry of Brian Turner and Hugh Martin (for a compendium of works, see Peter Molin's blog). At its best, this literature fully implicates us, as in Martin's poem, "Frisking Two Men in Sadiyah":

> . . . This man, maybe sixty,
>
> doesn't take his hazel eyes
> off my face & as I reach where

my right knuckles brush
the scrotum's loose weight, he doesn't
blink.[6]

This moment places us discomfitingly in the position of a soldier whose job it suddenly becomes—in the surreality of war and military occupation—to place his palms inside this man's clothing and touch his genitals. Those are American hands, following American orders. They are our hands, violating this man's privacy.

But too often in the classic war story, Iraq and Iraqis often are merely the exotic backdrop or inscrutable bit players in the journey of an American bildungsroman. If you can swap out the scenery and dial back the technology and be back in Vietnam or Iwo Jima, then you haven't ever arrived in Iraq. You're in the War Zone. It's a place that doesn't exist except in our imperial imagination. According to Ellen Shohat and Robert Stam, the imperial imaginary sustains a way of viewing the other through the lens of technological and ideological domination. In works of the imperial imagination, "The viewer is forced behind the barrel of a repeating rifle and it is from that position, through its gun sights, that he receives a picture history of western colonialism and imperialism."[7]

Inside the imperial imagination, we don't see, for example, as Nuha al-Radi writes in 1991, "Suha and I spen[ding] the day merrily painting in my studio while the war was going on full blast outside. I wonder where this detachment comes from, whilst others are gnashing their teeth with fear. This afternoon we saw a SAM missile explode in the sky. I also caught Mundher Baig riding around on his grandson's tricycle, scrunched up with his legs under his chin."[8] What an image: a war going on, and Suha painting, and a grandfather riding a trike.

Back in Bloomington in the late 1990s, Shakir and Nawal Nasrallah and Amy Breau and I would share meals together, prepared by Nawal, who was working on an epic and lovely 600-page cookbook, *Delights from the Garden of Eden* (2003). Years later, when the next war was five years old, Shakir would go on to publish *Contemporary Iraqi Fiction: An Anthology* (2008), required reading for anyone who wants to get out of the literature of the War Zone.

I'd also meet Salih Altoma, an Iraqi scholar who'd come to translate scores of poems by contemporary poets, decrying the economic sanctions that led to the deaths of countless Iraqis and decimated the middle class. Working with Kadhim Shabaan and local peace activists, we did numerous protests, demonstrations, letter writing campaigns, and fundraisers—to provide medical supplies to Iraqis, which Shabaan would pack in tremendous suitcases on his way back to his native country. He'd return with astonishing stories—of people removing all their glass windows and leaving only the frames, or professors selling all of their books—simply to feed their families.

One day, I went to my mailbox in Ballantine Hall, where I'd first met Shakir, to find a letter from Iraq—a young Iraqi scholar writing about the poet Elizabeth Bishop. Due to economic sanctions, she could not get the latest scholarship on Bishop. Could I help, she wondered? I literally couldn't mail a package to Iraq without breaking the law. Prior to the internet, in the middle of the sanctions regime, Iraq was terribly isolated. Going there would have been like visiting the moon.

I wanted to see it for myself, of course, to bear witness to what was happening, to what I could only imagine—but I never did. As a graduate student, I simply couldn't afford it, and then the week after I began my first academic job, the Twin Towers came down. My friend Christopher Allen-Doucot, cofounder of the Hartford Catholic Worker, did visit Iraq in 2000, and witnessed the deplorable conditions at Basra Pediatric Hospital, where the destruction of Iraq's electrical grid and U.S.-imposed economic sanctions meant that even the morgue would lose power a few times a day, and the bodies would begin to smell. Still, he tells of one family's efforts to bury their child:

> The day Binit Ukhti died, the morgue had 15 boxes with 15 babies that had been unclaimed because their families couldn't pay to bury them. The family of Binit Ukhti raised the 5,000 Iraqi Dinar, roughly $2.50, for burial. Back at the cemetery, the worker placed the naked body of Binit Ukhti, umbilical cord still attached to her belly, on a three foot square stone slab at the rear of the chamber as carefully as if he were placing her in a bassinet. The man filled a plastic pitcher and a teakettle with water. He measured the child and cut a length of white linen from a bolt kept in a satchel. The aunt then joined the man at the rear slab and together they gracefully washed the body with a yellow bar of soap and a cloth. The woman rinsed the girl with the water in the kettle.[9]

After 9/11, the neocons in the Bush administration decided to punish Iraq one more time, cooking up a war with stories of dangerous yellowcake in Niger and a soup of ridiculous conspiracies between Saddam and al-Qaeda. The inventors of their own reality somehow were astonished that they weren't greeted with flowers. When Zaid Mahir was stopped by the U.S. military in Baghdad during the Shock and Awe invasion, the U.S. soldiers themselves were shocked he could speak English. The force commander informed him that "this is a war zone, and you're a university professor. You shouldn't be here now."[10] The War Zone is a highly controlled space, where a thinking person, apparently, is not allowed. As he tells it in *The Way to Baghdad (Day 18 of the War)* (2011), Mahir replied: "Baghdad is my hometown. It is the capital of Iraq, and Iraq is my country. That is to say, *my* territory."[11] (Years later, Zaid and Shehla would treat me to an unforgettable Iraqi feast in their home in Warrensburg, Missouri, in their new territory, because of that war.)

In the internet age, Iraqis like Riverbend and Salam Pax now would be able to talk back to the empire via their blogs. On "Where Is Raed," Iraqi writer Salam Pax would respond to commenters who found his posts violated their narrative of the war. For example, to "Jack," "the newest member in the shut-up-and-say-thank-you club," Pax informs Jack how little he knows about the bomb shelter situation in Baghdad, and quotes *The Quiet American*: "He was incapable of imagining pain or danger to himself as he was incapable of conceiving the pain he might cause others."[12]

The invasion—originally called Operation Iraqi Liberation, until its acronym spelled out more than it intended—was followed by an occupation, botched spectacularly by the Bush administration when they decided to outlaw any member of the Ba'ath Party from participating in the new government. At the risk of simplifying a tortuous story, occupation led to resistance, which led to sectarianism and civil war, the breakdown of the central government, and the rise of ISIS.

In 2004, a drone-plotted attack in Iraq led to the killing of Iraqi American artist Wafaa Bilal's brother Haji. Shortly thereafter, Bilal created "Domestic Tension." In *Shoot an Iraqi* (2008), Bilal describes how for this monthlong, live-streamed performance piece, he lived "in a makeshift room set up in the gallery, going about [his] daily routine with a robotically controlled paintball gun aimed at [him], which people could shoot live and over the internet, 24 hours a day."[13]

In his poignant account, Bilal felt "guilt-ridden and ambivalent about my pleasures and successes."[14] After all, he'd emigrated to the United States, a refugee of the Gulf War, while his family remained under sanctions and bombings. In an act of radical identification with his brother, Bilal placed himself in a simulated War Zone, inviting us to confront our fantasies of domination and to reflect on "the nature of modern technological warfare, in which a soldier, sitting in comfortable safety somewhere in the United States can drop a bomb causing death and destruction in remote locales."[15]

People from 136 countries fired over 65,000 shots at him, though they mostly came from America and Europe. Not surprisingly, he encountered enormous sadism from the safety of disembodied anonymity. Though trolls taunted him to show his head when he crouched beneath the line of fire, he quickly realized that the point was to live under fire: "the point is, in Iraq . . . you don't jump in front of a gun asking to be shot."[16] He also exposed people to the impact of that shooting, engaging with shooters in a live chat room and posting daily reflection videos. When Digg.com publicized the project, someone created a script to enable rapid fire shooting. Soon, he began to develop PTSD symptoms.

"Domestic Tension" laid bare the imperial imaginary and pointed toward what was outside its limited view. Despite the violence, something beautiful happened. People online began to work to protect Bilal, creating what he called a "Virtual Human Shield" in an act of cyber resistance. In his words, "While Domestic Tension draws out the misanthropic and brutal elements of cyberculture and human nature, it also highlights the ways in which the internet has become a forum of community resistance and empowerment."[17] We are not doomed to remain inside the imperial imagination, though we're invited inside it every day.

In an empire as virtual as it is territorial, with the War on Terror now a chronic state, the whole world now risks becoming a War Zone, in which a drone missile can kill anyone anywhere. In *A Theory of the Drone* (2014), Grégoire Chamayou argues that the quasi-legal concept of "kill box"—a conceptual space of the War Zone—can, in the logic of imperial counterinsurgency, "*ideally* be reduced to the body of the enemy or prey."[18] If anyone can be in the War Zone, none of us are safe, and all of us are targets. This is the world we now live in, where anyone can be reduced to a target. The rhetoric of our contemporary Trumpian moment hauntingly correlates to the kill box mentality. Of course, some are more likely to be targeted than others.

Meanwhile, outside the imperial imagination, Iraqi writers testify to a complicated reality. The problem is that, from our distance, we read or see something about Iraq and presume it speaks for the whole. I quote Helen Benedict quoting Hasan Blasim, author of the unsettling *Corpse Exhibition* (2014): "each one of us picks up one shard and thinks he sees the whole picture."[19] Five years ago, *World Literature Today* published an issue called "Iraq, Ten Years Later" that offers a broader view, not limited to war stories—even if the war hovers in our imagination, and theirs.

Iraq is, at least in part, a fiction, an invention of map-making European powers after World War I. Just as America is a fiction. But Iraq also is the site of world civilization, where writing itself began, where the first laws were written, and where reading was an honored pastime. As an Arab saying goes, "Cairo writes, Beirut publishes, and Iraq reads." We have yet to read Iraq.

That's why I keep going back to Iraqi writers, so many of them exiles remembering and imagining their own Iraqs: Dunya Mikhail in *The War Works Hard* (2005) and *Diary of a Wave Outside the Sea* (2009), and her nonfiction book, *The Beekeeper* (2018). Sinan Antoon and his novels *I'jaam* (2007) and *The Corpse Washer* (2013). The poetry of Saadi Youssef, Fadhil Al-Azzawi, Sargon Boulus, and Amal al-Jubouri. The powerful collection *We Are Iraqis: Aesthetics and Politics in a Time of War* (2013).

Earlier this year, I received an email inquiry from Arwa Aldoory, a scholar living in Jordan who is working on a dissertation about Arab American poetry, and had some questions about *Sand Opera* (2015)—my book about the Iraq War and the War on Terror. I thanked her for writing about it, so that the voices of Iraqis who were tortured at Abu Ghraib could be heard. She shared that she was Iraqi, and I then apologized for what my country had done to hers. This was her response:

> Dear Professor Metres, you needn't apologize for a crime you are not responsible for. We are all victims of abhorrent policies and false propagandas. A relative of mine passed away six months after he was set free from Abu Ghraib camp. He was a very talented and respectable University Professor, but something changed in him. I could see the pain in his eyes, though he kept silent all the time until his death. Your book

> enabled me to understand his internal conflict. I realized after reading your book that the trauma of torture and of his humanity and manhood, which had been raped, haunted him until he passed away. Thanks for your book, which has spoken the unspeakable.[20]

I have never made it to Iraq, but somehow my work has. That someone who witnessed the impact of Abu Ghraib on her own family would read this book and find in it some use lessens the overwhelming guilt I feel about what has been done in my name, that I could not stop—not with marching or petitions or poems. Herodotus once wrote his *History* to prevent the events of his time from drifting into oblivion. If only our writing could not only aid memory but also attend to the wounded, the silenced, the erased, and offer some small balm, an opening for language, a little bit of fire to see each other again.

Ten years ago, at the Radius of Arab American Writers conference, we sat in a darkened theater in the basement of the Arab American Museum in Dearborn, Michigan. Above us, we could hear the screeching of chairs and tables being set up for a wedding in the main hall. Beside my wife and two daughters, Shakir and Nawal sat. Shakir wrote my daughter Adele's name in Arabic in her notebook. Then the exiled Iraqi poet Fadhil al-Azzawi—with translation from Khaled Mattawa—took the stage, regaling us with his poem "Toasts." On the anniversary of the invasion, that's what I want to remember. In the underland of exile, Shakir and Nawal laughing in two languages, toasting an Iraq that I may never see, and will never really know:

> Even though I am drunk and sad and can barely talk
> please allow me to propose another toast:
> A toast to the blind who see in the dark
> A toast to the mute who talk to God on the mountain
> A toast to the deaf who listen to the music of eternity
> A toast to the poet who steals fire from the gods
> A toast to God to create a better world the next time around
> A toast to Satan losing his bet and returning to hell
> A toast to the mother under whose feet paradise lay
> A toast to the beloved waiting on the shore
> A toast to the friend who does not abandon us

even when the rooster crows thrice
A toast to the deceiver who does not whisper evil in people's hearts
A toast to the noose that bends to the hanged man's neck
A toast to the torturer who flogs himself
A toast to the victim who rises from his torment
A toast to the bird that leaves the cage
A toast to exile that does not defeat our will
A toast to the homeland with rivers running beneath
A toast to freedom until the end
A toast to a world for all in collectivity
A toast to the despots we hire as museum guards
A toast to the tree with roots deep in the earth
A toast to the moon listening to lovers' laments
A toast to the sun in the bitter cold of February
A toast to the planets still rumbling about since the Big Bang
A toast to heaven on earth
A toast to hell pouring concrete over her closed gates
A toast to the past as it tells us its memories
A toast to the present gushing like a river in the streets
A toast to a future we climb without ladders
A toast to this beautiful, short life.[21]

2018

II.
On Palestine

CHAPTER FOUR

The Wall of Silence

> *The fact that we are here and that I speak these words is an attempt to break that silence and bridge some of those differences between us, for it is not difference which immobilizes us, but silence. And there are so many silences to be broken.*
>
> —AUDRE LORDE, FROM "THE TRANSFORMATION OF SILENCE INTO LANGUAGE AND ACTION"[1]

In his provocative 2005 Christmas card, Banksy paints in pastel a familiar biblical pastoral scene, but with a modern twist. Joseph, holding a shepherd's crook, and Mary sitting on a donkey, pause—their way to Bethlehem obstructed by a massive, forbidding wall. The wall—replete with a modern observation tower and brushed by faint graffiti—rises so high they can't see what's on the other side. Beyond the wall, in the distance, a star rises. The actual wall that Israel began to build in 2002 not only divides "sides," it also snakes through towns like Bethlehem, separating people from each other, from their own land. It's been called many names, depending on your point of view: security fence, separation barrier, apartheid wall.

This wall is the visible sign of another wall, built in equal parts of silence and noise, which separates the United States from the realities of Palestine and Israel. What words can one summon that might circumvent that wall? The truth is that the question of Palestine is far closer than many of us might have ever imagined or admitted.

Ever since my sister studied at Bir Zeit University in 1993 and came back with haunting stories about the brutality of life under military occupation, I have been trying to find ways around that wall, to ask the question of Palestine. A few years later, I found myself interviewing a young Palestinian from Gaza who had become a graduate student at our Midwestern university. I emailed him a draft of my news story about the tortuous journey of some Palestinians to attend graduate school. He read it carefully and asked to meet again at my house. After sitting and having tea, he set aside the cup. With a mix of fear and sadness in his eyes, he said that he needed to be written out of the story. The details about his journeys to college and then to graduate school—some of which skirted Israeli rules—could be used against him and others.

It struck me with such force—that the very details that demonstrated the absurdity of the Palestinian situation and the capriciousness of Israeli power would have to be removed from this story. But I wanted to help him, not render him and people like him even more vulnerable.

In situations of oppression, people find in silence a form of tentative protection. It's a provisional and temporary safety, of course, but the risks sometimes seem far worse. In colonial contexts, and in situations where states extend their power into the private lives of those they rule—from the Soviet Union to China, from Northern Ireland to Palestine—public speech goes into hiding. In Northern Ireland during the Troubles, where paranoia and terror were permanent guests, silence was the golden rule: "whatever you say, say nothing."

What I'm interested in exploring is another kind of silence. Whenever I share something on social media about matters relating to Palestinian rights, history, or the quest for freedom, it is greeted by another kind of silence. Is it the silence of apathy? Confusion? Fear? Or the sense that taking any position could lead to hurting someone else? Our peculiar moment, in the new Age of Distrust, in the land of social networks, seems to offer us only polarizing extremes—on all manner of issues. For example, "You're with X or you're against us." Your choice is to like this post or not like it—and you will be judged. The posts that move the fastest and farthest run on the fire of hot takes. The silence about what's happening in Palestine-Israel, or Israel-Palestine, in the country of argument, in the land of free speech, in the birthplace of Twitter, is what I want to open.

I have wanted to parse out that silence for a long time now, and it is partly the reason for my writing *Shrapnel Maps* (Copper Canyon, 2020), which gathers over a decade of poems, texts, and images that concern Palestine and Israel. It was a difficult book to write. To speak publicly about it involves a measure of risk—in a time when conversation itself is often weaponized or perceived as violent. But silence's safety is provisional and its own kind of danger.

Audre Lorde writes: "What are the words you do not yet have? What do you need to say? What are the tyrannies you swallow day by day and attempt to make your own, until you will sicken and die of them, still in silence?"[2] The question I ask myself, over and over, is: Who will be lost in my silence? What sort of words do I need to open it?

When my sister first arrived in Palestine, the first Intifada, an uprising against the Israeli occupation, was ongoing. As she went shopping in Ramallah, an Israeli settler drove down the street. "He was in a big truck," she recalls, "and he had his head out the window and he was shooting a gun wildly into the air. Some Palestinian grabbed me and pulled me into a shop, and they were all laughing. That's when I learned the Arabic words for 'what happened' and 'settler.'"

She was there to study Arabic language, but her education was far more than about past and present tense. She kept telling stories that seemed like they were written in a sci-fi dystopia: stories of torture of prisoners, indefinite detention, humiliating checkpoints. I wondered, given what I'd learned about the persecution of Jews, about antisemitism and the Holocaust, whether she'd drunk some radical Kool-Aid. I struggled to listen. Wasn't Israel the expression of Jewish nationalism, the creation of a national home? After all, how could a people who have faced exile and concentration camps and inhuman brutality turn to exiling, imprisoning without charge, corralling people into ghettos, torturing prisoners? At the time, it made no sense. But my sister stood by the truth of what she witnessed, what she'd come to understand, and so I had to embark upon my own journey of self-education.

I began to fill in the gaps of my understanding, which were not mere absences in my education, but part of a structure of active silence and noise. Attending conferences hosted by organizations like the American Arab Anti-Discrimination Committee; finding graduate courses like "Resistance Literature" taught by Purnima Bose; joining the Committee for Peace in the Middle East; and building friendships with Palestinians, I began to see other realities. The work of Palestinian scholar Edward Said was a touchstone for me, especially *Orientalism*, *Culture and Imperialism*, and *The Question of Palestine*. When, in 1995, Edward Said delivered his lecture "On Lost Causes" to a packed auditorium at Indiana University, the only thing I remember was how Said kept getting interrupted by protestors, often standing up in the aisles, shouting at him. Every nation, of course, has its saints and psychopaths—and most of us stand somewhere in the middle.

Despite the shouts of those protestors, the intentional silence or outright anger that would greet me and the others who worked to raise awareness about the issues that plague Palestinians—from home demolitions to indefinite detention, from refugee rights of return to killings at the hands of Israeli Defense Forces—we kept trying to change minds and change policy. We showed films, circulated petitions, wrote letters to the editor, invited Ali Abunimah to speak, organized street marches, did poetry readings, and raised funds for organizations working for peace, justice, and human rights. Mostly I just tried to show up, to learn from Palestinians, make friends, and to be part of building something bigger than our small voices.

In graduate school, I read the haunting *Men in the Sun*, by Palestinian writer Ghassan Kanafani, which narrates the journey of three Palestinians who risk illegal transport to Kuwait to earn money for their families. The most dangerous part of their multipart journey will be to climb inside an empty water tanker as it crosses a border. The conditions inside the tanker are suffocating, but the Palestinian driver Abul promises the stop will be short. Once inside the checkpoint office, however, the border guards tease him about his virility (he's been castrated by a war injury), and he pauses, trying to defend himself. By the time he drives them past the border, all the men have perished inside. Abul laments what's happened but blames the victims:

> The thought slipped from his mind and ran onto his tongue: "Why didn't they knock on the sides of the tank?" He turned right round once, but he was afraid he would fall, so he climbed into his seat and leaned his head on the wheel. "Why didn't you knock on the sides of the tank? Why didn't you say anything? Why?"—The desert suddenly began to send back the echo: "Why didn't you knock on the sides of the tank? Why didn't you knock on the sides of the tank? Why? Why? Why?"[3]

But it was never that simple. The choice was far starker for the Palestinian migrants inside the tank. If they knocked, they could get discovered and deported, or worse. And maybe, in fact, they did knock, but he could not hear them—lost inside the office or locked in his own shame.

Men in the Sun depicts the extreme precarity of Palestinian existence and the outrage of their suffocation inside a prison not of their own making. And, if that weren't humiliation enough, they are blamed for their own deaths. The driver rationalizes his own failure to move quickly enough. Perhaps the question isn't "Why didn't they knock on the tank?" but rather "Why did no one listen?" *Men in the Sun* cuts in all directions—against Israel and its displacement of Palestinians; against the Arab countries that treat Palestinians as noncitizens or worse; and against Palestinians themselves, who might believe that their silence might protect them. But I thought most of all about my position as an American citizen, in a country that has never treated Palestinians as equals to Israelis, about whether I was more like the driver who, in a fit of distraction and shame, would simply forget about Palestinians suffocating inside their metal prison—either crying out and not being heard, or trying to be silent to survive.

A prolific fiction writer, Kanafani also became the spokesman for the Popular Front for the Liberation of Palestine in the last five years of his life, a resistance organization calling for a single binational state. After some particularly bloody PFLP operations, including the Lod airport massacre, Israeli agents assassinated him at age thirty-six, along with his seventeen-year-old niece, in 1972. Kanafani's path to resistance—the "commando who never fired a gun," as one obituary wrote it—had begun when he and his family fled Acre and became refugees in 1948.

For many reasons, his path was not my path. What I am interested in is forging a nonviolent way to engage in the struggle for justice, freedom, and equality—as do most Palestinians. In 1990, as the U.S. beat the drums of war against Iraq, I wrote a conscientious objector statement to declare my philosophical and religious (not to mention political) refusal to bear arms. But stateless refugees face a far grimmer reality, and far starker choices than my staying home in a time of distant imperial war.

Ten years after my sister's first summer at Bir Zeit, she returned. In a whirlwind romance with a man she'd met a decade earlier, she got engaged. Our family made the trek across the world for the wedding in a little village in Palestine. It was surreal and magical—to be in the place that I'd heard and read so much about. I tasted a tiny bit of the bitterness of living under military occupation, alongside the savor and sweetness of

Palestinian family life in the village. I had guns pointed at me at checkpoints, saw the separation wall that devoured part of my brother-in-law's land, and roads torn up by military bulldozers. But I also danced the *dabke*, ate until I nearly burst, and felt the love of a family who accepted our family as part of their own. Though we met only once, I have never forgotten them.

At John Carroll University, I developed a course called Israeli and Palestinian Literatures that explores, in a contrapuntal structure as Edward Said proposes, the predicament of this co-claimed land. I wanted to do what I could not to propagandize my students, but to offer them ways to understand the origins of this problem, to be implicated in it in the way that the U.S. is implicated in it—and, if possible, to participate in changing the future. My approach, from the start, was dispassionate. Although I was passionate about it, I've always believed that the best way to teach is to create spaces for students to have their own experiences, create their own questions, come to their own conclusions, and make decisions based on that process of discernment and praxis.

That's why, the following year, when a local Orthodox Jewish woman inquired about my course, my first impulse was to invite her to be a guest speaker in my class. After all, my goal was to offer students a range of inputs, and I knew from our email conversations that she could represent a certain view in a way that would be more difficult for me to pull off—to make a religious case for Israel. She declined my invitation, saying she couldn't come to my class because, in her words, Palestinians are not a people. After she sent me an ongoing series of inflammatory emails, my patience waned, and I said I couldn't communicate any further with her. In my one mistake in tone, I told her that I wished her well "but not her racism."

This response triggered a series of emails to the president and every member of the administration at my university, accusing me of antisemitism and preaching hatred toward the Jewish people, asking that my course be canceled immediately. I was, of course, horrified and afraid—afraid for my future. Had I stepped over an invisible line of silence that I would pay for with my job? Mostly, though, I was horrified, because I'd made every attempt to create space for a variety of Jewish narratives and perspectives on Israel, and because I took the accusation of antisemitism seriously. Had I not been fair enough to her, to her cause, for Israel? Israel, after all, is full of its own stories and narratives worth hearing—but had I not explored that complexity fully enough?

In the end, I was deeply gratified that the administration, after studying my course materials, supported the course and my progress toward tenure. I was lucky. Other faculty whose work was arguably more threatening to the status quo on Israel have not fared so well. In 2007, Norman Finkelstein, the child of Holocaust survivors, was denied tenure at DePaul, despite department and university committee votes in his favor and having numerous books and articles to his credit. Some have surmised that Finkelstein's takedown of Alan Dershowitz's *The Case for Israel* as a plagiarism of a hoax text (Joan Peters's *From Time Immemorial*) led to Dershowitz's direct intervention on the tenure case. Seven years later, after outside intervention, Palestinian scholar Steven Salaita was "unhired" by University of Illinois on the basis of "uncivil" tweets during Israel's latest war on Gaza—a war that killed over a thousand civilians, destroyed forty mosques, targeted crucial infrastructure like water filtration plants, and set Gaza on a path to being uninhabitable. Evidence suggests that donor pressure led to the decision to remove Salaita. Did I like Salaita's tweets? His tone is not my tone, but that doesn't mean they were grounds for firing. And what if incivility in the face of barbarity is actually more human than silence?

The work of organizations like the Anti-Defamation League and the Lawfare Project has actively suppressed speech about Israel and Palestine. Faculty and students alike have been defamed and sued into silence. At the same time, states have begun to pass laws that outlaw support of the Boycott, Sanctions, and Divestment (BDS) movement, a nonviolent strategy to pressure Israel to change its policies toward Palestinians. Americans have literally lost their jobs for failing to sign a loyalty oath to another country. While I understand that some fear that BDS is a strategy of demonizing Israel, I am reminded of Colin Kaepernick's dilemma, when American football fans became outraged after the quarterback took a knee during the national anthem to protest police violence against Black people: In what way can Palestinians protest their unjust treatment that would somehow not be deemed offensive or dangerous? In what way can Palestinians cry out against the impossibility of their lives as disposable persons, people without a country?

Some years after that unforgettable visit for my sister's wedding, I began trying to find a shape against my own silence. I had little thought of what was taking shape as I wrote the first poems about that wedding and all that we'd witnessed in "A Concordance of Leaves." On the final day of my course, I always wanted to share something personal about why I felt responsible to teach this conflict, to share something of what I'd witnessed in my time there. What began as a short slide show became a long poem. Over the years, other pieces of the shrapneled map that is Palestine and Israel would reveal themselves.

Since *Shrapnel Maps* was published in April, I have given a number of Zoom readings. Often, I begin with this one:

[Family]

At the Catholic university, a speaker clicks through slide after slide of barbed wire, cattle-chute checkpoints, and walls. His mantra is occupation. What threatens the Christians, he concludes, is what threatens Palestinians. A woman stands up. *I wanted to let everyone know,* she says, *that this talk was FULL of SPIN.* (I can't see her, she's behind me, I'm afraid to look back.) *The truth is the OPPOSITE.* (My heart goes out to her, standing in the heart of another country.) *The reason for the wall was that people were being ATTACKED,* she says. *BY TERRORISTS. After all, the Arabs sold the land, it was too much trouble.* (I shrink back in my seat, shake my head.) *And at a Catholic school, you should KNOW what the Church has done, especially during World War II!* Then a man gets up (I can't see him, he's behind me, I'm afraid to look back.) *The Jews bought a tiny bit of land, but the rest, the rest was STOLEN!* (My heart goes out to him, standing in the heart of another country.) *BUT!* he says. *THEY did not buy everything, even if they buy Congress!* (I shrink again.) She says, *YOU have FOURTEEN ARAB countries! Can't we have just ONE? THEY should take you in.* He says, *but this is OUR land! Why should we have to leave? Because EUROPE took it from us? That is why we fight!* (*What about peace?* someone mumbles.) He says, *how can you negotiate over a pizza when one side continues to EAT!* She says, *how can you negotiate over a pizza when one side is trying to STAB you with knives!* It goes on like this for a long time. Years. Decades. Generations. I sit like a child at the table, watching parents grip utensils, spit words like shrapnel. I hate

how I love them.
Ashamed, I look down, unable
to bury the hot metal.[4]

This poem, in the form of the Japanese haibun, recounts an incident that happened at my own campus, when a local community member gave a talk about the challenges facing Palestinian Christians. Much of it is nearly verbatim. I live in University Heights in a predominantly Jewish Orthodox neighborhood. Every day I'd encounter my neighbors, in awe of their rituals and community, and trying to understand them when differences arise. Israel was nearby, in more ways than one. Many of my neighbors have come from Israel or will be moving to Israel.

In the poem, I wanted to capture that deep discomfort that accompanies many public conversations in the U.S. on Palestine and Israel. As a poet, I wanted to sit with that discomfort, inside the stories of these two people, to try to imagine with compassion their worlds. That night I heard the pain of the Jewish woman as she asserted her own story, but also how that pain caused her to rationalize the suffering it caused Palestinians. I heard the pain of the Arab man as he rebuffed the Jewish woman's narrative, and how his pain seemed to rebuff the Jewish woman's story. Finally, I heard my own pain, my inability to react to the situation as it unfolded.

"Family" also confronts the silence of the bystander. Of the three responses to threat—fight, flight, and freeze—the bystander is the one who freezes. Freezing is a self-protective reflex, but in the end it obstructs intervening in what is a situation of conflict or violence. As someone who instinctively prefers peace over conflict, I recognize that I have sometimes stood back, freezing in fear, rather than moving forward to play a more constructive role. I don't want to condone a peace without justice, which in the end only serves the powerful. The poem acknowledges that insufficiency of this silence, but does not offer another way. (Other poems in *Shrapnel Maps* try to do that work.)

Of course, during the real life incident, I froze. Instead, I wish that I had welcomed my Jewish sister at my university and thanked her for her perspective. I know how important it is to make spaces safe for Jews and Jewish expression, and to oppose anti-Jewish hatred. I wish that I had welcomed my Palestinian brother as well, to thank him. I know the history of Orientalism and anti-Palestinian hatred, and if we want to create a just peace, we must grapple with the legacy of empire, colonial erasure, and demonizing.

What would have happened, if we had been able to talk afterward? Their stories are so different, grounded in two different realities. In a material sense, they are. The state of Israel is prosperous, privileged, militarily strong. That doesn't mean that Israelis don't have their own struggles and history of traumas—both caused by the Holocaust and by expulsions from Arab countries after the founding of the state. They face their own kind of precarity, and the general threat of the "neighborhood." The psychic map of that reality looks something like the map from the Israel Information Center, which features a tiny blue silver (Israel) in the wide swath of Arab states, from Mauritania to Oman.

However, most of Israel's non-Arab citizens largely conduct lives in which Palestinians are an abstraction, part of a generalized sense of a world that opposes them. Palestinians, on the other hand, always have to deal with the reality of Israel—whether they are refugees, Israeli citizens, or living under military occupation. The Israelis they meet today are nearly always military figures imposing their will on their lives. For Palestinians, the Nakba of 1948—the catastrophe that led to the dispossession of over 700,000 Palestinians, the destruction of over 400 villages, and an ongoing exile—continues. Year by year, Israel annexes more land, dispossessing more Palestinians, and diminishing future Palestinian sovereignty. Their reality is expressed in those maps in which the green of Palestine is gradually swallowed by the white of Israeli colonization.

Neither of these maps tells the "whole" story (and perhaps there is no "whole" story anyway)—but they are the images that rhyme with the dominant narratives carried by each people.

In the United States, we are moving into a moment in which, paradoxically, we're more polarized than ever, yet at the same time, we're confronting the very basis of our history. I recently saw a map GIF that struck close to home, and echoed the map above, of the disappearance of American indigenous territory, bit by bit.

What the Dakota Access Pipeline protest and Black Lives Matter movement have done to transform the U.S. conversation about white supremacy and colonialism is what many groups are working to do to understand the U.S. role in Israel and Palestine over the past century. We need to understand systemic and legalized oppression and violence. Most violence doesn't begin at a traffic stop or with an itchy trigger finger, but goes all the way back to legislative assemblies, corporate boardrooms, and executive offices—a kind of ongoing set of protocols of control that lead, invariably, to spiritual and physical death. We need to find ways of calling for accountability, constructive engagement, and nonviolent means of persuasion.

Silence is not just my own personal failing. It's a national condition, this silence about the long-standing, univocal, and unconditional U.S. support for Israel. Reasonable people can disagree about foreign policy. But to completely neglect human rights and the political implications of this policy for Palestinians is to ensure that the U.S. stands against an occupied and stateless people, who have no leverage in its negotiations with its ally. This is, in part, how violent resistance comes to seem like the only option. There is almost no debate about the billions and billions of dollars of U.S. military aid to Israel offered without conditions. And despite the fact that Trump was uniquely damaging to the cause of Palestinians—from the move of the U.S. embassy to Jerusalem to the so-called Deal of the Century to the legitimizing visit of Mike Pompeo to an illegal Israeli settlement in the West Bank—a President Biden administration does not offer Palestinians much hope either.[5] Thus far, the empire has spoken only one story.

How do we break the wall of silence that empires and states build, to hear other stories? I wanted my book *Shrapnel Maps* to be more than a book of poems, but another key to open a door in the wall of silence. Given the predicament it explores, and the lives impacted by our own national silence, and yet knowing the deep pain of both Jews and Palestinians, I wanted it to become a careful invitation to a conversation. In my own position as an Arab American, as a Catholic, as a poet—someone outside but proximate to these identities and experiences—I've tried to inhabit a stance that would model a way of listening to Palestinians and to Israelis.

In *Shrapnel Maps*, I also wanted to shine a light on Palestinian and Israeli activists whose courageous work for a just peace offers us another path. People like Rabbi Arik Ascherman, who cofounded Rabbis for Human Rights, and whose defense of defenseless Palestinians is highlighted in "According to This Midrash." People like Huwaida Arraf, who cofounded the International Solidarity Movement, and whose outlandish bravery is captured in "The Dance of the Activist and the Typist."

Friendships became the ground of much of *Shrapnel Maps*. My friendship with Nahida Halaby Gordon, one of the many regular visitors to my course to share her harrowing story of exile and erasure, led to the poems in "Returning to Jaffa." It was from her that I learned about the disappearance of the Jaffa municipal archives during the Nakba, which ensured that Palestinians would not be able to confirm their right of return to the most populous Arab city in 1948. My friendship with Fady Joudah, an incredible poet and translator of exquisite grace, opened my eyes to what I could not see. Even his email, which includes the name of the village that his people were expelled from, became a key to a door of the history of the Nakba.

As I was completing the book, I recognized the many silences, the many blind spots, which the work would invariably contain. I wanted to create a text that might create spaces where silences could be broken, where people could be seen. As I write in "Future Anterior,"

> 13. *What do you want others to know?*
>
> Tell them that we exist.
> That we exist,
>
> even between the words of their text.[6]

That includes, of course, my own text. The response to *Shrapnel Maps* has been various. There have been some beautiful, heart-opening responses from all corners of the world. One, among many, shared that "the written, that is to say unspoken, Hebrew word for 'hope' is the same as the word for 'despair.' This is a brave book." A poet from Gaza named me a Gazan for its depiction of Gaza. And there has been at least one deeply critical review, that compelled me to come to grips with the traumatic pain that many Palestinians feel, as they are disappeared even by supposed allies.[7] I understand all the reasons for such criticism, and feel sorrow that the work failed to reach them.

So how can we make our way around the wall, and encounter Palestinians and Israelis working for justice and peace? The COVID pandemic, paradoxically, has opened up new pathways of engagement and encounter. From your own home, you can "travel" beyond the walls and into the streets and homes of those impacted. The U.S. organization Eyewitness Palestine has created virtual delegations to visit its partners on the ground, from Jerusalem to Bethlehem to Jaffa. Breaking the Silence, an organization run by veterans of the Israeli Defense Force, continues to share its research on the impacts of the military occupation on the lives of ordinary Palestinians. The progressive Jewish organization Encounter offers programs designed to invite Jewish leaders to "expand their view of the Israeli-Palestinian conflict and to be a positive force for communal change." Progressive organizations with cultural or religious ties—from Jewish Voice for Peace (JVP) to Friends of Sabeel North America (FOSNA), a Palestinian Christian organization—shares ways to learn more and get involved in making change. Human rights organizations from Al-Haq to B'Tselem monitor Israeli human rights violations. Al-Shabaka's new podcast *Rethinking Palestine* explores political analyses.

For those interested in Palestinian writers, the 2020 Palestine Writes Festival featured an extensive program of Palestinian writing, in English and in Arabic, as well as radical luminaries from Angela Davis to Robin D. G. Kelley. I asked fiction writer Susan Muaddi Darraj, one of the organizers, what it meant to be part of this festival. She noted that the online format enabled triple the registrants to sign up, to "welcome all people in the diaspora to participate." She noted, poignantly, that "Palestinian people are a living poem . . . we encapsulate so much beauty and tragedy and power. I'm excited to join everyone this week and celebrate that." Naomi Shihab Nye wrote that the festival "means the world. It's our big, wide, deep family."[8] Tariq Luthun called it "a reunion of sorts . . . that allows us to celebrate our culture first and foremost, but also enters the archival discourse to further assert our place in the world."[9] Similarly, George Abraham shared that it was "a space which connects us despite the crimes against our diaspora, especially within literary institutions; it has been a revitalizing and grounding force for me, in a time that seems never-ending in its distancings."[10] One of the first events, moderated by Lena Khalaf Tuffaha, featured two éminence grise writers, Ibrahim Nasrallah and Mahmoud Shukair, whose lives have spanned the entire Palestinian Nakba. Nasrallah nodded to the predicament of diaspora, telling us "it doesn't matter if you've never been to Palestine. You live in your homeland as long as it lives in you."[11]

In the poetry reading at the festival, I found myself moved by spoken word poet Rafeef Ziadeh's "Three Generations," by Fady Joudah's original poem in English and his self-translation, by Fargo Tbakhi's futurist visions of a Palestine in 2148, by Dareen Tatour's impassioned explanations of the condition of imprisonment. Tatour had become a cause célèbre when she was arrested and imprisoned for incitement due to a poem that she had written, "Resist, My People, Resist Them."[12] But here she was, not a cause or a concern, but a flesh and blood writer, sequestered at home with a headset, trying to explain what words struggle to depict—the mostly invisible, silencing condition of carceral discipline that the colonized face and sometimes internalize. And there, as well, was Jahani Salah's notion of "writing the world to right the world."[13]

Suddenly, Palestinian writers have breached the wall of American literary acclaim. Adania Shibli's harrowing *Minor Detail*, translated by Elisabeth Jaquette, was a finalist for the National Book Award for Translated Literature in 2020. Naomi Shihab Nye was named the Young People's Poet Laureate in 2019. The debuts of poets George Abraham (*Birthright*) and Jessica Abughattas (*Strip*) and fiction writer Zaina Arafat (*You Exist Too Much*) all emerged in 2020. The wall is beginning to show cracks.

When the wall is breached, the question of Palestine will not be some distant enigma. It will seem as close as our own American history. As we begin to break the silence of our own history and systems of control, we will begin to see its projections and erasures all around us. What walls in us are ready to be broken? What fields will be visible unfolding before us? Can we reach a place where all can be seen, and all can belong? How will we speak of it?

2021

CHAPTER FIVE

Beyond the Familiar Landscape of Violence

A conversation with Philip Metres about *Shrapnel Maps* by Milena Williamson

MILENA WILLIAMSON (MW): Let's begin at the beginning, with the title of your latest book, *Shrapnel Maps*. After looking up "shrapnel" in the *Oxford English Dictionary*, I learned that the term came from Henry Shrapnel, a British army officer, who invented what was otherwise known as the spherical case shot.[1] I wonder how the etymology of "shrapnel," its transformation from a name into a weapon, might reflect some of the concerns in your book? Names or naming are central to *Shrapnel Maps* and its cartography of violence. What may be the relationship between names/naming and violence?

PHILIP METRES (PM): Milena, these questions strike to the heart of the matter. Names are not inherently violent, but they're also not neutral. Who gets to name, and who gets named? In the case of the place we know by various names—Israel, Palestine, Holy Land, Canaan, etc.—each name is not just a name, but a doorway into a whole architecture of narratives and realities. Say *Israel* and get whisked into one reality, say *Palestine* and you're in another one. The trouble, of course, is that those realities are mapped onto the same place. On old maps, there is a key to understanding the map: a legend. The problem is that the legend nearly always tells a single story. A single story is a dangerous story. The violence comes when a hegemonic story begins to erase the other stories, and with it, the people who hold it dear. The title of the book, *Shrapnel Maps*, attempts to capture the polyphony of the book—how maps (invariably authored by the West) set up violent conditions that take apart local and national realities. The maps shrapnel, and shrapnel maps result: in language and in life.

MW: An idea you suggest with one of the book's epigraphs, from Mahmoud Darwish, a Palestinian poet: "—I don't get the meaning" "—Nor do I, my language is shrapnel."

PM: That's right, and Darwish is certainly one of the muses for this book, whose existence was defined by the new state of Israel as a "present-absent alien" when he and his family fled Birwe north into Lebanon and then returned as refugees before the border had hardened. What sort of poetry proceeds from a person whose very existence is a "present-absence"? As in *Sand Opera* and really everything I've written, I've always been interested in rendering visible the nexus between huge political decisions and systems and their lived experience on the ground by those who bear their brunt. A map is drawn in another country, and suddenly bulldozers come to build a wall between a village and their olive orchard, to use another example. It's Colonialism 101. One rabbit hole for this question that I won't go down too far is to consider the British role in encouraging the Zionist movement—from the Balfour Declaration through the appointment of Herbert Samuel, and onwards. As in Northern Ireland, India, and South Africa, the British Empire needs to be held to account. Another rabbit hole is to acknowledge how Christian Zionism also played (and continues to play) a significant role in the erasure and displacement of Palestinians.

MW: I'd say this is an excellent first attempt, not only at answering my questions but also at illuminating the many big questions in *Shrapnel Maps*. So what are the dangers of divergent single stories that contradict one another—as you say, Israel in one reality and Palestine in another—and how do these one-sided narratives differ from polyphony? Specifically, I'm thinking of something Ciaran Carson once said, how mapping "tends toward a kind of entrapment" and ultimately "danger therefore lies in the impulse to replace the oppressors' map with your own mirror-image of it; this may merely replicate, and so confirm, the original labyrinthine entrapment."[2] How does one break the cycle of making maps and mirror-image maps, of replacing one legend with another, of victims becoming oppressors?

PM: I think of Darwish's lines from *Journal of an Ordinary Grief*: "What is homeland? The map is not the answer."[3] Maps are not the answer to the question of belonging. Yet it's clear that the practice of mapping and countermapping are ways of visualizing territory and realities that are sometimes difficult to see. Take the "Visualizing Palestine" project, and its attempt to map "a rights-based narrative" using data science and technology.[4] For me, the point is not to dispense with maps and visualizations (no one interested in power or justice should), but to be attentive to what maps can't see. On another plane of narrative, Israeli and Palestinian historians collaborated in an attempt to create a single binational history. They failed to do so, but ended up creating a text called *Side by Side*, which includes on opposite pages two ways of telling the same story. At least they're within a single spine. They each acknowledge that there's another way of seeing and telling these stories. In an interview, Palestinian poet Ghassan Zaqtan proposed that "if you want to belong to this place, you have to belong to all of its history and respect 10,000 years of several civilizations."[5]

Zaqtan calls us to a wider memory, and a wider sense of belonging, where no one is erased by another's dream of a place. So Ciaran Carson is correct, that the danger is simply replacing one hegemony with another. No doubt, that is what Protestant Unionists fear about a united Ireland; will we be subject to the same secondary status that we subjected the Catholic/Nationalist/Republicans in Northern Ireland? Or worse, will we be subject to the same attacks that our ancestors bore during the settlement, and over the centuries, by the Irish Republican movement? Will we ever be safe if we're not in charge? These are the same questions that fuel the Zionist imagination: although we are in charge in Israel, we are surrounded by those who wish us to disappear or die. Should we forget Shoah, the pogroms, the Persian rule, the Babylonian exile, the Roman oppression, etc.? These fears are easily justified, given the history. I've been thinking a lot about how every narrative (as with every name) is a reduction as well as a realization. There's no way around it. *Shrapnel Maps* is inspired by practices like Edward Said's concept of contrapuntalism, where the work of the intellectual (or, in my case, artist) is to be able to bring together, in counterpoint, these different realities, narratives, maps, and names—not to render a false equivalence—but to imagine a way that they can be held together in relationship, a dream of a wider sense of belonging, where one's belonging doesn't exile another's.

MW: In the first poem, there is a neighborly dispute about a tree: whether it should be saved or torn down, and who has the right to tear it down. While the speaker's wife is adamant that the tree should be preserved, the speaker seems inclined to keep the peace: He thinks, "Must I fight for my wife's desire for yellow blooms when my neighbors' tomatoes will stunt and blight in shade." I am fascinated by this moment, which considers—what are one's responsibilities to people and what are one's responsibilities to the people we love? What are the dangers of separating people into those categories? I'm thinking of how this moment echoes throughout the book to another moment with another neighbor. When the speaker asks why his daughter cannot play with the Orthodox Jewish neighbor's daughter, the neighbor says, "My wife . . . she grew up only around our kind." What's the dialogue between these two poems?

PM: *Shrapnel Maps* is definitely a book obsessed with the question of neighborliness. Not only who is my neighbor, but what do we owe our neighbors, and what do we owe our beloveds? Growing up in the Catholic tradition is where I first heard this question articulated, and the ethical injunction to "love your neighbor as yourself." Both, it turns out, are difficult loves. For some, it's hard to love our neighbor. For others, it's hard to love ourselves. Both are necessary but sometimes come in conflict. It's also true that the speaker (who is also some reflection of me) seems to prefer a kind of peace that seems to be conflict-avoidance. He would give something up rather than struggle for it. In a way, that's a failure to love oneself. In the three religions of the Book, and indeed perhaps at the core of every religion, is the question of how we welcome the stranger, the other. The Torah calls the people to welcome the stranger thirty-six times, more than just about any other commandment. The Quran also speaks about hospitality; after all, these three religions emerge from a desert culture where hospitality was not an affectation. It was a necessity to stay alive. The great Jewish philosopher Emmanuel Levinas writes that "to approach the Other in conversation is to welcome his expression, in which at each instant he overflows the idea a thought would carry away from it. It is therefore to receive from the Other beyond the capacity of the I, which means exactly: to have the idea of infinity. But this also means: to be taught."[6] To encounter the other is to risk vulnerability. In that vulnerability, that openness, is something that is found in few places.

That said, every religion also contains the opposite of this welcome of infinity. Exclusionary interpretations of faith come out of fear and shut people out from each other, and arguably, from the Infinite. In the case of the second poem, I imagine that my particular neighbor was trying to observe *kashrut*, to keep her house kosher, and having my daughter there made it difficult for her. It caused me pain to see my daughter excluded. But it's also possible that this response comes out of a history of violence against Jews, a deep distrust of the non-Jew. When I told this story to a Jewish friend, the look on his face was horror and shame. I have felt that same shame hearing "traditional" Catholics sometimes talk about LGBTQ+ people, a woman's right to choose, or religious traditions.

MW: I can relate to this given my own complicated feelings about Judaism; I have long struggled with what it means to be half-Jewish, both personally and in relation to various Jewish communities. For example, how am I meant to feel when a few people told me to "marry Jewish" given that my very existence depends on my mother's defiance to do just that. What does it mean for me to identify as half-Jewish when, according to Jewish customs, I am undeniably and fully Jewish as determined by the matrilineal line. Perhaps my complicated Jewish identity explains why I so love the poem "[The Daily Contortions]" in which, after some initial reluctance, the speaker's daughter Adele receives a piece of pretzel from the Jewish neighbor because "Adele's almost Jewish . . . Aren't you, Adele?" In 2015, when I traveled to Israel on Birthright, I encountered a kind of Orthodox rhetoric that I never had before. I was deeply unsettled to hear people my age who were American, but had grown up in Orthodox Jewish communities in New York City, talk about Israel as home. When I asked about the parallels between Native Americans and

Palestinians, I was dismissed. How could some narratives of colonialism be condemned while others were rationalized? A rhetorical question I know . . . the blind spots of one's own identity, I believe.

PM: Thanks for sharing that about your own journey. We're all on journeys to understand. One of the things I hope that Jewish readers get out of *Shrapnel Maps* is the sense that their suffering is seen and heard—the suffering of a long history of persecution, of an ongoing situation of precarity in a world where antisemitism is a very real threat, and the pain of struggling to belong. But recognizing that precarity doesn't mean erasing Palestinian realities, and I realize that there may be discomfort for some readers in recognizing Israel is not a state beyond reproach. I once had a public talk canceled in Cleveland because the title of the talk was "The Colonial Dimension of Israel/Palestine." Without even knowing the content of my talk, there was a huge outcry about it. Even the thought of Israel and colonialism in the same sentence was too much to bear. In *Shrapnel Maps*, I also wanted to highlight the work of courageous Jews who have acted in solidarity with their Palestinian neighbors, people like Rabbi Arik Ascherman and Jeff Halper.

MW: Unfortunately, that sounds all too like the heart of America's current political difficulties—refusing to engage with material that might be challenging or upsetting, even if the refusal is a method of self-preservation, still means a lost opportunity for dialogue.

PM: I agree. The divides are everywhere, and the polarization is as fierce as I can remember. This book's ostensible subject is Israel/Palestine, but it's about the predicament of every nationalism, every people writing a story about a place. It's also about America. Writing this made me want to delve into the erased histories of the places I've lived in the states, the missing indigenous cartographies and stories, the class and racial divides in our cities, and between our cities and the country—all the ways that people are segregated from each other.

MW: You mentioned that you hope Jewish readers may take away from *Shrapnel Maps* the sense that their suffering is heard. I also found myself wondering what Jewish readers might take away from the book. I could imagine a pro-Israel voice (based on those whom I've met, even those in my own extended family) saying, "yes, we are seen and heard in these poems, but we are not seen and heard enough," which perhaps suggests a dangerous slippage between "enough" and "exclusively"—a difficult boundary to maintain for anyone who has suffered so much.

PM: I'm looking forward to what dialogues *Shrapnel Maps* calls forth, particularly from Jewish readers. What you describe, of course, is a concise version of the Palestinian/Israeli predicament. Two peoples—(Palestinian) Arabs and (Israeli) Jews—who have experienced a history of oppression, marginalization, and erasure. Both—in different ways, of course—have been wronged. Palestinians would rightly remind me that the asymmetry of power makes such equivalency false and dangerous, and Jews would rightly remind me of the history of their vulnerability. Both strive to be seen, to be recognized, and recognize themselves in the way their stories are being told in the world. The problem, as you note, is when the narrative that one holds *necessitates* the erasure of the other. Narratives, when they fall into the "single story" trap, can be enormously violent. In some sense, the lyric impulse insists on particularities that the single story cannot suffocate.

Others would say, as well, that playing the representation game is a trap. There is never a perfect representation. On some level, representation always misses, ossifies, and diminishes. This is perhaps why some poets (and sometimes whole coteries and even generations of poets) decide to move into abstraction, or reject persona poetry, or the imagination, or metaphor—as an attempt to take an ethical and political stance in poetry. It helps explain various modernisms and postmodernisms, including Language Poetry. I understand that insofar as my poems attempt to represent the complex realities of Israelis and Palestinians, they participate in an imperfect project that has failure built into it. I cannot write perfect poems. I can only write poems. I have tried every means available to me to bring this reality closer to my own awakening. Still, the mimetic impulse is deeply human as well, and powerful. How important it is for people to see themselves and be seen in works of art!

The two poems you mention, incidentally, come out of small incidents in my own life and neighborhood, which is predominately Jewish Orthodox. Instinctively, as an Arab American, I saw them as metaphors for the wider question of states and nations, of Israel and Palestine. Imagine if the stakes were not about a tree and a garden, or a child entering a home, but a refugee and a former refugee, or a farmer separated from their olive orchard?

MW: For me, some of the most powerful lines in *Shrapnel Maps* come from the poetic sequence "Theater of Operations." In this section, a set of parents describe the death of their son in a suicide bombing, and their subsequent decision to donate his organs, to "resettle in alien skin" some parts of him:

> . . . & now inside "the enemy" you rise
> behind the lines of inside / you live
>
> & see for yourself what none of us can see
> ourselves / ourselves from the outside[7]

The harrowing nature of this image hovered in my mind for days after reading. Would you elaborate a bit on it? I also wonder if this passage could be a philosophy of poetry, perhaps your poetry specifically, which so empathetically examines painful histories, the erasure of "what none of us can see." Your poetry, like a prism being turned in the light, reveals "ourselves / ourselves from the outside."

PM: I found writing "Theater of Operations" incredibly difficult, but vital to the fabric of *Shrapnel Maps*. Because I knew the arguments for armed resistance as a right to those under military rule, and because I'd seen and known the suffering of Palestinians, I could feel in myself an emotional distance toward Palestinian attacks against Israelis. I could never approve of them, but I sensed I could be lulled into a rationalization of them as a mere consequence of oppression and injustice. What I wanted to do, by writing that sequence, was to look into the heart of the darkness of violent resistance, to refuse to separate myself from its great harm (both individual and social injury, to Israelis and to Palestinians). I researched and read everything I could about Palestinian paramilitaries, with a particular emphasis on the dread tactic of suicide bombing that emerged with vicious regularity during the Second Intifada.

While all the poems in the sequence are inspired by real life events, the poem you quote is based on the story of Ismail and Abla Khatib, who donated their twelve-year-old son Ahmed's body and organs to Israelis, after he was shot to death by an IDF soldier. When interviewed, the father said that "this kind of action is a form of resistance. Six Israelis have a part of a Palestinian in them and we don't think those people would come to kill a Palestinian person. And I don't think their family members would kill a Palestinian child," he says.[8]

I don't think I need to explain the metaphor from the poem above, once you know the story. But I believe you're right, that poem articulates the heart of what I was trying to do in the poems—to enact the moral imagination, to engage in a radical act of imaginative empathy that might itself be an absurd impossibility. The poet Solmaz Sharif has argued strongly that empathy is always a sort of liberal colonizing endeavor—and she's not alone in her critique. There is a provocative body of argument in psychoanalytic theory about identification as a devouring activity. So I'm not saying that I have any access to knowing how the other (or anyone else) actually feels to be themselves. But I'm trying to dilate my own feeling about what it might mean to be otherwise than myself, and in the process, become human in a way that I have not yet been.

MW: "To receive from the Other beyond the capacity of the I" as you quoted of Levinas earlier. Or as Muriel Rukeyser writes, "We would try by any means / To reach the limits of ourselves, to reach beyond ourselves, / To let go the means, to wake."[9]

PM: That's precisely what poetry can do. It can be a technology of waking, of receiving the other as neighbor.

MW: One of the ways *Shrapnel Maps* attempts a radically expansive representation is through the inclusion of artwork, specifically the Visit Palestine posters. Funnily enough, I encountered the original image for the first time in the summer of 2019 when I was staying in an Airbnb with my family. I should note that none of us were familiar with the backstory of the poster, although I have since done my research. My father, who is not Jewish, and I looked at the poster through a contemporary lens. We thought that by using the term "Palestine," the poster was advocating for the country and the people living under Israeli occupation. It was clearly pro-Palestine, we said. On the other hand, my mother, who is Jewish, saw the poster as an idyllic image, one that used "Palestine" as the term for the ancient region that included the Kingdoms of Israel and Judah. It was clearly pro-Israel, she said. I have since learned that we were both right and both biased, and nothing was terribly clear. Could you tell us more about the history of this image and perhaps some of the other images in *Shrapnel Maps*?

PM: I love your parents' polar reactions to the images! Of course, it's both. I was astonished by these posters, which I discovered in a number of places online as I was researching the representations of Israel-Palestine particularly during the British Mandatory period (1920–47). I found it intriguing how they appeared on both Palestinian sites—trying to reclaim the name Palestine—and Israeli sites, as vintage culture. They were made by a Jewish American commercial artist for a tourist agency during that period, alongside many other posters and postcards trying to encourage Jewish tourism and immigration. The images themselves are stylized, fantastical—not representations per se, but imaginative renderings. As with the poems, I'm interested in images that trouble and complicate, even when they appear clear. I could say more, but I want the readers to have a chance to wrestle with the images (some of which I've cropped and edited) and their implications.

MW: As a poet myself, I'm intrigued by the concept of merging multiple chapbooks (*Returning to Jaffa*, 2019, and *A Concordance of Leaves*, 2013) into a book. Could you talk about this process? Did individual poems change due to the new framework of this book? Or was it more about finding a way to slot poems together like puzzle pieces? What was the editorial process like at Copper Canyon Press?

PM: I've been writing poems about the Palestinian/Israeli predicament for as long as I've been a writer. My first book of poems, *To See the Earth*, featured four poems: "Letter to My Sister," "The Familiar Pictures of Dis," "Installation/Occupation," and "Two States." I'm surprised to see so many, and each of them would be at home in *Shrapnel Maps*. I believe the first project that led me to think that I might write an entire book was what became "Theater of Operations," written in 2009, as a series of sonnets around a suicide bombing. Then came "Concordance of Leaves," meditating on my time in Israel/Palestine when my sister Katherine married Majed in a small village in the Jenin district. At some point, the mapping poems of "Unto a Land I Will Show Thee" emerged in the mid-2010s, and "Returning to Jaffa" came in 2019.

The whole concept of a chapbook as a unit has fascinated me. I've always been drawn to poetic sequences, serial poems, long poems—and a chapbook can be a brilliant sanctuary for such a singularity composed of parts. Invariably, I have continued to revise those poems, condensing, revisiting, and repurposing, as they come into dialogue with other parts of the book. *Shrapnel Maps*, as it happens, is a double album (well over 160 pages). Michael Wiegers and the team at Copper Canyon Press have embraced this book from the start, and encouraged me during its growth in size and scope.

The order of the manuscript is complexly dialogic. As with *Sand Opera*, the book is not chronological in historical or compositional time. I would hope that everyone reads the book—and really, all of my books—from beginning to end. To be honest, the structure is a bit of a mystery to me that I don't want to understand. I know I wanted to take myself and the reader on a journey of encounter, a series of engagements that will invite, bewilder, challenge, provoke, and perhaps even provide some hope—even if it's a "hope against hope."

MW: In your book *The Sound of Listening: Poetry as Refuge and Resistance*, you write: "Perhaps it's true, as Seamus Heaney wrote, that 'no lyric has ever stopped a tank.' But as Dave Lucas once noted, we don't know the futures that our poems create."[10] It's an impossible question, I know, but what do you hope is the future that your poems will create?

PM: I believe that poetry can be a technology of remembering the past, but not be suffocated by it. To listen to the ancestors in the spirit world, but not worship them or be imprisoned by them. A technology to dream the future, but not be destroyed by it. To remember what we have not yet known. To accompany through the imagination and in reality the people in this world whose lives have been shattered by violence, injustice, and despair. Poetry as a dream space to wrestle the present and imagine beyond the past.

This is what John Paul Lederach suggests are the peacemaker's disciplines in his book *The Moral Imagination: The Art and Soul of Building Peace*: "the capacity to imagine ourselves in a web of relationships that includes our enemies; the ability to sustain a paradoxical curiosity that embraces complexity without reliance on dualistic polarity; the fundamental belief in and pursuit of the creative act; and the acceptance of the inherent risk of stepping into the mystery of the unknown that lies beyond the far too familiar landscape of violence."[11]

Regarding the future of Israel/Palestine, conversations tend to revolve around (or get reduced to) whether the political solution is two states or a single binational state. It's not for me to decide, and in the end, the most important questions cannot be reduced to nationalisms and statehood. We have a planetary climate crisis that all of us share, and of course the poor and dispossessed will bear disproportionately. We all need to figure out how to belong in ways that are equitable, just, and sustainable. No flag will create potable water for people in Gaza. No national anthem will undo PTSD or raise the dead. No border guards will bake the bread. No tank can feed an infant at its breast, and no drone can teach literature or draft the floor plans of the imagination. Humans are probably better at surviving than loving, but perhaps poems can widen the circle of that love.

2020

CHAPTER SIX

Vexing Resistance, Complicating Occupation

A Contrapuntal Reading of Sahar Khalifeh's *Wild Thorns* and David Grossman's *The Smile of the Lamb*

The main battle in imperialism is over land, of course; but when it came to who owned the land, who had the right to settle and work on it, who kept it going, who won it back, and who now plans its future—these issues were reflected, contested, and even for a time decided in narrative. As one critic has suggested, nations themselves *are* narrations. The power to narrate, or to block other narratives from forming and emerging, is very important to culture and imperialism, and constitutes one of the main connections between them.

—EDWARD SAID, *CULTURE AND IMPERIALISM*[1]

Two children of the same cruel parent do not necessarily love each other. They often see in each other the image of the past oppressor. So it is, to some extent, between Israelis and Arabs: the Arabs fail to see us as a bunch of survivors. They see in us a nightmarish extension of the oppressing colonizing Europeans. We Israelis often look at Arabs not as fellow victims but as an incarnation of our own past oppressors: Cossacks, pogrom-makers, Nazis who have grown mustaches and wrapped themselves in keffiyehs, but who are still in the usual business of cutting Jewish throats.

—AMOS OZ, *UNDER THIS BLAZING LIGHT*[2]

Sumūd is watching your home turned into a prison. You, *Sāmid*, choose to stay in that prison, because it is your home, and because you fear that if you leave, your jailer will not allow you to return. Living like this, you must constantly resist the twin temptations of either acquiescing in the jailer's plan in numb despair, or becoming crazed by consuming hatred for your jailer and yourself, the prisoner.

—RAJA SHEHADEH, *THE THIRD WAY*[3]

Religious War. Suicide Bombers. Unwanted. PLO. Arafat. Aggressive. These were among the initial (and anonymous) free associations for the word "Palestinian" that my students wrote down and shared during the first day of my course on Palestinian and Israeli Literatures in 2006. How do earnest and often thoughtful Midwestern college students at a fine liberal arts university come to such reflex impressions? We need look no farther than our mass media. Take, for example, a recent issue of *Newsweek*, during the recent battles for control over Gaza between Palestinian factions Hamas and Fatah. The cover photo shows a Hamas fighter, dressed in black and face hooded except for his eyes, straddling atop a tank and holding an AK-47 aloft in the air (pointed, ironically, right to "JOLIE," whose name and story graces the header title: "ANGELINA JOLIE TAKES ON THE WORLD." The main title—"Why Gaza Matters: NEW VIOLENCE, OLD HATREDS AND A GROWING RADICAL THREAT TO AMERICA'S HOPE FOR THE MIDEAST"—attempts to situate the conflict in Gaza as part of *our* concern, *our* hopes for the Middle East (for democracy, ironically, given our complete embargo of the democratically elected Hamas government). The image is menacing, phallic, and almost faceless.

Inside the magazine, the photos that illustrate the story fall into all-too-familiar categories of Orientalist images of Middle Eastern life: masked fighters, the dead, mourning *hijab*-wearing women, and swarming crowds. All these images, save one, are images of people without faces, whose faces are occluded, shut off, or lost in crowds. If the face-to-face encounter is, to paraphrase philosopher Emmanuel Levinas, the ethical moment, the moment in which we encounter the radical and irreducible otherness of another person, we can say without hesitation that the images displayed in these photographs render such an encounter almost impossible.

There is one exception to this Orientalist display, however. It appears in the blurred face of a Palestinian youth turned toward the camera as he helps others lay a bleeding Palestinian man onto a gurney in an emergency room. His face looks like it's pleading, as if in terror. In this moment, we as viewers are interpellated into the scene, and find ourselves in the moment that Levinas describes as when "the face is the other who asks me not to let him die alone, as if to do so were to become an accomplice in his death."[4] For all the possibilities that this photograph invites, it also invites the uneasily imperial response—*we must save these people from themselves*—rather than ask, "How has it come to this?"

Forty years after the 1967 war (known as the June War, or the Six-Day War), the Israeli military occupation of the West Bank and Gaza Strip (now under nominal Palestinian control) continues. Yet the costs of that occupation—economic, cultural, political, and moral—to both Palestinian and Israeli societies have not gone unnoticed. In marked contrast to the American media's often depthless, distanced, or worriedly "balanced" stories, Palestinian and Israeli writers have courageously scrutinized and exposed their own nation's myths about occupation and resistance in the post-1967 situation, and have invited readers into the complex lives that confront and are confronted by such political turmoil. Two novels, *Wild Thorns* (1976) by Sahar Khalifeh and *The Smile of the Lamb* (1982) by David Grossman, both set in 1972, five years after the Six-Day War, dramatize the social and personal crises that the occupation (and the violent resistance to it) has fomented in uncannily similar ways; for the Palestinian Khalifeh and the Israeli Grossman—both of whom came of age in the post-1967 landscape—the very possibilities of a home/land as a site of peace and security have fractured. For both Israelis and Palestinians, in Khalifeh's and Grossman's telling, the old ways—the traditional social structures of gender and class, the old stories and myths that have constructed the present—no longer suffice. Yet these novels, addressing primarily their national audience, also differ in some critical ways: (1) how the story is told—that is, their generic choices of narrative style; (2) how the occupation registers existential crises for Israelis and Palestinians; (3) how each represents "the other"; (4) how each demonstrates the possibilities and perils of identifying with "the other"; and (5) what possible new formation(s) might result from this slow-burning catastrophe.

Contrapuntal Reading and the Novel: Strategies of Reconciliation or Resistance?

To provide an antidote to pervasive Orientalism, Edward Said proposes in *Culture and Imperialism* that scholars actively engage both Western canonical literature and the Orient's self-representations through a method called "contrapuntal reading." Employing a musical term that denotes the interplay between two "independent but harmonically related" melodies, Said's notion of contrapuntalism rides the tension between being a totalizing theory of global cultural harmonic interdependence and one that emphasizes disjunction and polyphony. At first, Said's usage of the term appears to emphasize and even embrace a vision of a total culture, by

> reread[ing] [the cultural archive] not univocally but contrapuntally, with a simultaneous awareness both of the metropolitan history that is narrated and of those other histories against which (and together with which) the dominating discourse acts. In the counterpoint of Western classical music, various themes play off one another; yet in the resulting polyphony there is concert and order, and organized interplay that derives from the themes, not from a rigorous melodic or formal principle outside the work. . . . It should be evident that no one overarching theoretical principle governs the whole imperialist ensemble.[5]

Here, Said's notion of contrapuntal reading affirms a fundamentally "organized interplay" between imperial narratives and other narratives (resistant or complicit), even if such interplay is marked by multiplicity and ambivalence. Said thus balances his own double investment and dual identity as philologist and global scholar invested in both Western and non-Western culture alongside his long-standing investments as a Palestinian Arab, exiled from a country that is not recognized.

Later in the book, however, Said reasserts the need to see contrapuntal reading as one that asserts particularities rather than erasing them. Rather, "this global, contrapuntal analysis should be modeled not (as earlier notions of comparative literature were) on a symphony but rather on an atonal ensemble,"[6] one that "emphasize[s] and highlight[s] the disjunctions, not to overlook and play them down."[7] Said's contrapuntal reading strategy thus attempts to avoid the pitfalls of a fundamentalist resistance that demonizes the West, at the same time that it highlights the disjunctures and fissures within imperial culture—that which has been "forcibly excluded."[8] Said wishes to pose an alternative to the emergence of fundamentalisms as a tactic of resistance (particularly religiously coded fundamentalisms)—whether Western neoliberalism or Islamic fundamentalism.

Despite the potentially negative effects of reading literature infected by Orientalism, Said suggests that reading how the Orient "talks back" to Western representations might provide a deeper understanding of Western literature and its epistemological limits. But what might "contrapuntal reading" yield in the Israeli-Palestinian context, given that Israeli literature is both informed by Western ideologies (most evident in the Zionist project that led to the creation of Israel) and non-Western thought? Israelis, as both victims of the West and beneficiaries of Western guilt, inhabit a liminal space between the West and the non-West. Palestinians, as victims of the West (the Balfour Declaration, U.S. unconditional support of Israel, and so forth) and the beneficiaries of Arab and Muslim outrage, would seem a simpler case; yet the years of exile have created a substantial polyphony of Palestinian voices, inflected as much by Western discourses of human rights and international law as by more homegrown articulations of resistance.

Reading Palestinian and Israeli literature contrapuntally requires acknowledging, first and foremost, their fundamentally asymmetrical power relationship—that the state of Israel (despite its security concerns) wields a military might that makes it virtually impervious to what was called "the existential threat." The cultural work, therefore, in which each novel attempts to engage will be different. In Said's words, "a contrapuntal perspective [is] able to think through and interpret together experiences that are discrepant, each with its particular agenda and pace of development, its own internal formations, its internal coherence and system of external relationships, all of them coexisting and interacting with others."[9] Thus, contrapuntal reading enables us to grant to each discourse its own internal logics, but pushes onward to consider its coexistence with other logics and its impacts on others. In the contrapuntal reading of Israeli and Palestinian literature, then, we must account for the particularity of each literary tradition, but refuse to leave it at that, and consider how this literature gets enacted at the level of praxis, of social and political implications.

Contrapuntal reading is complicated further by genre, by the myriad formal possibilities and ideological limits of the novel. On the one hand, as Said, Fredric Jameson, and others have noted, the rise of the novel was coterminous with, and perhaps even pivotal to, imperial culture—Said calls the novel "*the* aesthetic object" of imperial cultures in Britain and France.[10] Despite its origins, and its ideological contours, the novel has figured importantly as what Barbara Harlow calls "'acculturated forms,'—western genres like the novel or autobiography which have been adopted or adapted by writers in colonized cultures."[11] In *Resistance Literature*, Harlow makes the case for the novel as one of many narrative sites of resistance:

> Narrative . . . provides a more developed historical analysis of the circumstances of economic, political, and cultural domination and repression [than poetry] and through that analysis raises a systematic and concerted challenge to the imposed chronology of what Fredric Jameson has called "master narratives," ideological paradigms which contain within their plots a predetermined ending. The use by Third World resistance writers of the novel form as it has developed within the western literary tradition both appropriates and challenges the historical and historicizing presuppositions, the narrative conclusions, implicated within the western tradition and its development.[12]

In other words, resistance writers have adapted the novel form as a way of telling other stories, not only sapping its former hold over their own destinies, but also by changing the way the stories are told, and what possible endings might emerge from them. This final point is one I will return to at the end of this chapter, when I consider what these two narratives, *Wild Thorns* and *The Smile of the Lamb*, might offer us in terms of imagining the occupation and bringing to light the ways in which each citizenry might resist the logics of unending conflict and move into mutual futures.

Resistance and Its Discontents: *Wild Thorns* and the Struggle of Sumūd

Despite the fact that Palestinian writing has frequently appeared in the vanguard of resistance literature and its theorizations—the name "resistance literature" itself was coined by Ghassan Kanafani in the 1960s—Palestinian literature has questioned, complicated, and sometimes rejected romanticized representations of the resistance fighter. In poems such as Rashid Husein's "Against," Palestinian writing often demonstrates the struggle within Palestinians between an abhorrence of violence and the necessity to defend one's rights and homeland:

Against my country's rebels wounding a sapling
Against a child—any child—bearing a bomb
Against my sister studying a rifle's components
Against what you will—
But even a Prophet becomes powerless
When his visor takes in the murderers' horses
Against a child becoming a hero at ten
Against a tree's heart sprouting mines
Against my orchard's branches becoming gallows
Against erecting scaffolds among the roses of my land
Against what you will
But after my country, my comrades, and my youth were burnt,
how can my poems not turn into guns?[13]
(translation by May Jayyusi and Naomi Shihab Nye)

Sahar Khalifeh's novel *Wild Thorns* compellingly dramatizes the struggle within Palestinian society, within families, and within individual characters to articulate and participate in a meaningful and productive resistance to occupation. Telling the story of a West Bank Palestinian, Usama, who has returned after five years to engage in violent resistance against the occupation, Khalifeh shows how Usama must confront how life under occupation is different than he imagined, but not the simple defeat and humiliation that he views it. Khalifeh's novel offers a range of responses to military occupation—all of which suggest that we need to complicate our notion of resistance as only armed resistance. From Usama's guerrilla tactics to Abu Adil's courting of journalists, from Basil's youthful radicalism to Zuhdi's emotional reactivism, to Adil's resistance through steadfastly refusing to leave Palestine, Khalifeh dispels Orientalist views of Palestinian society, while dramatizing the struggle of individual Palestinians to come to terms with their own predicament. Khalifeh's novel proposes no easy answers about the question of resistance, but suggests that the old ways (represented by the downfall of the house of Karmi) no longer suffice.

But what do we mean by resistance? As Diane Elam has noted, although "the concept of resistance enjoys a privileged status in contemporary criticism,"[14] resistance as a term is both ubiquitous and theoretically uninterrogated. (Even the use of a term like "interrogated" in the context of Palestinian or Arab experience more generally demonstrates the abyssal distance between contemporary theoretical discourse and what is going on in prisons around the world.) Resistance as a critical term crystallized in 1966, when Palestinian writer and secular revolutionary Ghassan Kanafani theorized "resistance literature" as literature that was part of the "arena of *struggle*."[15] The struggle for Palestinians has been various and multiform—but the national struggle has been one for the recovery of land lost since 1948 and for the creation of a modern Palestinian state. Since Palestinian literature has emerged in the wake of suffering, exile, and occupation, one of its cultural projects has been to recover the repressed (or suppressed) facts of Palestinian life. What Edward Said has called the "permission to narrate"—what has been most denied to the Palestinians by the international media—was simply the power to communicate their own histories both to themselves and to the world outside hypnotized by the Zionist narrative of "a land without a people for a people without a land." Seizing this "permission to narrate" itself has been an act of resistance and an act of cultural survival, given the pressures to conform to Israeli narratives and laws or to the narratives and laws of host Arab nations.

Harlow's *Resistance Literature* (1987) expanded Kanafani's term into a theorization of the literature of national liberation movements from El Salvador to South Africa, and invited us to see these struggles as parallel revolutionary movements. Indeed, the literature shared a political and politicized raison d'être. It was frequently explicitly political, even partisan; often a force for eliciting and mobilizing "collective response" to oppression; and "a repository for popular memory and historical consciousness."[16] Yet Harlow's suggestive argument also implicitly and explicitly links resistance literature as an arm of *armed* struggle. After all, Kanafani's term *muqāwama* implied nothing less than armed struggle. For Harlow, the "resistance writer, like the guerrilla of the armed liberation struggle, is actively engaged in an urgent historical confrontation."[17] At times, Harlow's empowering and celebratory tone belies the bloody contradictions at the heart of national liberation struggles based on armed revolution, and the tensions played out for writers between their imaginative labors and their intellectual and political investments.

Palestinian writer Sahar Khalifeh's *Wild Thorns* (*Al-Subar*), published in Arabic in 1976, is a novel that, in its heterogeneous representation of Palestinian life under Israeli occupation, enables a revaluation of resistance as a critical term, inviting a broader conception of resistance that may include armed struggle but also a host of nonviolent responses to occupation. For Harlow, *Wild Thorns* "both vestiges the scenario of liberation and armed struggle scripted by the resistance movement's leadership in exile and critiques the atavistic structures of traditionalism that continue to resist social changes from within."[18] While Harlow captures the double movement of the novel, it does more than vestige and critique the poles of revolutionism and traditionalism; through its employment of the novelistic form, *Wild Thorns* dramatizes the damage that each polarity wreaks upon the present and future. Yet the novel offers no easy solutions. Set in 1972, *Wild Thorns* tracks the lives of a number of Palestinians whose lives are intertwined, and whose fates are ultimately inextricable from each other. *Wild Thorns* is a remarkably self-conscious novel, embodying the "permission to narrate" as both a creative act of literary imagination and a representation of the nation to itself and to the outside world. Because it begins in the point of view of Usama, a Palestinian romantic turned revolutionary who has been living abroad and is unused to life under military occupation, the novel invites and interpellates the reader—regardless of national origin—into the subject position of the exile.

We see this new reality through Usama's eyes, heightened by his (and, arguably, "our") relative innocence regarding the mechanisms of occupation. Chapter 2 introduces Usama and us to the humiliations of checkpoints—confiscations of banned goods, strip searches, and verbally abusive interrogations, as in: "Who's Usama al-Karmi?" "I am." "You are, huh? Why didn't you answer? You were in the toilet. How was it, filthy dirty as usual? Dirty Arabs! We build spotless sweet-smelling toilets and you fill them with shit!"[19] As Usama is interrogated about his reasons for returning, he can hear the screams of a young Palestinian woman who is being slapped around and probed between her legs for smuggled contraband. Anyone who has gone through Usama's experience more than once probably wants to forget and repress it; yet Khalifeh's narration of it—as if for the first time—summoning the sounds, sights, and smells of border control and checkpoints, must be seen as an act of testimony, of imaginative witness, and itself a resistance to the numbingly daily act of crossing borders for Palestinian workers and travelers. As such, it brings us—those of us who are not privy to this reality (or even only glancingly)—into imaginative confrontation with the implications of occupation.

Yet Khalifeh's novel is not a mere protest against Israeli abuses, but a dramatization of how Palestinians themselves attempt to survive the depredations of occupation. Usama's first act of resistance is a nonviolent one—a struggle of naming. During the border interrogation, Usama informs the soldier that his mother moved to Nablus. Here is that moment:

> "My mother moved to Nablus."
> "Why did your mother move to Shekem?"
> "She likes Nablus."
> "Why does she like Shekem?"
> "She's got lots of relatives in Nablus."
> "And why have you left the oil countries to return to Shekem?"
> "I'm returning to Nablus because my father died."[20]

Usama steadfastly holds to the Palestinian name Nablus, despite the soldier's attempt to erase that name and its reality by calling it Shekem, the Israeli name for Nablus. Usama refuses to cede the name, even though it might mean his interrogation lasts longer, because he refuses to cede Palestinian reality. His version of reality may be misunderstood, misnamed, but it is his and he won't let go of it.

Khalifeh's novel suggests that we need to see such daily acts of resistance as courageous—perhaps even more courageous than acts of armed insurrection. In this way, the novel becomes a dramatization of the trials of *sumūd*, the steadfastness demonstrated by Palestinians who refuse to give up their cultural identity or leave their homeland. Yes, the novel begins with Usama's return to the West Bank, and follows him as he plots an act of violent resistance. Yet rather than romanticizing Usama and his mission (which is to blow up buses of Palestinian workers heading for work in Israel to stop their complicity with the occupation), Khalifeh paints him as a vexed, naïve, and deeply dangerous romantic who feels he must eviscerate himself of his own dreaminess and, in his thoughts, "become a rocket, a guided missile."[21] Usama's impetuous actions (stabbing an Israeli soldier, then bombing a busload of Palestinians heading to Israel) cause reverberations that lead, in the end, to the destruction of the house of his uncle, Abu Adil Karmi, by Israeli soldiers—and, in some sense, to the death of his uncle as well.

Thus, Khalifeh weaves Usama's return into the stories of the formerly aristocratic Karmi family, who are the center of this novel, in their various struggles to survive amid the new realities of occupation. Abu Adil, the family patriarch, can resist only through words; yet his daily sessions with journalists seem to lead nowhere, and dramatize the seeming futility of language and narration. To make matters worse, Abu Adil requires the services of a costly kidney dialysis machine; his body is sucking the family dry. His aged and infirm body—like the infirmities of the patriarchal culture that Khalifeh increasingly addresses in later novels—becomes a figure for a language without vitality, a system whose inequities have become exposed by the occupation as empty. Though Zuhdi, like Adil, will say, "words are our only weapon,"[22] in an echo of Kanafani's famous novella, *Men in the Sun*, Zuhdi also laments: "We speak, but they don't hear us. Who can we speak to? For God's sake, who can we speak to?"[23] Khalifeh, like Kanafani, sees the older generation's reliance upon words alone to be insufficient; in this metafictional moment, Khalifeh articulates the fundamentally interpellative longings of Palestinian narrative—that it cease being merely an aesthetic object, and become a hailing of those others who might make its language into reality.

Wild Thorns thus depicts the traumatic changes to Palestinian life as a result of occupation, and the difficulties of Palestinians to make their way in the new landscape—both political and geographical. *Wild Thorns* is a thick description of place—not of a romanticized land about which the exiles like Usama have fantasized, but of a human geography. Yet, at least at one point, the translation saps the thickness of description. In an intriguing endnote, Nejd Yaziji remarks that "this passage [describing the now-desolate land of the abandoned Karmi farm], which goes on for a whole page in the Arabic original, is reduced in the English version to a four-line paragraph."[24] What interests me more than a critique of the novel as *genre* is how this particular novel—and its translation into English—creates new ways of seeing the occupation, and what such elisions might tell us about the distance between Palestinian realities and our own. This translatory elision of description of the land might have been due to excessive particularity, with a host of native terms that seemed unnecessarily detailed for the English reader; it may have been deemed a distraction from the plot. And yet, we might also ask, Does not the thick description of the land render more poignantly the heart of the Israeli-Palestinian conflict—who gets to own the land, to be stewards of the land? That the Karmi farm is in desolation suggests that the very "land rhetoric" that underlies Palestinian resistance ideology could not compete with Israeli economic opportunities for the attention of the Palestinian peasant.

Adil, the eldest son and cousin of Usama, has given up working the ancestral farm and is secretly working in Israel to feed his family and his father's kidney machine. Thus, on the surface, Adil is a collaborator, a cynic who sacrifices his dignity and will simply to keep up appearances for his father. In Usama's eyes, Adil and the rest of Palestinian society "inside" the occupied territories have disintegrated, and have lost the will to resist. In a conversation between Usama and Adil, Usama vents his anger at the filthiness and lassitude of Palestinian life: "Is this an occupation or a disintegration?"[25] He asks Adil what he's doing "to oppose what goes on inside."[26] Adil responds, "the same as what you've done to oppose what's outside." Usama, ever the Manichean thinker, who believes you're either with us or against us, replies: "The picture's perfectly clear, can't you see that?"[27] Khalifeh counterposes Adil's more authorial point of view: "Flicking the flies from his face, Adil replied, 'There's more than one dimension to the picture.'"[28] In this utterance, in this refusal of the absolutism of Usama's view, Adil embodies Khalifeh's novelistic embrace of the multiple yet bound fates of Palestinians; in her imagined world, all characters have human contours—Usama's tragic idealism, Adil's heartbreaking weariness, Basil's youthful radical fervor, Zuhdi's reactive passion, and so forth—and each attempts to survive as they can. Yet even Zuhdi, a friend of Adil's, who is distrustful of revolutionaries while in prison, and resists the resistance, gets sucked into battle when he finds himself blown off the bus and next to Usama as he fends off Israeli soldiers. Zuhdi's sudden transformation from a *sāmid* (one who practices *sumūd*) into a "wild thorn," into one who resists, demonstrates how the occupation draws normally nonrevolutionary people into violent acts. By contrast, Adil's resistance is *sumūd*—survival, staying put, simply not giving up and leaving, is his resistance to occupation, his final stand.

Yet for Khalifeh, Palestinian life is full of contradictions, of "impossible choices," between family and nation, between individual and family, between self and self. And this is precisely why a rigidly revolutionary reading of the novel misses the novel's traumatic kernel. The ultimate brutality of the occupation is that no one is spared from ethical taint; for Usama's act, and for the complicity of Adil's sister holding weapons in the house, the house of Karmi is demolished by the Israeli military. In the waning moments before the destruction, Adil attempts to take out some personal belongings of the family, and ends up consciously leaving behind the kidney machine. He does it, even though he knows his father will die:

> Would you kill a man, then? Kill your own father? But men are always being killed. And if my father goes on living, we'll all die. . . . Me, Nuwar, the children. Haven't we lost enough already? Usama, Basil, the family estate. And all in self-defence. In defence of a dignified, honourable life. Let my father die! No let him live! If you save him, you'll save your own soul from the damnation of a terrible crime.[29]

Though Adil is, in my reading at least, the hero of this novel, he is a troubling one; his refusal of armed resistance does not leave him with any greater moral clarity or authority, and leaves more questions than answers. Adil's complicity in the eventual death of his father suggests that the occupation leaves no hands unbloodied, and that the old order of Palestinian society that Abu Adil represents cannot survive. But what will be there to replace it? Will it be born in the youthful radicalism of Basil, who escapes into the city—a cipher for the increasingly radical generations that have succeeded this novel's historical moment—essentially anticipating the Intifada? Will it emerge from those moments of cross-national identification, when Adil carries off the Israeli child who has witnessed the murder of her soldier-father by Usama,[30] or the weeping of Israeli prison guards over the tearful reunion of an imprisoned father and his son?[31] Or will it be more mundane than that, in the daily persistence of survival that the novel ends with, as "people [go] about their business, buying vegetables, fruit and bread"?[32] Thus, Khalifeh's novel functions as both resistance literature and a literature resistant to singular and fundamentalist notions of resistance. Khalifeh helps us see how radicalism is bred out of conditions of extreme privation and humiliation, and the multiplicity of Palestinian responses to those conditions. Finally, Khalifeh confronts the ways in which Palestinians struggle to fill their personal or familial needs against the national needs—and how sometimes the claims of human relations move us beyond the bounds of national allegiance.

Adil's example shows how Palestinians see the humanity of Israelis, even though they often see their worst in the context of military occupation. Yet, arguably, the novel ultimately points to the impossibility of any permanent solidarity, at least under the present conditions of occupation. Adil might see the Israeli soldier about to demolish his house as his father, but in the end the soldier will destroy the house anyway. One can critique Khalifeh's novel for what might be seen as stock Israeli characters, and yet she offers an imaginative portrait of how the fates of Israelis and Palestinians are bound. Whether they are bound to end with the bullet or by mutual recognition remains to be seen.

The Israeli Dilemma: Jewish Conscience and the Arab

If the struggle for Palestinian writers has been to gain the "permission to narrate"—to articulate their personal and national stories in ways that will function as both cultural repositories for the dispossessed and interpellative acts to hail the international community to intercede on the behalf of Palestinians—for Israeli writers, the struggle has been to tell the story of this nascent nation-state in ways that might suture the gap between the diasporic religious, literary, and cultural traditions and the new realities of Israeli life. Even in works where the Arab was little more than a stock figure, stories such as S. Yizhar's "The Prisoner"—written and published in the middle of Israel's War of Independence—demonstrate how Israeli writers have engaged in unsparing moral questioning and critique of the abuses of power by an occupying army. Thus, Israeli writers have functioned vitally as bearers of conscience and prophets for social justice, even during the moments when the nation-state's very existence seemed in question.

Yet, according to critics Menakhem Perry and Barbara McKean Parmenter, the early Zionist imagination and in Hebrew literature at least until the 1960s was suffused with the representational repertoire that Said termed Orientalism. Israeli representations of Palestinian Arabs tended, ambivalently, either to idealize them as closer to the land with what Parmenter calls "a clear and condescending paternalism"[33] or to demonize them as threatening forces ready to destroy Jews. In Perry's words, "Whenever the Arab *problem* is the issue, Hebrew literature has acted as an opposition to the conservative national concensus [*sic*]. When, on the other hand, we examine the concepts involved in the characterization of the *Arab himself*, sometimes by the very same authors, we can only be amazed by the preconceptions derived from nineteenth century European romantic colonialism."[34] This contradiction strikes at the heart of Israel's response to the conflict. The question for Israeli literature, reading contrapuntally with Palestinian literature, becomes: Can the dynamic, probing, vital moral strength demonstrated in the Jewish tradition overcome the tendency to read the Zionist Imaginary onto the Arab people and the land?

Given the ongoing dynamics of Israeli literature's ambivalent relationship to its Arab co-inhabitants, David Grossman's novel *The Smile of the Lamb* (1982) (and subsequent nonfiction *The Yellow Wind*) marked a pivotal moment, where the primal encounter of Jews and Arabs, Israelis and Palestinians seemed to release its reader from yet another traumatic repetition of inexorable and unending conflict. Part of a vanguard of Israeli writers who emerged after the Six-Day War, Grossman demonstrates an unsparingly honest and self-critical examination of the psychological and moral damage of occupation on Israelis and Palestinians. Grossman illuminates a complex and painful portrait of how a homeland for the Jewish nation, and a triumphant victory for its vulnerable state, has meant suffering for a dispossessed people. Rather than glossing over that pain, Grossman's conscience-rich narrative hearkens back to the Hebrew prophetic tradition and extends the vein of Israeli literature of conscience manifested in the works of Yizhar, Amos Oz, and A. B. Yehoshua into a fuller representation of the Arab. By giving voice both to an Israeli soldier in a moral crisis (Uri) and an Arab outcast outraged by the death of his son (Khilmi), Grossman's novel opens up the possibility of cross-national identification in ways that echo and extend Khalifeh's novel. In some sense, *The Smile of the Lamb* reads like a response to *Wild Thorns*, insofar as it, six years later, engages in the parallel cultural work of imagining the lives of the Israeli soldiers on the other side of the occupation—but with a similar degree of sympathy and heartbreak. In the following analysis, then, by focusing on narrative technique, character, representations of the occupation and the other, and identification, I will explore Grossman's achievement and test its limits against Khalifeh's version of the occupation.

***The Smile of the Lamb*: Extending *Al-Subar* to Sabras**

In contrast to Khalifeh's poetics of everyday life under occupation, *The Smile of the Lamb* is a fractured, self-conscious modernist tour de force told from four different narrative points of view in alternating chapters, four monologues of characters undergoing existential crises in the two days covered in the story. *The Smile of the Lamb*'s central drama—at least for the concerns of this chapter—concerns the interweaving of the voices and fates of two Israeli soldiers (Uri and Katzman) and an old Arab man (Khilmi). These four narratives encapsulate four ways of telling a story—Uri's stream of consciousness, Khilmi's fabular magical realism, Katzman's third person noir, and Shosh's confessionalism—and dramatize a world in which unitary, stable meanings have broken down. In each narration, tellingly, the characters have both lost faith in the fictions of their fathers, and have betrayed (or will) their own adoptive sons.

Uri begins the narrative, in medias res, at the point when Uri has finally left the Israeli Defense Force for good and rushed to Khilmi's side, to share with him the news of the death of his son Yazdi, and, we learn, to offer himself up as a sacrifice for his loss. The youthful Uri (whose name means "light" in Hebrew) comes from a Sephardic background, and has a kind of open-heartedness and idealism that startles and attracts the more defensive characters around him, especially the cynical Katzman. Uri's longing for a enlightened occupation, for one that helps the Palestinians, founders when he finds himself unable to counteract the bruising inhumanity of collective punishment that occupation requires; the final straw—the murder of the son of his friend and adoptive father-figure Khilmi—causes him to rush to Khilmi's side, and to offer himself as a hostage to end the occupation. Uri embodies the idealism and longing for social justice that Israeli writers have promulgated; his leap, however, from longing to crossing over, might suggest Grossman's own desire to overcome the impasse between Israelis and Palestinians.

Katzman, Uri's friend, by contrast, is thirty-nine, and transformed himself from a Polish immigrant to a Sabra through sheer force of his own will. His belligerent and self-protective cynicism, he acknowledges, crystallized during his traumatic experience as a young boy hiding in what he calls "the pit" with his father and mother during the Holocaust.[35] For Katzman, despite his questions about the morality of the occupation, there is no safety in the world.[36] Still, he marvels at Uri's astonishing openness to the world, and is drawn to his love.[37] Dramatizing Katzman's own notion of selfhood as opaque, Grossman tells Katzman's story from the distance of the third person, a story that embodies Israel's post-Holocaust trauma that inflects its fierce warrior ethos and occasionally defiant Nietzschean antagonism with world opinion.

Khilmi (Arabic for "gentle"), an aged Palestinian man who is an outcast in his own society, is a dreamer and storyteller who weaves fabulous tales in order to fend off the brutalities of life—whether from a humiliating social culture or from military occupation.[38] Like a male Scheherazade, Khilmi tells his stories as an act of survival, a defense against a murderous world where powerful people threaten without remorse. He tried to teach his bastard son, Yazdi (whom he has adopted), a private language that only they would share, to protect him, but Yazdi ultimately rejects his father's fantasies as the helpless dodderings of an old fool, and joins the resistance forces:

> Father, he says, you dream. We have important things to do. We have to fight.
>
> They are very powerful, I answer, and cannot be beaten by force.
>
> By what, then? By silence? By dreams in a barrel?
>
> How he spoke. How ugly the word "barrel' sounded coming from his lips.
>
> No, not by silence; but by being softer than a feather. More fragile than an egg.
>
> It won't do any good, *Ya ba*. They understand only the language of power.
>
> This will be a different kind of war. Long and arduous. And for weapons we will use stubborn patience and infinite weakness. They will not be able to bear it.[39]

Yet this method of "stubborn patience" (Khilmi's articulation of his own kind of *sumūd*), cannot withstand the crushing force of betrayal. With the death of Yazdi, Khilmi threatens to give up storytelling and to take up violence as the only remaining means of response.

Through the character of Khilmi, Grossman richly explores "concrete details of everyday life in the West Bank and has a variety of Palestinian characters, folkloristic anecdotes and even a detailed 'semiotics' of plants that are unknown to the Israeli reader and called by their Arab names."[40] Khilmi's presence, for Perry, "is exciting and exceptional among Arab characters in Hebrew literature. Nevertheless, it seems impossible to avoid stereotypes in describing the other. In Grossman, too, Hilmi [*sic*] the Arab is close to nature, speechless, occupied with fantasies and daydreams, passive and insane."[41] Given the critiques of representations of Arabs in Israeli literature, Grossman takes a risk by representing the only Palestinian character as a half-mad, half-blind holy fool who eats soil and rubs himself with lemons to reduce his stink. There is something so excessively Orientalist about the brute facts of the character, stated in this way, and yet Grossman fully imbues Khilmi with a kind of humanity that is undeniable. By making Khilmi an outsider to his own culture, and by making his novel about fictionality itself, Grossman's portrayal inoculates against the criticism of representation that a more realist novel would fall prey to. Some years later in 2006, David Grossman's son, Uri Grossman, was killed in the war with Hezbollah. In a story in the *Guardian*, Hillel Schenker quoted Grossman: "I once thought of teaching my son a private language, isolating him from the speaking world on purpose, lying to him from the moment of his birth so he would believe only in the language I gave him. And it would be a compassionate language. What I mean is, I wanted to take him by the hand and name everything he saw with words that would save him from the inevitable heartaches so that he wouldn't be able to comprehend the existence of, for instance, war."[42] In other words, Grossman imbued this desire to protect his son in Khilmi.

For Rachel Feldhay Brenner, *The Smile of the Lamb* is partly a story of how children reject the stories of love and social harmony that their fathers instilled in them, in favor of the intoxicating brew of militaristic domination and social cohesion offered by the state. For Brenner, the fathers' stories attempt to

> rewrite the traumatic effects of defeat and dispossession . . . mental and physical abuse (Khilmi), and the Nazi decree of annihilation (Katzman's father) into stories aimed at forging relationships of love and trust. These tales teach neither submission nor violent opposition to oppression . . . [they instead confront] the dominating system with a story of love and poetic imagination. It is this message of love that the heirs to the stories are meant to communicate to the victorious mainstream, nurtured by stories of militancy, war, and domination.[43]

Read back from her accounts of social justice by other Jewish and Israeli writers, this reading caps her compelling account of a tradition of writers whose works point toward coexistence. In a sense, however, *The Smile of the Lamb* both contains this reading and its opposite. The storytelling of the fathers, Khilmi and Katzman, functions paradoxically. On the one hand, as Brenner rightly suggests, they provide a way for the father to protect the son from the depredations of the war and its ways of domination; on the other hand, they also insulate and sometimes even traumatize the child with the single-mindedness of their visions, visions that are incommensurable with the realities the children later face. Thus, Katzman feels as if his father betrayed him. In other words, the trauma experienced by the fathers is thus communicated through the stories, the stories become a kind of reaction-formation to the world. In the end, the sons reject these stories because they find them insufficient to the world that they face. They refuse to be sacrificed upon the altars of their father's imaginations. *The Smile of the Lamb* is a novel about a child's rejection of a father's sacrifice, a father's attempts to placate an implacable God. It is a fiction at war with fictionality.

Here I have restaged the critical debate, then, between Brenner's notion of fiction as a liberating site of possibility and Perry's notion of the characters' fictions as ultimately being illusions: "The fact that several characters are involved in weaving a network of lies—including lying to themselves—or a network of fantasies, adds to the difficulty [of this novel]."[44] Grossman's novel, as stated earlier, holds both of these points of view, in a productive tension that allows for what fiction can enable—in both senses of the term. Fiction clearly has aided and informed the Zionist project of statehood, for example, even as it has turned one eye away from its effects on its Arab co-inhabitants. As Perry notes, "personal life and West Bank problems are inseparable. There is an integral Israeli-Palestinian totality reflecting a single set of tendencies,"[45] though those tendencies are about how characters lie to themselves and others in ways that will destroy them. In the end, though, these lies do not destroy the state, but actually seem to underwrite it. The state reasserts itself in the end, in part because the lies are fantasies that have no power beyond the few that they have entranced. Still, for Perry, "The fabricated stories are something positive, a journey several people take together, of their own free will, to a 'better world.' But Hilmi's [*sic*] last deed resembles the lies of others. In a desperate attempt to preserve his own world he must act according to the rule opposed to his world."[46]

Grossman stages debates within Israeli society about the occupation through the conflict between Katzman and Uri. During the Six-Day War, Katzman protests the absurd violence of warfare by shelling Kalkilya too much; Katzman, like Grossman's portrait of Moshe Dayan, intimates the critique of the warrior trapped in his own cage of paranoia: "Dayan was like a trapped wolf scurrying around his cage. His whole life had been a nervous repetition of this behavior. In his youth, defying death or the battlefield, he had never known what was impelling him . . . the cage that held Dayan was infinitely elastic."[47] The cage, in a sense, is a figure for the psychic oppression that the occupation creates for the occupier.

Neither Katzman nor Uri believes in the occupation—in contrast to the messianic Israeli settlers who believe the West Bank is their birthright. Katzman, toward the end of the novel, says that the occupation turns everyone "into hostages,"[48] but he rejects Uri's acting through the radical notion of "absolute justice": "[Khilmi and Uri are] talking about absolute values. Either the army withdraws from all the territories or else—Uri dies."[49] For Katzman, absolute justice is a "cowardly evasion of commitment . . . an invention of weaklings . . . a hormone secreted from my brain."[50] Katzman believes that absolute justice paralyzes people from what needs to be done to secure oneself against the world. At this moment, Katzman—oddly enough—begins to look more like Adil in *Wild Thorns*, and Uri more like Usama. While Uri clearly is a character with whom it may be easier to identify (after all, he is the peace activist of the work), his passionate, naïve idealism causes danger for others as perilous as Usama's. Grossman's novel complicates a liberal longing for the heroic, conscience-muscled Jew who follows universal values against the will of the state; the ending solidifies that perhaps those willing to break the impasse may not be the ones whom we expect.

Though Katzman believes Uri is after absolute justice, the novel suggests Uri's outrage against the occupation comes from his own profound experience of helplessness at the collective punishment leveled against ordinary people. When youth of the town of Andal where Uri works throw a stone and strike an Israeli soldier, Katzman orders that the donkey that the soldiers kill in the ensuing "battle" should remain in the center of the town. The decaying donkey becomes, in Uri's eyes, the stinking embodiment of the occupation, whose stench is an undeniable truth. The dead animal, the mute creature unable to speak through its pain, becomes too much for Uri to bear: "I could forgive [Katzman] everything except the donkey."[51] Yet arguably what drives Uri equally crazy is how the Palestinians seem to put up with this festering presence:

> Once, just before sunset, a man in an undershirt walked over with a sack and began to winnow flour right in front of the donkey, flour for baking pita bread. Then an old woman led her husband out to sit beside the man, and a few minutes later they were joined by three old men. One was smoking a hookah, and I could almost hear the water bubble in the pipe. Fine white flour flew in the evening breeze and landed gently on the donkey carcass. Another old man rolled himself a cigarette. He sealed it with the slow movement of his tongue. Two little schoolgirls wearing uniforms skipped gaily past the donkey. I started the jeep and took off, oblivious to everything.[52]

The scene of everyday life continuing, despite the donkey corpse at the center of everything, disturbs Uri to the point of deserting the army and giving himself up to Khilmi. Rather than seeing the actions of the Palestinians as a profound act of survival, of maintaining daily life despite the butchery at the center of life—another articulation of *sumūd*—Uri (like Usama in *Wild Thorns*) appears to interpret it as a kind of submission and defeat.

While for Uri, the donkey becomes the traumatic embodiment of the occupation, and turns him to rebel, for Khilmi, the death of his son Yazdi brings him to reject his formerly "passive resistance"[53] and remove himself from the legal web of occupation—"those poisoned webs they weave around us, more deadly than naked hatred"[54]—and burn his *huwiya*, the identity card that grants him legal status under military law. Like Antigone mourning her brother, Khilmi removes himself from the web of symbolic order to weave his own web of narrative and, now, agency through violence. Though Khilmi has threatened, since the beginning of the novel, to cease his storytelling, his incantatory narrative persists—though now it is filled with a catalogue of humiliations that life under occupation entails. In this contradiction, again, Grossman dramatizes fiction's power and danger—that, in becoming an organizing principle of understanding the world, fiction can exclude that which runs counter to itself. In this heteroglossic novel, Grossman attempts to forge a fiction that can contain, but not domesticate or destroy, the multiple truths interwoven at the heart of the conflict between Israelis and Palestinians.

Toward the ending, Khilmi tells a story of having flown that reveals a stunning metaphor. The story itself is Khilmi's fabular way of describing how, years ago, a dynamite truck of oil speculators blows up and kills all the men of the town. This story contains the image of a map that covers everything in his town and world. This map, an image of Cartesian notions of spatial control, industrial capitalism's thirst for oil, and Zionist desire for the land, and of fictionality itself, captures the novel's ambivalence about its own claims for truth:

> a kind of silken map, which the four white youths unfurled . . . the map spread endlessly . . . the map continued to unfurl in their soft hands, and a shadow fell across the crowd as the map flew above them, and the four youths separated father and farther, climbing over hill and dale, and through the silken map with its red arrows and shining stars. . . . I realized I, too, was under the sheer silk, yet I could see above it and watch the youths vanish to the four winds of heaven, and like mildew spreading, there appeared on it a silhouette of the iron monster [the train]. [55]

Like fiction itself, like all grand narratives, the map both locates and threatens to suffocate Khilmi in his town. Yet the map, and the whole town, explodes when a bystander lights a match. In Khilmi's story, Grossman attempts to give voice to the subaltern, to the one who is being mapped, whose stories cannot be heard.

The Smile of the Lamb, in this way, advances farther than *Wild Thorns* in its imagination of characters from both nationalities. Yet Grossman's authorial identification with these characters does not preclude his admonition about the dangers of identification. Identification, as a psychological process of imagining oneself in the life of another, has powerful political possibilities; yet, as the criticisms of identification have shown, identification can be a powerful way of erasing the other. In Uri's powerful identification with Khilmi, Grossman dramatizes how such identification can lead to powerful cross-national acts of solidarity, or—more menacingly—to one's own death (as Khilmi has resolved to kill "adoptive" son Uri rather than let him go, as he let his own son go). Similarly, in *Wild Thorns*, when Adil suddenly recognizes his father's face in the Israeli soldier about to demolish his house, he decides to leave his father's kidney machine behind, leading to his death. Identification's peril—like fiction's peril—is that in imagining the other we risk erasing the other, we risk erasing ourselves.

For all of Grossman's labors on behalf of protesting the occupation and imagining the possibilities of cross-national identification, *The Smile of the Lamb*'s conclusion courts a return to the same problematic dynamic inherent in Israeli literature. Katzman, in what can only be described as an act of sacrificial love—an act of the father sacrificing himself for *his* symbolic son, Uri—storms Khilmi's cave alone to save Uri, and is shot dead by Khilmi. Yet, just prior to the shooting, Uri does not look any longer like a lamb: "It isn't the smile of the lamb anymore, it's a grimacing mask of evil."[56] Brenner argues that "Uri ultimately fails to transform the legacy of love into a stepping stone enabling a dialogue between the warring parties . . . [and] though the two characters have exchanged positions, the positions themselves have not changed."[57] Whether we read the ending as Katzman's successful transformation into a loving being or Uri's regression to monstrosity, we must also consider Khilmi's fate; as in the ending of Yehoshua's "Facing the Forests," the Palestinian is dragged away by law enforcement, while the symbolic exchange between Uri and Katzman remains central. Thus, the Palestinian becomes simply the obstacle that an Israeli character requires to find redemption.

The final sentences of the novel return to the oppressive image of spatial control. In analyzing the land rhetoric of Israelis and Palestinians, Parmenter argues that "the idea of land transformed into a topographic map constitutes a profound negation of rootedness."[58] Grossman pursues and develops that image to one not simply of topography, but one of the complex distancing apparatus of military surveillance, of land as a set of squared coordinates: "As they make their way down the path, someone runs up carrying a folded stretcher, and far away, in the city of Jerusalem, a helicopter takes off and the pilot traces the little squares on a military map with his finger, searching for Andal."[59] At novel's end, then, we have the inexorable reassertion of military distancing, of a seemingly impossible gap between Israeli and Palestinian realities. The city of Jerusalem—the spiritual heart of both Israeli and Palestinian life—here signifies the center of state power, from which the apparatus of control extends. The pilot's finger may be able to locate Andal, the small Palestinian town, on his map, but Andal will not be found.

Endings (as) Beginnings

Ironically, then, while *The Smile of the Lamb* arguably extends the possibilities of cross-national identification and solidarity implicit in *Wild Thorns*, Grossman's novel does not offer any imagination of what coexistence might look like. In both *Wild Thorns* and *The Smile of the Lamb*, the final scenes leave us with a powerful sense that nothing has changed. While *The Smile of the Lamb* represents the reassertion of military order and domination, *Wild Thorns* ends with a scene of life in the marketplace that is a precise repetition of one that occurs toward the beginning of the novel. However, what has changed as a result of each novel is, perhaps, the reader's understanding of the situation—by imaginative identification, by the virtual *living-through* that novels enable. As Brenner has shown in her profound study, "These literatures [dissent] from the widely accepted ideological propagation of the irreparable antagonism between Palestinian and Jewish national groups" and show that "the two literatures affirm a complex yet indissoluble affinity between the two communities."[60] The very fact of the numerous parallels in these novels—their careful and critical dramatization of life under occupation, their imaginative attempts to leap into understanding the heterogeneous subjectivities who must cope with the effects of occupation, their longing for images of coexistence—suggests a solidarity between (at least some) Israelis and Palestinians that most media narratives obfuscate.

Further, these novels speak not only to Israelis and Palestinians, to readers of Hebrew and Arabic, but also to all of us who read the works in translation. Implicitly, each of these novels bridles against the limited way that these national readers might conceive of their nation's dilemmas, and imagines and appeals to an international audience as well. Though the cultural work that each novel engages is slightly different, when we read contrapuntally, we can see how *Wild Thorns* represents Palestinian life not only to Palestinians, but to Israelis or American as well—showing the pain of occupation but also the complexity of Palestinian responses to it, and posing multiple modes of resistance against each other. Khalifeh herself once remarked that "you cannot liberate the Arabs without liberating the Israelis; you cannot liberate the Israelis without liberating the Americans."[61] Ultimately, while Khalifeh "does not present a viable alternative to the nationalist vision," she does dramatize the irreconcilable elements of the nationalist rhetoric with the experience of those whom that rhetoric seeks to employ as victims for the patrimony of the generation of 1948.[62] We can see how *The Smile of the Lamb* presents a dramatic argument for the way in which the traumatic past of Jewish suffering and the reactions to those traumas has led to an occupation that has made Israelis prisoners to their own military victory.

Perhaps Emile Habiby is correct when he says that "the literary portrayal of Jews and Arabs, each in the works of the other, will not change even when we know one another better and write about each other as individuals—the change will occur only after a political solution is found, which will bring normalization and peace between the two nations."[63] At the same time, these novels have acted as a kind of vanguard for a future coexistence, insofar as they not only dramatize the hectic present, but humanize the peoples that it represents. Sadly, some thirty years after the publication of *Wild Thorns*, and twenty-five after the publication of *The Smile of the Lamb*, the novels continue to speak to the ongoing conflict grinding on in Israel and Palestine, and to the largely absent coverage of the human tragedy that falls beneath the politically charged narrations and mappings of the conflict in the United States.

What Khalifeh's novel offers us today, in its recognition of the economic interdependence of Israel and Palestine, is perhaps a rejection of the short-sightedness of the two-state solution, or at least a rejection of the idea that Palestinian sovereignty is the ultimate positive goal for Palestinians. What we need to see is not the extricability of the Palestinian state from the Israeli occupation of the West Bank and Gaza, but the inextricability of Palestinian and Israeli futures. Though there are many reasons to reject a single democratic state, the notion of a single democratic state option that once was "formally introduced by al-Fatah . . . in 1968,"[64] is again being proposed by such intellectuals as Ali Abunimah. In the two-state solution, a traditional (in both senses of the term) nationalism suggests no transformation of society, but a retrenchment of old values; it fails to recognize what has been called "the facts on the ground": that 20 percent of the Israeli population is Arab, and that a sizeable portion of the

West Bank has been annexed through an aggressive policy of settlement by Israelis. Much work remains to be done—work that necessarily implicates the United States, given its historic role in complicating the peace process by abetting the military occupation and settlement of the West Bank simply to initiate the first steps toward mutual recognition. Mutual recognition would move beyond a grudging delivery of land or peace. It must include and become a postnationalist articulation of the common goals of cultural survival. In the end, it may be that the walls of nationalism need to be erected, in order that, at some future date, they will be seen as no longer necessary—and will fall almost of their own accord. Yet the probings of the common life done by Khalifeh and Grossman are suggestive of the initial imaginings of two nations in search of a common future.

2007

CHAPTER SEVEN

"Nothing Will Stop Me from Writing What I See"

An Interview with Sahar Khalifeh

Sahar Khalifeh is the author of eleven novels in Arabic, translated into English, Hebrew, Italian, French, German, and other languages. She has received numerous awards, including the Fulbright, the Peace Award from the Women of Color Association of Iowa, the Alberto Moravia Award for International Fiction, the Qassim Amin medal for Women's Writing, the Naguib Mahfouz Award, the Simone de Beauvoir Prize, the Dubai Al-Thaqafiya Magazine Prize, and others. She is a finalist for the 2019 Neustadt Prize for International Literature, also known as the American Nobel.

Khalifeh is among the finest Arab women novelists in the twentieth century, shining a light on the struggles of Palestinians—particularly Palestinian women—under military occupation and patriarchy. Born in Nablus in 1941, Sahar Khalifeh was the fifth girl to arrive to her parents, who saw her as a burden. She sought escape from the strictures imposed upon her by reading, painting, and writing. She was subject to an abusive arranged marriage that lasted thirteen years and produced two cherished daughters. Finally able to extricate herself, Khalifeh made a radical decision. At age thirty-two, she went back to school. She would earn her bachelor's degree from Birzeit University and then, after publishing her first books, including the classic *Wild Thorns*, received a Fulbright to study at the University of Iowa's International Writers Workshop. She would go on to receive her master's degree from the University of North

Carolina and her PhD in Women's Studies and American Literature from the University of Iowa.

Al-Subar (translated into English as *Wild Thorns*), published in 1976, was an instant classic. Characteristic of all her work is its intimate descriptions of the predicaments of ordinary Palestinians, struggling against traditional values and military occupation. Her controversial *Bab al-Saha* (translated into English as *Passage to the Plaza* in 2020), published in Arabic in 1990, is equally a classic—a vivid and unforgettable depiction of the difficult lives of women living under the double oppression of military occupation and patriarchy. After helping to found the Union of Palestinian Writers in the years before the Intifada, she left after bruising criticism from male leftists and Islamists, and decided to study in the United States. She returned to Palestine in 1988, and founded the Women's Affairs Center in Nablus, West Bank. She opened additional branches in Gaza City, the West Bank in 1991, and Amman, Jordan in 1994.

The interview was conducted via email in August-September 2019.

PHILIP METRES (PM): Do you remember the first story or stories you wrote? What drew you to writing in the first place? How did it feed something in you?

SAHAR KHALIFEH (SK): I started with poetry. It was immediately after we were occupied by the Israeli army in June 1967. The defeat, occupation, and my discovery of our incapacities as a nation shook me so much, it was like an earthquake. For the first time in my life, I mingled with our refugees who were driven by the Israeli army from their villages. Three days after our defeat, we woke up to find Nablus full of those villagers. Hundreds of them took refuge under the olive trees that surrounded my home. Children, old men and women, dogs and donkeys, all were sleeping under the trees, under the bare sky, for weeks. They were without food, water, or shelter. It was just horrible. I, with a group of volunteers, had to offer help. That was the time I discovered our Palestinian reality, our real reality. A few months after that I started writing poetry. After writing a dozen poems, I realized that poetry was not enough. It did not satisfy my anguish. A complex, devastating situation like ours with so much fear, anger, helplessness, and agony needed a wider, deeper, more explanatory type of writing. So I moved to the novel. In the novel, one is an artist, but one can also be a social scientist, a politician, and a psychiatrist. This is where I found myself. My first novel, which was about the first weeks of occupation, was never published. The original copy was confiscated by the Israelis and the draft was confiscated by my husband, ex-husband. It was lost, forever lost. But that was the beginning.

PM: That is a loss indeed. Yet your second published novel *Wild Thorns* (*Al-Subar*) is such a strikingly polyphonic dramatization of the Palestinian predicament living under Israeli military occupation. Of the many textured characters, Adil seems to be at the heart of the story. When he counters his radical cousin Usama with the admonishment, "There's more than one dimension to the picture," he embodies your kaleidoscopic way of seeing and being as a Palestinian. Adil's resistance is *sumūd*—his steadfastness, his staying put, simply not giving up and leaving, is his resistance to occupation, his final stand. Existence is resistance, as the motto goes. Yet he also decides to leave his father's kidney machine in the house, which would lead to his father's inevitable death. The novel is, frankly, a devastating tragedy, and I've taught it every year that I've taught Palestinian and Israeli literatures because, forty years after its publication, it still feels timely and prophetic (about the Intifada). In a sense, the novel shows the two sides to *sumūd*. On the one hand, Adil persists. On the other, Adil's reality is no different at the end of the novel. Does the novel feel even more prophetic, as Palestinian armed resistance fails, and the nonviolent *sumūd* is co-opted by the Oslo Accords of 1993 between Israel and the Palestine Liberation Organization?

SK: Yes, for Adil, existence is resistance. The first thing we learned from the 1948 catastrophe is not to leave our homes and our land. The moment we left, strangers from Europe, America, Australia, and Africa came and kidnapped those homes and usurped our land. Their excuse for that theft is that those homes and land have been theirs three thousand years ago. Who believes that? Even their leaders who started the whole process of establishing Israel did not believe it. They were secular. They were not religious at all. Most of those leaders were socialists, starting the kibbutz system where people live a shared life, including raising their children.

They were the ones who made the Soviets believe that Israel will be a socialist state. That is why the Soviet Union was among the first in the world to recognize Israel as an independent state in 1948.

On the other hand, if we accept the Israelis' claim that they were the grandsons and daughters of the Jews who lived three thousand years ago in Palestine we can also adopt that claim. Why? Because no one in Palestine knows for sure who his ancestors are. Who are the ancestors of the Christians? Were they Jews or what? And who are the ancestors of the Muslims of Palestine? Christians or Jews or both? Who can tell? Who can absolutely be sure? All we are sure of now is that we Palestinians, Muslims and Christians, have been living in this land for thousands of years. Who are our ancestors? We don't know. Who cares to know? All we care about now, including my character Adil, is to have our right to live in this land as real human beings and enjoy our human rights. Is this possible under Israeli military rule? Of course not. So, among us are those who believe we have to fight for those rights and others who can see that we are not yet qualified for that fight. We Palestinians, and Arabs in general, are at the moment very weak and divided. Unless we are strong and united, we can never be free. This is how I see things. This is how people like my character Adil see things too. That's why Adil left his father's kidney machine in the house, which would lead to his father's death. His father is the symbol of the rotten patriarchal Arab regimes and system. Only when we get rid of those regimes and that system we will never be free, even if we were liberated from Israeli military rule.

As for Oslo, it was a stupid move on our leaders' part. If they studied Israeli history and the Zionist plans they would have known that the Zionist goal is to devour all Palestine. The Israelis will never give up any part of Palestine as long as we are so weak and divided. Do you think that men like Adil's father can succeed in obtaining a part of Palestine through Oslo or something similar to Oslo? Of course not. They are so shallow and ignorant. They are not qualified to be the head of the family nor the head of our people. So the kidney machine must go. Adel's father must die. This process will take time. It has already started in different parts of the Arab world. Can you see that?

PM: I'd like to add a follow-up about Adil's decision (or lack of decision) to leave the kidney machine in the house before it is demolished. It happens right after he seems to have mistaken the Israeli soldier for the general that Usama (Adil's militant cousin) had stabbed earlier in the book: "That face! That man! You carried his daughter on your back! You stripped off his stars and carried his daughter. You carried a human being. And you felt your own sense of humanity swell and deepen as you became aware of the Israeli officer as a human being. You father, too, you've carried him for a long time. " I've always wondered whether this misidentification—and his empathy—leads to his decision that things needed to be changed. If I've read it correctly, is it safe to say that the novel forces us to confront how empathy is both dilatory and dangerous?

SK: Yes, you are right. Empathy in such cases is dilatory and dangerous. When it comes to fighting for liberation, unless one is naïve or stupid, one would not empathize with his enemies. We should never empathize with a dictator or an occupier. For example, I cannot, and should not, empathize with the Jews when it comes to crushing us and stealing our homes and land. I cannot. I should not say: because the Jews suffered in Europe and because they were annihilated by the Nazis it is okay if they annihilated us. The Jews of Palestine were living among us just like the Christians, as part of our social network until the Zionists invaded us. Jews of Palestine were our friends and neighbors. When the Zionists came into Palestine, those friends and neighbors turned to occupiers. How can I empathize with Jews coming from Europe or Jews living in Palestine when they turn to occupiers? Besides, it is not Palestinians or Arabs who made the Jews suffer. Europe did that. If Europe wanted to solve the Jewish problem and make up for their sins, why should we pay the price? They could have given them a part of the British Empire or a part of France or even a part of the USA. Would the Americans accept giving them California or Florida or even the small state of Rhode Island or Delaware? Of course not. So why should the West think that we accept? Frankly, we don't. And, frankly, we know that we are not strong enough to change what has been done. We also know that the balance of power will not go on unchanged forever.

That is why we are calling now for a sustainable solution that works for both Palestinians and Jews. We are calling for a humane solution that stops the ongoing crimes and bloodshed. One state for all, this is the real, correct, humane, sustainable solution. This might sound ridiculous.

But mind you, history is not counted by decades, not even by centuries. Eventually, this is what will happen despite differences of religion, color, or race. The US is a very good example. Our one state solution in Palestine is even better because we and the Jews have the same ancestors and the same race. I hope you agree.

PM: It's interesting, because I think that your work is deeply imaginative and even empathic, and its depictions of Israelis—particularly in *Of Noble Origins*—is textured and complex, even if they are not at the center. But your perspective reminds me of an interview with Toni Morrison, in which she is asked by a reporter when she will write about white characters in a more substantial way. Morrison responded: "You can't understand how powerfully racist that question is, can you? You could never ask a white author, 'When are you going to write about Black people?'"

SK: I believe that we should know our enemy. We should understand how our enemy thinks, plans, and the ways he uses to implement those plans. How could we defend ourselves if we do not know all that? We should even learn from the Israelis. They are ahead of us in such cunning ways in dealing with the international atmosphere and the international media. We have to learn. Our leadership, ignorant as they are, corrupt and self-serving, should be made aware of their ignorance. Our duty as writers and artists is to draw their attention to such matters. We Arabs have to learn how to maneuver, how to plan, and how to deal with our problems in similarly cunning ways. It is not enough to say: because we have the Right, we will eventually get our rights. Or to say like naïve religious people: God is with the Righteous. God has never been with the Righteous. As far as I know, God has always been with the strong, with the clever, with the cunning.

This is what I mean: to learn from our enemy. In order to do that, we should really know our enemy inside out. I started the process. In our Palestinian literature, and Arab literature in general, as far as I know, no writer had written about Israeli characters. No one had tried to delve into the complex psyche of Israelis. It is not easy to do that. On one hand, one has to exert a lot of effort like reading, researching, and encountering to be able to do that. On the other hand, writers might be afraid of being accused of treason, which is what happened to me. Back to your question about empathy, I realize now that I made a mistake. I mistook the word *empathize* with *sympathize*. I agree with you. I did empathize with Jewish characters. I really tried. But this does not mean I sympathize with them. Look how I portrayed the farming professor at the kibbutz in *Of Noble Origins*. From the outside, he looked kind and polite and cooperative. But deep inside, he is a liar. Being such an expert in technology and farming, couldn't he see that the olive trees they were cultivating were very old, hundreds of years old? He kept saying that the Jews who established the kibbutz only a number of years ago were the ones who planted the olive trees. The olive trees were almost as old as Jesus Christ. Yet he insisted that the Jews planted those trees. My Arab character knew the professor was lying.

In contrast, the Israeli officer who was stabbed in *Wild Thorns* was in a different situation. He was wounded, a powerless human being. Here is where sympathy applies, an honest sincere reaction one feels toward the helpless. This has happened several times in real life. Once, an Israeli general, the military governor of Nablus, was bombed while he was driving his car. He was severely wounded. Palestinians hurried to his rescue despite their hatred of his post and his cruel deeds. They carried him and took him to the hospital. Another incident, in fact several incidents, where Israeli drivers, while passing through the occupied territories, had terrible accidents and were injured. The same thing happened. People, my people, hurried to their rescue. And there is another interesting story which is worth telling here. A group of settlers, vicious settlers, had repeatedly attacked a Palestinian village at night and stole goats and cows, and slayed donkeys that refused to be driven out of their barns. One night, the villagers trapped those settlers and caught three of them. Those three settlers were terrified to the extent that they were crying like children. They sat on the ground and started begging and kissing the feet of our villagers and swearing not to steal animals from that village again. Our villagers felt pity for them. They sympathized with them and released them. Here's where we use the word sympathy but not empathy.

PM: Do you ever receive criticism based on how your work centers Palestinian experience, with Israeli Jews at the periphery?

SK: Of course I did. A number of narrow-minded critics did accuse me of treason for doing that. They could not tolerate my objective way of looking at us in a way different than the way we traditionally look at ourselves. In *Of Noble Origins*, I simply made a comparison between the clever up-to-date Jews coming from the West and the naïve, simple-minded, out-of-date Arabs. Those critics were angry because I showed how Israeli agriculture is healthier and the Israeli fruits are bigger and nicer. Coming from the West meant that Western Jews had access to Western, modern ways. While Arabs, living under the archaic rule of the Ottoman Empire for more than five hundred years, made them slow and out-of-date. Those critics did not understand my intentions. They were angry because in comparison with the Jews, my Arab characters sounded slow-minded and helpless. But we are helpless. In reality, we are still helpless. One has to be blind not to see that. I am not blind. So let those critics write and say what they like. Do I care? Of course I do. But this will not stop me from writing what I believe is right.

PM: I'm very excited about the forthcoming publication of the first translation of *Passage to the Plaza* (*Bab al-Saha*). Set during the First Intifada, the novel takes us into the world of three women—Nuzha, a sex worker who has been ostracized by the neighbors; Zakiya, an elderly midwife and a person of faith; and Samar, an educated scholar studying the impacts of the uprising on women. It is a very courageous book, unflinchingly exploring the dark side of patriarchal oppression in Palestinian villages. Yet it also feels like the other "wing" of the Palestinian bird, a sort of feminist mirror to *Wild Thorns*, which is really about Palestinian masculinity. The book asks: What is Palestine, in the end, if Palestinian women are not liberated as well? Was it a difficult book to write, and how was it received?

SK: The book was not received with the same enthusiasm as *Wild Thorns*. But that was at the beginning. Things have changed a little since then. Many writers, artists, academicians, and educated people have changed their views since then. The number of educated, enlightened women has risen too. Women became more active socially and politically. They became more aware of their status as second-class citizens. But still it is a long way to go. Oppression against women is everywhere in the Arab world and not just in villages. Women are still killed or ostracized whenever they are suspected of having sexual or emotional affairs. The social system, family system, even the judicial system are all prejudiced against women. It is not easy to be a woman in the Arab world. One has to be a real fighter to work for change. For many years, I have been criticized because of my feminist views. Even by women, many of whom thought I was out of my mind. I was with only a few women like Nawal El Saadawi and Fatima Mernissi who started writing and fighting for women's rights. The number of women fighters has multiplied since then.

Passage to the Plaza was written during the First Intifada, almost thirty years ago. We have a new generation of highly educated women now. But the situation and the status of women have not really changed. So you can imagine how this book was received at that time. If this book did not talk about Israeli occupation too, it would have been completely ignored. But since it talked about the different layers of suppression women suffer from, including the Israeli occupation, our political and social leadership could not tell our readers to stop buying it. Now *Passage to the Plaza* is among my bestselling novels. I also receive positive comments from university students, especially girls. Many academic studies have been done about this book. I am grateful. Back to your question whether it was difficult to write: my answer is definitely not. In fact, I enjoyed writing it because I know most of its characters. I depicted real characters from real life. I empathized with them. In fact, I am one of them. I wanted to defend them and defend myself. I too, as a woman, have suffered a lot from our social system and our out-of-date values. Things have to be changed. Someone has to lead the way. I am glad and proud of being among those who started the process.

PM: Is the predicament of Palestinian women similar to the events depicted in *Passage to the Plaza*, nearly thirty years later? (We recently read the news of the murder of Israa in Bethlehem, allegedly at the hand of her brother.) I know you have been centrally involved with supporting Palestinian women with your work in Women's Affairs Centers in Nablus and elsewhere. Can you talk about that work? And how has life changed on the ground with women?

SK: Israa is just one victim of our value system. Thousands of women through the ages have been killed for similar reasons. Under the pretext of defending the family's honor, women are beaten, imprisoned at home, pushed into forced marriages, or killed. This has been going on for ages and no one has been able to stop it. Even when thinkers like Qasem Amin called for women's liberation, very few have listened. No one among the ruling class men really cared. Unless women themselves fight for themselves no one is ready to fight for them. To fight means to pay the price. That price would include being ridiculed, ostracized, or even physically beaten. How many men are ready to do that for women? Even among the best of them men are reluctant and ashamed of doing it even if they believed in it. They are afraid of being frowned upon. They are also afraid of losing their privileges as men. Now many women are aware of that. They finally know that if they did not fight for themselves no one would really do it.

The question was: Should we fight as individuals or on the communal level? Our fight started with individuals who became role models for others. A number of individuals had the means and guts to start associations, clubs, centers, or just active groups where women meet, discuss, learn, and apply. I was among the first who started the fight. In the centers that I established and worked for, I started by teaching young women, university students, to make studies and research about women in different fields. I wanted those women to learn how to be specific in dealing with their own problems. I wanted them to see for themselves that all women in different fields and different backgrounds are being dealt with as second-class citizens, and many, the majority, as slaves. Even women of the ruling class do not enjoy equality or respect. Look at what is happening to Princess Haya bint Hussein. Look at what is happening to her husband's daughters. Princess Haya ran away from her cruel husband in Dubai, but his daughters are still in jail. Have a look at the internet and read what is happening to those women who are supposed to be rich and powerful. I am only giving examples of what's really going on, not only in Palestine but in the whole Arab world.

In our situation in Palestine, we are living in a unique situation under military rule and the international media focuses on the Palestinian militant women. Ironically, we are only militant against the Israeli soldiers, but not against our dictatorial fathers, brothers, husbands, and even sons. I tried to show this reality in *Passage to the Plaza*. Of course, men did not like what I showed. I paid the price. But now, I am earning a different price: awards, admiration, and positive comments.

PM: I loved the historical texture of the novel *Of Noble Origins* and its window into the British Mandate period. It is a highly researched and also imaginative account of the 1920s through the '40s. It's also remarkably nuanced, with its rounded depiction of the (unnamed) British governor, an English feminist, the Jewish daughter of a Hollywood movie magnate, an Arab Jewish family, and other historical figures such as David Ben-Gurion and Ze'ev Jabotinsky. I'd love to know about your process of research for this book, since it brings to life the ambivalence of Palestinians as they faced the radical changes from Jewish immigration and ongoing British rule. And will there be sequels (as it was planned as a trilogy)?

SK: Let me begin by saying that the two sequels are already published in Arabic, and one will come out shortly in English. As for the research I made for *Of Noble Origins*, I had to read and read. I tried to teach myself to write about a period I did not live through. Unlike my other novels, I did not witness what went on during the 1920s through the '40s. I was not born yet. To make up for what I missed I had to read what other witnesses, historians, journalists, and writers have written. To be able to be objective and see things from different angles I had to read what historians and writers from different backgrounds had written: Arab diaries, Arab journalists who lived through that time, Israeli diaries, Israeli historians, and British ones. It was a long difficult process. Many were not readily available. I had to run from one place to another to find them. Finally, after all my reading, I could imagine what went on. I wanted to show others—Palestinians, Arabs, and non-Arabs—what really went on. I wanted to show the stupidity of the Arab ruling class and the exploitative maneuverings of the British mandate. I wanted to show the racist attitudes of the Jewish Zionists. I wanted to show how men and women on both sides, Palestinian and Israeli, deal with their lives within their families and how they deal with each other. How women within the Arab family are victimized and how Israeli friends and neighbors turned into enemies.

All these issues are difficult, complex, and sometimes boring. I had to find artistic ways to make the reading of such a book smooth and appealing. I was not sure I would succeed. Some critics have liked what I have written. Others, a few with reactionary ways of looking at things, accused me of treason. The comparison I made between the European up-to-date Jews and the out-of-date Arabs made them angry. I am used to such narrow-minded reactions. But to be honest, at that time, the reaction upset me. Being a committed writer who worked most of my life for the Palestinian cause made those accusations and insults very painful. In the book I am writing now, I discuss in detail what I felt at that time and what I think now. I also say in my new book, as I always say and do, that nothing will stop me from writing what I see, what I believe. Nothing.

PM: You've recently published your autobiography, and I'm aware that it's being translated. I'd love to know a bit about the impetus for writing it, and what the process revealed to you about your own life and your life work.

SK: My first impetus is to reveal secrets. My secrets as an individual and those of my community. I wanted to tell women, young and old, that breaking the rules is not a crime. Rebelling against our chains is the way not just for liberation, also for creativity. Look at me, before breaking my chains I was an oppressed wife, a narrow-minded being. I was unhappy, miserable, poor, and worth nothing. Now I am a well-known writer, admired, respected, and powerful. My power is in my voice. Others listen. The voiceless can have no audience, no power, no respect, and no fulfillment. Try to do likewise. Here I am in front of you. Take my experience and follow my lead. Those of you who do not like what I say or do, stay where you are but look around. Things are changing. In the age of the internet and social media, where barriers are removed between individuals, communities, and nations, you can't stay hidden, untouched. Here are stories about the brave. I am not alone anymore. There are many brave women who have rebelled and moved forward. Read, open your eyes, open your heart and soul. If I did it and many like me could do it, you also can. Life for the brave is worth living. Step out of your closed homes and look around. There is so much to learn and enjoy. Life is wide and beautiful. Don't stick to your chains. This is what I wanted to say.

PM: How have you changed as a writer over the years, in terms of your approach or style?

SK: I am not sure. When I revise my older novels and see how I developed my characters, I wonder whether I would use the same style and technique in portraying them if I rewrite them. Would I use the same monologues and dialogues? Would I use the same descriptions? Would I use the same vocabulary? For me, the character is the center of the novel's universe. How they talk, how they move, how they think, in which background, the rhythm of life, all should relate and be attached to the character to make it more touchable, more lifelike. The main thing is to balance form and content. When I develop a character from the working class, I should be sincere to his language, his behavior, the rhythm of life that surrounds him. It is different from developing a character who is educated or from the ruling class. Have I succeeded? It is not easy for me to judge. I leave this to my readers and critics. I know that my style, over the years, might have slightly changed but not immensely. Perhaps it has become more subtle and refined, more calculating, because of the numerous revisions I make before I submit my work to publication. Whether this is good or bad, I am not sure. Probably it is good.

PM: What do you value most in terms of your craft? Your translator Sawad Hussain shared that she loves your colloquial use of words, which was surprising for Arabic literary fiction.

SK: What I value most in my craft is my ability to turn politically complicated subjects into smoothly readable works of literature. The simple but multilayered language I use makes my work easy to read despite the difficult questions I raise or the grim atmospheres I portray. My characters are so alive, so convincing, you can almost touch them. This is what most of my readers say. I often receive questions like: Is this character that particular person we know? Is Zakiyya that old midwife who lives on that street? Is Rafif, the educated rebellious woman, a copy of you? I feel great when they ask me such questions because I know then that I succeeded in making my readers believe my fiction. After all, fiction is the game of making believe.

PM: What is a day in the life of Sahar Khalifeh like? What gets you up in the morning? And what keeps you writing?

SK: Now I am retired from working for the Women Affairs Centers. So I just focus on my writing. I wake up very early in the morning, around six a.m. I write while I am still in bed. Most of the time I write with an old-fashioned pencil. While I am half awake, half dreaming, I write fiction. If I need to write nonfiction, I do that out of bed while I am fully awake. I spend around three to four hours writing. I have my coffee while writing. In the middle of writing, I have a short break, only a few minutes to have a small breakfast and then go back to writing. When I finish writing, I do my errands, house chores, things like that. After that, I leave to do exercise in a nearby club. I am aware of my need for being physically healthy. At noon, I have lunch, a good nap, and around five p.m., I start reading. I read for at least two hours. I spend my evenings mostly alone with my TV listening to the news and watching a movie or getting together with my two daughters and two granddaughters who live in the same building. I live a very limited social life. When I was younger, I was socially active. Now I don't have that luxury. I save my energies for the next day to wake up early for writing. It is a simple, well-organized, well-programmed life. I am satisfied and in a way happy.

PM: What advice would you give to young writers, particularly writers from marginalized groups?

SK: Make your writing your priority. Put your heart and soul in your writing. Write what you believe is right and beautiful. Be a professional. Live a programmed, organized life. Writing is not just entertaining. Of course, art has to be entertaining. But this is not all. Good writing, serious writing should be entertaining and meaningful. Sometimes, when you have a cause, your writing includes fighting. Be ready to do that and be ready to pay the price. Writing also includes reading, a lot of reading. We need to keep learning from other experiences, from different ways of looking at things, and following up with new styles and techniques. This is the advice I keep reminding myself of. Sometimes I fail to stick to my rules. This is natural. But I keep trying. I hope this works for you as it worked for me. Keep trying.

PM: How would you like to be remembered?

SK: As a writer who spoke for the voiceless, the powerless, the beaten, and the ostracized.

2020

CHAPTER EIGHT

Teaching (Beyond) the Conflict

A Contrapuntal Reading of Savyon Liebrecht's "A Room on the Roof" and Ghareeb Asqalani's "Hunger"

> There were no guns at the PLO Research Center, no ammunition, and no fighters. But there was evidently something more dangerous—books about Palestine, old records and land deeds belonging to Palestinian families, photographs about Arab life in Palestine, historical archives about the Arab community in Palestine, and, most important, maps—maps of pre-1948 Palestine with every Arab village on it before the state of Israel came into being and erased many of them. . . . You could read it in the graffiti the Israelis boys left behind on the Research Center Walls: *Palestinian? What's that?* And *Palestinians, fuck you*, and *Arafat, I will hump your mother.*[1]

At the heart of Palestinian narratives is the question of the "permission to narrate"[2] itself. In the face of the Zionist narrative—backed so fiercely by United States imperial interests and institutions—Palestinian stories seem to disappear. This erasure was made literal again in 2014, when Diane Sawyer reported that Israelis had been attacked by Palestinian bombs, while CBS showed footage of Palestinians in Gaza being bombed by Israel.[3] Yet even Thomas Friedman, long an imperial cheerleader, notes that the very facts of Palestinian history presented such a threat to Israel's narrative that, upon invading Lebanon in 1982, the Israeli Defense Force headed first to the PLO Research Center to abscond with its archive.

This perverse situation animates my ongoing thinking of how I teach Palestinian literature—and how this literature comes to be produced, circulated, and received. Since 2006, I have been teaching a course called

Israeli and Palestinian Literatures in a contrapuntal way. Yet the continued dispossession of Palestinians has caused me to question continually the impression that the course gives students. Although I began teaching Israeli and Palestinian Literatures with the purpose of highlighting the moral imagination evident in both literatures, and with the possibility that literature might offer a vision that the so-called peace process had not, I became increasingly uneasy that I was leaving students with the false impression that the conflict was as symmetrical as the authors' exercise in moral imagination. I found that I needed to foreground the tension between exploring the moral imagination and accounting for the vast asymmetry of power between Israel and the Palestinians. Not surprisingly, because of an increased attention on social media, larger numbers of students are entering the class with knowledge of the Palestinian story.

This chapter explores, first, the rationale for teaching Palestinian literature using a contrapuntal method and makes a case for a peacebuilding pedagogy that still accounts for the fact that Israel maintains almost complete hegemony over Palestinian life in Israel and the occupied territories. Second, I demonstrate the possibilities of contrapuntal analysis of Savyon Liebrecht's story "A Room on the Roof," told from the point of view of an Israeli woman who hires three Palestinians to build a room for her, alongside Ghareeb Asqalani's story "Hunger," which tells the story of Sa'id, a Palestinian worker, from his point of view. Finally, I render explicit the promise and perils of teaching Palestinian literature in this way, highlighting the complication of "teaching while Arab" in the United States, which has itself changed since I began teaching. Through a critical reflection on my experience teaching this class and on the ways in which I have been situating myself in relation to the material, I hope to provide a resource to others who would like to teach Palestinian or Israeli literature from a framework that looks for and anticipates a transformation of the conflict and the establishment of a just peace.

Why Teach Palestinian and Israeli Literatures Contrapuntally?

Because I focus on Palestinian and Israeli literatures together in my class, I actively court cognitive dissonance—my own and the students'—enacting what Edward Said, in *Culture and Imperialism*, calls "contrapuntal reading."[4] Said's contrapuntal reading represents a third way of reading postcolonial literature and the literature of empire, the first two being the politics of blame and the politics of colonial triumphalism. Said articulates a path that will enable us, reading the story of Palestine through Palestinian and Israeli literature, to see how "intertwined and overlapping histories"[5] already exist and to offer ways to begin imagining a just peace.

His contrapuntal reading rhymes well with John Paul Lederach's *The Moral Imagination*, whose subtitle is "The Art and Soul of Building Peace." Lederach enumerates the moral imagination's four disciplines as

> the capacity to imagine ourselves in a web of relationships that includes our enemies; the ability to sustain a paradoxical curiosity that embraces complexity without reliance on dualistic polarity; the fundamental belief in and pursuit of the creative act; and the acceptance of the inherent risk of stepping into the mystery of the unknown that lies beyond the far too familiar landscape of violence.[6]

Lederach's emphasis on the need for cultivating empathy, curiosity, creativity, and courage might appear to be ineffectual liberalism, given the obstacles that Palestinians face. But his work reminds us that peace requires as much preparation as war. In fact, peacebuilding is probably more difficult, given the human propensity for exacting revenge and acting out of fear. Said's contrapuntal reading and Lederach's theory of the moral imagination meet at the intersection where we "imagine ourselves in a web of relationships that includes our enemies." Including one's enemies, of course, does not require one to accept their conditions. In contrast to the mainstream liberal discourse of peacemaking, Lederach argues that we should resist the assumption that peacebuilding is merely a balancing of perspectives, that there can be no normalization or reconciliation without justice:

> We must understand and feel the landscape of protracted violence and why it poses such deep-rooted challenges to constructive change. In other words we must set our feet deeply into the geographies and realities of what destructive relationships produce, what legacies they leave, and what breaking their violent patterns will require . . . [and] we must explore the creative process itself, not as a tangential inquiry, but as the wellspring that feeds the building of peace.[7]

If we do not analyze fully and remorselessly the nature of destructive relationships, if we do not understand and address what has fueled the conflict and oppression, we risk moving too quickly to a false or unjust peace. To read contrapuntally is to hear with both ears, to see with both eyes, outside the frames offered by mainstream media or ideological propaganda. It does not mean, in the case of Israel/Palestine, to seek balance or coexistence at all costs; on the contrary, as Marcy Jane Knopf-Newman has explored in *The Politics of Teaching Palestine to Americans*, coexistence projects have tended to obfuscate the causes of Palestinian resistance, to undermine historical analysis, and to normalize oppression.[8] Peacebuilding must define peace through prisms of both justice and security. Situating itself critically and empathically at the point of intersection of national frames, it must resist the binarism that wars and sectarianism require.

Background Research

Israeli and Palestinian Literatures, an introductory-level course, emerged from my study and teaching of war literature, postcolonial theory, and peace studies. Through a contrapuntal reading of literary and historical narratives of Israel/Palestine, with a special emphasis on works that activate or embody the moral imagination, I try to model for students how literature might contribute to a real peace process, one that addresses the crucial final-status issues, especially the plight of Palestinian refugees. I want to show that understanding the politics of representation can provide a way to see that conflicts are not eternal and inevitable but historically specific and therefore resolvable.

In my initial research, I was stunned by the cultural intervention of both Palestinian and Israeli literatures. Considered together, they offer critical insights into how the relationship between the Israeli state and the Palestinians has affected and is affecting both sides. Because my focus in this chapter is on Palestinian literature, it is important for me to point to Israeli writers who have undergone unsparing self-criticism, bearing witness to the pain of Palestinian dispossession—beginning with the 1948 *nakba* (النكبة ; "catastrophe") and through the continuing occupation (particularly after the 1967 *naksa* (النكسة ; "setback")—becoming voices of conscience that hark back to the Hebrew prophetic tradition. S. Yizhar (the pen name of Yizhar Smilansky) in particular merits attention for his

Khirbet Khizeh (חרבת חזעה), an unvarnished portrayal of the destruction of a Palestinian village by Israeli forces in 1948. Other writers, such as Amos Oz and David Grossman, have explored the moral damage of the military occupation of the West Bank and Gaza Strip. At their best, they have not only represented the contradictions of Israeli society and the moral ugliness of occupation and dispossession but also, at moments, have challenged their own liberal Zionist (yet often Orientalist) frames of reference.

I disagree with Elias Khoury's incisive but perhaps dated and too quickly dismissive reading of Israeli literature's representations of Palestinians:

> How is the Palestinian represented? Either he doesn't speak because he is deaf and dumb and exists only in Hannah's dreams in [Amos Oz's] "My Michael"; or the Palestinians are part of the geography, as in Yizhar, or even for Oz in his short story "Nomad and Viper." In Yehoshua, the Palestinian is mute or a child, like Na'im in "The Lover." Even with David Grossman—the most open of the writers—in, say, "The Smile of the Lamb," the Palestinian is an insane character.[9]

Khoury is largely correct but collapses the question of engaging otherness with the question of representing the other. Both "The Prisoner," by Yizhar, and "Nomad and Viper," by Oz, can be read easily as deconstructions of Israeli Orientalist attitudes toward Palestinians. Khoury's reading of Khilmi in *The Smile of the Lamb* is reductionist; Khilmi may be half-mad, but he's also a wise and loving proponent of nonviolent resistance (cf. "Vexing Resistance"). Khoury also misses key authors who have engaged Palestinian reality in ways that are far more nuanced, and show far more solidarity, than Grossman's portrayal, such as Savyon Liebrecht (in "The Road to Cedar City") and Aharon Shabtai (in *J'Accuse*). A contrapuntal reading of such works can be mobilized as part of an effort that goes beyond representing what has been called the "beautiful soul" of Zionism to explore the damage done by the racist othering of Palestinians.

Palestinian literature has struggled in its diverse locations against the dispossession, Israeli occupation, and the cultural, economic, and military siege that people have lived through since 1948. Palestinian writers such as Ghassan Kanafani, Emile Habiby, Mahmoud Darwish, Taha

Muhammad Ali, and Sahar Khalifeh, when read alongside Israeli writers challenging the official Zionist myth-narrative of Israeli history, illuminate the human cost of the conflict to Palestinians (and the moral cost to Israelis) despite the ongoing erasure of Palestinian history. These writers help us see the predicaments of Palestinian lives increasingly hemmed in by what Jeff Halper has called the "matrix of control"—his term for the legal, economic, and military frameworks that suffocate Palestinian existence in Israel, the West Bank, and Gaza.[10]

Palestinian writers dramatize how radicalism emerges from conditions of extreme privation and psychological humiliation. Kanafani's *Men in the Sun* (رجال في الشمس) and Khalifeh's *Wild Thorns* (الصبار), for example, confront how Palestinian politics has contributed to and complicated their suffering, how the struggle to satisfy personal desires or family needs can be in conflict with national aspirations. Finally, throughout the corpus of Palestinian writing—as Khoury has noted—we are witness to moments of the moral imagination in which the humanity of Palestinians and Israelis alike is represented.

Contrapuntalism in Practice

In the course, we alternate between Israeli and Palestinian texts and perspectives in specific periods: from the beginnings to 1948, 1948–67, 1967–93, 1993–2000, 2000 to the present. For the first period, we establish the complexity of the origins of the Israel-Palestine conflict, the problem of navigating radically different framings of that history. The first week, students read four brief accounts of Israeli history—a BBC article, an orthodox Zionist take, and that of Ilan Pappé, an anti-Zionist Israeli historian. They then read early Israeli patriotic war poems and Yizhar's story "The Soldier" and consider the debates in Israel regarding the narrative about what happened in 1948 and how Yizhar describes the Israeli soldier's treatment of Arabs. The following week, they read four Palestinian historical accounts of 1948, including the website complement to Walid Khalidi's *All That Remains*, a documentary history of the 1948 *nakba* and the hundreds of destroyed villages of Palestine. This exploration, laying bare the contestedness of history itself, is followed by poems and a story, such as Kanafani's *Men in the Sun* or *Returning to Haifa* (عائد الى حيفاء), which show how 1948 affected the lives of Palestinians.

For many years, students tried to guess my political points of view, but I avoided divulging them, often until the final class. (This semester, during the active genocide in Gaza, I have experimented with being more explicit in my views, while also sharing that I want the classroom to hold space for different views.) After all, reading contrapuntally and cultivating the moral imagination require an ethos of openness and a willingness to refuse the fatalism of received narratives. Though the course admittedly employs an aspirational frame—the final unit is called "Prospects for Peace"—it suggests that history is fundamentally contingent, always in the making; further, it proposes that our positionality is never neutral and that our empowerment involves the loss of the invisibility of United States privilege.

The contrapuntal strategy is valuable because students learn more when they are challenged with contrary viewpoints. They are given greater agency to explore the complex longings and sufferings of Palestinians and Israelis as fellow human beings. Contrapuntal reading also provides inoculation against the virus of racism (whether it be anti-Arab or anti-Jewish), not only because literature activates the moral imagination but also because, at its best, it creates characters irreducible to ideology and stereotype. At the end of my course, students will know the hunger and desperation of Said, from "Hunger," and the ethical uncertainty of the unnamed Israeli female narrator of "A Room on the Roof," who must confront her fantasies and fears about the Palestinian laborers whom she has hired. Students will know these characters better than they may ever know an actual Palestinian or Israeli.

A Case Study: The Post-1967 Occupation in "A Room on the Roof" and "Hunger"

In an article in the *New York Times* written nearly fifty years after the 1967 Arab-Israeli War, Judi Rudoren explores the "double-edged sword"[11] of Israeli jobs for Palestinian workers. If Palestinian laborers once helped build the state of Israel, now their labor supports the illegal settlement of the West Bank. Hassan Jalaita, a mechanic, repairs jeeps for the Israeli army in the Mishor Adumim Industrial Zone inside the West Bank. According to Jalaita, "I feel like I'm not a human being—we are serving the occupation."[12] This dilemma—between earning a living to support one's family and refusing to help an occupying power—has been an ongoing vexation for Palestinian workers. During the 1970s and 1980s, after the 1967 war and before the First Intifada, according to Suha Sabbagh, who uses 1989 figures, about "120,000 laborers were bussed daily to work in Israel, 55% of whom work in construction, the rest in agriculture and industry. Unskilled day labor from the West Bank and Gaza represents 6.5% of the total Israeli work force."[13]

Given the asymmetrical power relationship in which Israelis and Palestinians find themselves, it is not surprising that encounters between them tend to confirm stereotypes and biases about the superiority of one's own culture and the inferiority of the other. Liebrecht's "A Room on the Roof" and Asqalani's "Hunger" both undermine these stereotypes and biases, staging two different encounters, intensely subjective and politically inflected, between Palestinian construction workers and Israeli overseers, in ways that explore how people are challenged by the complex humanity of the other. In both stories, there are crucial moments in which the moral imagination burgeons, but no false reconciliations take place and no panaceas are offered.

In "A Room on the Roof," set in Israel after 1967 during the period of a housing boom, an Israeli woman hires Palestinian workers to build a room on her roof while her husband, Yoel, is away. The central drama of the story, told from her point of view, concerns her struggle to maintain her authority over the workers, whom she feels she cannot trust, and her desire at the same time to be generous to them. Her sudden interest in one of the Palestinians, Hassan, teeters on the verge of (and nearly falls into) romantic love.

"A Room on the Roof" clearly alludes to Virginia Woolf's *A Room of One's Own*, and the story revolves around othernesses—the otherness of female subjectivity in a patriarchal society, the otherness of working-class Palestinians in bourgeois Israeli society. It's almost too easy to read the main character as an allegory for the Israeli state. After all, her independence requires the constant assertion of authority, yet she is an insecure, vulnerable person who has difficulty showing kindness and generosity. She swings between wanting to offer the workers coffee and the use of her kitchen or bathroom and refusing them the money they need to complete the job.

At one point, she has let them use the bathroom but begins to fear that they are readying a terrorist operation, because the knapsack is "the kind that Yoel used to extricate from the storeroom when his unit was called up for maneuvers."[14] It turns out that they are going to a wedding in nearby Tulkarem. For most American students, the narrator becomes a kind of medium by which they measure their own fear of and fascination with the other. They see, in Liebrecht's selectively omniscient exploration of the Israeli woman's thoughts, their own socially constructed thoughts about Palestinians.

The woman slowly shifts from seeing the three Palestinians as "a single person"[15] to being stunned by Hassan's gentleness with her baby son, Udi:

> She heard Hassan talking softly to the baby in Arabic, like a man who loves to talk to his child, in a caressing voice, the words running together in a pleasant flow, containing a high beauty, like the words of a poem in an ancient language which you don't understand, but which well up inside you. Udi, lying tranquilly on his chest, reached out toward Hassan's dark face, and Hassan put his head down toward the little fingers and kissed them. She, stunned by the sight, stood where she was and looked at them, as the tremor inspired by fear gradually died down, and another, new kind of trembling, arose within her, seeing something that, even as it happens, you already yearn for from a distance, knowing that when it passes nothing like it will happen again. And, as though dividing themselves, her thoughts turned to Yoel, whose eyes examined his son with a certain remoteness. Since the baby's birth he had never clasped him to his body and was careful not to wet his clothes or have them smell of wet diapers.[16]

The woman, utterly taken aback by Hassan's interaction with her baby, sees how the baby doesn't care about his background, just his gentleness. Then she is surprised to learn that Hassan can speak English better than she can, that he studied it at the American University of Beirut, and that because of difficulties in life he had to discontinue his studies.[17] The "new kind of trembling" she feels is akin to the vulnerability of attraction. We sense that real change is possible in her, yet we are also aware of the distance that divides Hassan and her. Liebrecht, echoing the moral imagination of each of these characters, encourages the circle of humanity to widen, initiating possibilities of reconciliation.

Yet things go wrong. The Palestinian workers do violate some of her boundaries, and we never quite know if they've done it purposefully or, acting on their cultural codes, unconsciously. Are they cheating her, for example, or do they simply fail to understand her directions, or do they feel that she does not understand what the room addition requires? As she grows afraid of her own vulnerability and lack of authority, her distrust and hostility reemerge. Hassan, insulted by her treatment of him, leaves and doesn't return, and the story ends with the work finally done and the husband back but with her transformation incomplete. When Yoel comes home, she lies about having a "Jewish foreman" and hides the complexity of her feelings. She tells her husband about Hassan but doesn't name the man who "'spoke to [Udi] softly and kissed his fingers.'"[18] Her feelings shock her:

> Suddenly she noticed the softness flowing into her voice, betraying herself to herself, and she added loudly, more stridently than she intended, "But once they made some trouble about the money and tried to trick me by putting iron rods that were too thin. Arabs, you know."[19]

Although she knows better, she reverts to the stereotypes about Arabs prevalent in her culture, to reestablish solidarity with her husband and hide her emotional self-betrayal. This poignant ending shows the subtle ways in which people betray themselves and one another when they perpetuate the ethnocentric mechanisms of othering, the machinery of colonial oppression. But such introspection should not be fetishized: it can be merely a typical operation of the colonial imaginary and a demonstration of the colonizer's inherent moral and intellectual superiority to the colonized. For that reason, it is necessary to read Liebrecht's story alongside a Palestinian story that deals with the same scenario. A contrapuntal reading allows us to dilate that moment of epistemological opening.

Whereas "A Room on the Roof" depicts the complex ambivalence of an Israeli woman's relationship with Palestinians, Asqalani's "Hunger" dramatizes the complexity of the experience of workers who struggle with their complicity in a state-building project that ensures the erasure of their people. By seeing the inner and outer lives of Sa'id, a desperately hungry Gazan construction worker who labors in Israel, we understand better the behavior of the workers in Liebrecht's story. We learn about their physical exhaustion and angry helplessness—their struggle just to get to work every day. Most of all, we become aware of the social and spiritual shame felt by Palestinians who must work in Israel to feed their families. We see in a new light the hidden lives of Hassan, Salah, and Ahmad, who remain ciphers untranslatable to the Israeli woman.

"Hunger" capitalizes on fiction's ability to explore a character's inner thoughts, which the translation emphasizes by italicizing Sa'id's italicized inner monologue; it reveals that Said has been in prison and has a revolutionary past but feels he must prostitute his revolutionary values in order to feed his children. The italicized monologue dramatizes the gap between the stoic exterior of its main character and the pain that seethes within him. Palestinians in Gaza, the story tells us, are imprisoned, behind bars, not only physically but psychically as well.

In contrast to the Israeli woman's slow recognition of a diversity of character among Palestinians in Liebrecht's story, Asqalani thrusts us into the conflicts in Palestinian society—for example, between those who suffer hunger, like Sa'id, and those with jobs or power in Gaza who ask "with distaste and condescension, 'Why don't you work in *Israel*?'"[20] Asqalani introduces us to complexity in Israeli society also: Sa'id is hired by an Israeli foreman and contractor named Shlomo, an Ashkenazi Jew, and later works with Azra, a Yemeni Jew who "speaks Arabic better than [he does]."[21] The cross-national identification between Sa'id and Azra suggests how Israeli society has suppressed its Arab roots both in the Palestinian community and in the Mizrahi communities, which emigrated from the Arab world after the founding of Israel and often were treated as second-class citizens. Sa'id sees himself in Azra, whose pitiable, skeletal form feels like his own fate.

The skeleton motif, which weaves through the story, signifies both bodies and buildings, individuals and states. Avoiding the starvation of his children comes at an enormous cost for Sa'id: the building up of the state of Israel. When he recognizes Abu Mahmoud, a Palestinian foreman for whom he once worked, he feels the gulf between his ideals as a revolutionary and his reality as a father:

> *Abu Mahmoud, am I going to be sharing with you in the dressing up of this skeleton?* He remembered vividly the look of terror in the man's eyes

> the day he had torn up his work permit and thoughtlessly thrown it in his face. He had never attempted, that day, to hear his own stuttering, frightened words, nor had he sympathized with the terror he felt in his own heart. He had never realized, on that day, that the pain in children's eyes was stronger than a work permit and a measuring tape—stronger even than cement columns.[22]

Sa'id understands that in order not to have a skeletal body and family he must put flesh on the skeletons of buildings, on the bigger skeleton of Israel. These Palestinian construction workers are making houses on their former homeland, houses that they will never own and that will lessen the possibility of their return. He makes and is unmade by his labor; in his making, "he himself [will] become a skeleton withered by the wind."[23]

Interestingly, it is Azra who is the first to collapse from the work. Sa'id sees him as "this human skeleton"[24] who labors as the building rises, in stark contrast to the "fields of Majdal spread out like a green carpet that is forbidden to you." At the climax of the story, when the Yemeni Jew collapses, his body is "slumped over the cement mix, face downward."[25] It is as if the building itself came to drown him. Sa'id reflects later that between him and Azra "there's no difference, no difference at all." In this epiphanic moment, what binds the two men is not their language but their sharing in tormenting, oppressive labor, in which the workers literally are consumed in the process of building.

The story ends with Shlomo's firing of everyone—after his derisive comments about the crew and Sa'id's attempt to attack Shlomo physically in response to the insults. Yet, as in "A Room on the Roof," there is a glimmer of the moral imagination, and the possibility of a cross-national movement against economic and political oppression remains in the mind. Despite the smoke and dust that cover the workers from Shlomo's departing car—images of our greater human transience—Asqalani lays bare the pain of Palestinians living in statelessness—not without their humanity but with a keen despair.

Reading these two stories in a contrapuntal fashion compels students to engage critically with and feel empathy for the predicament of Palestinians and Israelis, through the irreducibly particular portraits of Asqalani's Sa'id and Liebrecht's unnamed narrator. It also reveals how the

United States and Israel are connected by privilege (and by blind spots). My predominately white students often identify with the Israeli woman's fascination with and fear of her Palestinian workers. Encountering an analogous story from the Palestinian point of view makes them question the epistemological limits that are inherent in political privilege.

The Perils of Teaching Palestine as an Arab American

At the Radius of Arab American Writers conference in 2010, Michael Malek Najjar articulated the parallelism between the outing of queer people and the outing of Arab Americans after the terrorist attacks of 9/11. Despite my own visible invisibility as a person who identifies as Arab but often is not recognized as such, I too felt exposed and vulnerable in those days in 2001. At the same time, 9/11 provoked me into action, into coming out publicly not just as a progressive but also as an Arab American who stands in solidarity with Arabs at a time when we have been the objects of suspicion and even hatred. My coming out was an experience both terrifying and empowering.

The level of fear that accompanied my entering the public sphere in the 1990s to protest the brutal economic sanctions against Iraq, and to decry house demolitions and land confiscations in Palestine, was considerable. I received a string of anonymous hate mail after being quoted in the local newspaper. Because of my personality, I dread the moment when an argument goes from a simmer to a boil or when a friend's face twists when I say something that disturbs his or her picture of the world or vision of me. I'm well aware of the deep division between my Jewish and Palestinian friends and of how the victims of history often don't feel saintly toward one another or toward themselves.

I bring together my personal, political, and pedagogical responsibilities through this course. I developed it despite my desire to run away and be invisible in my privilege of distance and unrecognizability—partly because, as Miguel de Unamuno once wrote, "Sometimes, to remain silent is to lie."[26] I bring out this example of myself both because it may help others in an analogous position and because the challenges we face when writing about erased histories in the academy are shared beyond our specific positions.

A peacebuilding pedagogy fosters future peacebuilders and encourages academic honesty and openness. In developing my approach, I have benefited from the work of other scholar-teachers who work in this field, Marcy Jane Knopf-Newman in particular. Knopf-Newman's strategies, articulated in *The Politics of Teaching Palestine to Americans*, differ from mine but have helped me sharpen my analyses. Her chapter "Separate and Unequal: On Coexistence" offers a valuable deconstruction of coexistence narratives that efface the radical asymmetries of power at the heart of the problem.[27] I continue to revise the course to reflect my evolving understanding of the conflict. I believe that a historical wrong was perpetrated against Palestinians and continues in the form of occupation and dispossession. I also believe that Israelis have an important story to tell and that anyone interested in Palestinian rights must also be interested in the human rights of Israelis and fight anti-Jewish and anti-Arab hatred wherever it is found. I believe that a just peace is possible.

The personal and professional risks of teaching courses in North American university classrooms dealing with the Palestinian experience are worth taking. As teachers we must plant the seeds for critically engaged and empathetic global citizens who are not afraid to ask difficult questions about the future of Israel/Palestine and the United States relation to the conflict between Palestinians and Israelis. Simply reading the literary and historical narratives of Palestine and Israel and discussing them in class will not solve the conflict, but it will offer students an intimate window onto the geographies of violence and, more important, into the moral imagination—how to become agents of change not primarily through coercion, but through metanoia—a radical turning of the heart. May fugitive moments of that imagination slip through the crevices of the walls promoted by ideologues and fundamentalists, and all those who benefit from perpetuating this excruciating yet seemingly intractable violence.

2012, 2022

CHAPTER NINE

Fidelity to the Unnameable

Zaina Alsous's *A Theory of Birds*

The title, *A Theory of Birds*, aligns two allegiances of Zaina Alsous's debut poetry collection—on the one hand, her rigorous philosophical critique of reality (in particular, its imperial and Anthropocene guises), and on the other, her longing to participate in the pure and instinctive song of birds, one of the oldest tropes of poetry. As she writes in "Being-Nothingness," "The dervish in me can't let go of my addiction / to theory."[1]

A Palestinian American poet and political organizer, Alsous takes the political nationalism of the Palestinian movement—glimpsed in an epigraph like "free the land"—and translates it as more than a call for a Palestinian state. It becomes, over the course of the book, an invitation to wider and more revolutionary forms of belonging, beyond mere ownership—visible perhaps because of the vision that dispossession paradoxically enables.

In the title poem "A Theory of Birds," Alsous wrestles with her relationship to "there," a Gaza city where "canaries are raised / for sale," a metonym for the bigger cage of Gaza, often called the biggest open-air prison on the planet. Shifting scenes, she imagines in a cardinal the spirit of her grandmother. The poem ends:

> . . . I have
> wanted love more
>
> than history;
> to be chosen

by another bird,

an arranged cluster
of sunflowers, breeding
more sun,

a sun race,
maybe then
a return,

maybe wingspan,
elsewhere.
I am not

a proud beast.
these feathers
are merely pinned

amidst shoulder,
mimicking the sound
of dusk. Soon, soon.[2]

The predicament of Palestinian exile compounded by exile offers the poet the longing without the satisfaction of arrival. It's why, perhaps, that the Palestinian story is compelling, even romantic, to thinkers and writers (and, ironically, homologous to the Jewish story of longing for a homeland prior to the founding of Israel). The story of exile is fundamentally an erotic story, about loss and longing—and therefore, the poetics of unattainability is seductive for outsiders but useless for the people living in it. Alsous's approach to the problem explores her own discomfort with the idea itself. She doesn't relish the romance. She refused to buy the myth. She feels like a fake bird, her wings unworkable, a mimic, a theory of a bird.

Alsous's poems are at their most exciting when brilliance of thought meets the sheer dizziness of style, when language deforms into a new door. I think of "Description de l'Egytpe," which refers to Napoleon's imperial project of gathering information about the Orient. More than a mere rehearsal of Saidian critique, the poem falls down the well dug by the epistemic violence of naming:

> One morning my birth is an ink line
> in the language of plantations
>
> I grow to watch the memory assemble me:
> a fiction of poppies and idolatry,
>
> gradient in supernumerary fervor,
> bloody at the footnote. There is a door that betweens
>
> me and then, the authors say the door is always open,
> the ghosts say the door is not for us.[3]

Just listen to the music: the assonance of "language of plantations," the "w" sounds in "grow" and "watch," yielding to the assonance and rhyme of "memory assemble me." This is the birdsong drunk on the song. I love that use of "betweens" as a verb, as it is the liminal space that Alsous wants to create in her poems, where so much resides. She knows the hold of the past on us, and feels stuck between entering into it and knowing that it is itself another fiction that owns us.

The figure of the dodo recurs in her work as an image of extinction and ghostly persistence. In some sense, the dodo became one of the first touchstones of a world culture aware of its ability to erase entire species, a first sign of the Anthropocene. The dodo lives, paradoxically, as a ghost-guilt of imperial power. What a perfect bird to become the spirit animal for a poet concerned with the nexus of imperial naming and disappearance. In "Notes from the Gallery of Evolution," describing her seeing the skeleton of the dodo, she writes:

> To look remains
> first person. Unclassified, to be determined. I have come
> as vocabulary. I will report back what I was told.
> The beast picked apart was an intention towards peace. I did
> not press my nose to the glass.[4]

As Orientalism makes clear, the production of knowledge itself can be a violence, insofar as it attempts to re-create a preset version of reality, where Arab women are slaves who need to be saved (and thus, will likely be destroyed). As Alsous writes in "'Arab Making'," which seems like a version of Amiri Baraka's controversial "Somebody Blew Up America,"

> Who is my name
> Who painted Gerome's fingers
> as poppies crowding my throat
> Who marketed Mia Khalifah's penetration
> Who made me watch
> Who filled my cervix with sand
> Who nocturned us desert and film
> Who invented me begging
> softly to be destroyed[5]

Alluding to a Lebanese porn actress who got famous for wearing a hijab in a sex film, Alsous captures the predicament of the Arab woman, caught amid so many images and projections, and her own complicity in watching this unfold.

In poem after poem, Alsous brings to light that which is unnamed. In "Translator's Essay," for example, she wrestles with the "professor," the "artist," and the "grad student"—men who prey on women, from Christopher Columbus to Pablo Picasso, who she will not dignify by naming. No, she wants to remember, in this poem, Bhanu Kapil, Ana Mendieta, and the monstrous Medusa. Alsous is not a poet who righteously condemns and cries out for the missing. Her stance is self-indicting, confessional, and yet that vulnerability feels like a kind of power. She stands for the missing, struggling with her own desire to be among the lost: "Every time I look for women, I become more bird."

In an extant poem not in this collection nor available online, Alsous writes, "I never find a picture frame for my arm hairs." It's a great synecdoche for the general argument that representations don't capture our creaturely wild selves, who we are beyond the versions of us promulgated by an Orientalist vision. Which is to say: I don't see myself in any of these depictions of me and where I'm from, how it feels to be me.

There is a strong longing in the book, expressed earlier by the image of pinned wings, for finding revolutionary power in herself. As she writes in "Violence":

> In a high-school history class, white children raised
> their eyebrows when I raised my voice.
>
> I don't know what they thought I was capable of;
> I wish I was more capable of it.[6]

There is something wild and a longing for the wild that makes these poems so vital, so important, and bring me such hope. At its best, Alsous's poetry does not settle for gestures of brittle rebellion. It emerges from and unfolds into a postgrief ferocity, a steady fidelity to the unnameable, what cannot be domesticated, stripped, and destroyed.

It is postgrief because she knows what she (and all of us) are capable of, have done. As she writes in "Arabidopsis,"

> My first surrender was the need to be understood.
> My first failure: domestication, an inheritance of kingdom.
> I was too wet in the summer to yield saffron. I was too angry
> to mom. Too demographic for rurality. Too middle class
> for truth.[7]

That grief is a step to something else. As she writes, in "birds survive the death of Nature": "Everything they teach about enlightenment leaves / prisoners or my mother out. To answer your question: / I refuse." What precisely will be the next steps is not quite clear. To a descendant of refugees, what can return look like, to a land where one has never lived? What if return could mean something else entirely?

Which leads us back to the epigraph of *A Theory of Birds:* "free the land." What first looks like a political gesture of national liberation for Palestine, by the end of the book appears to be something far more complicated and radical—a call to liberate the land, to free earth, from all of our projections and dominations, not just Zionism's. It's intriguing to me that her work, like George Oppen's (another political organizer), doesn't strain to be "political." For Alsous, poetry is a dreamspace to wrestle the present and imagine past the past.

Her work heralds a new vision, alongside other young Palestinian American poets like George Abraham, Hala Alyan, and Noor Hindi (not to mention my generation's poets Fady Joudah, Deema Shehabi, and Lena Tuffaha), of a new way of thinking and writing diaspora, (Palestinian) exile, and our planetary future.

The poem "bird survive the death of Nature" provides a clue to Alsous's thinking. It ends: "*Listen*, next time, the flowers are naming themselves."[8]

2021

CHAPTER TEN

Of Seeing, the Unseen, and the Unseeable

Technology, Poetry, and "When It Rains in Gaza"

1. I Tap My Cell to See

In the beginning, I did not see but heard: news over the radio about the bombing of Gaza in 2014, triggered by a whole series of events—we say "triggered," as if history itself were a weapon ready to be fired. Voices untranslated, the tone of panic rising, sometimes breaking into anguished cries, the wail of air raid sirens, and the smooth voiceover of journalists, trying to tuck the adrenaline beneath the language, trying to strike a tone that seems fair and balanced.

Gaza I have never gazed with my own eyes. Only through screens have I seen غزة. The G in "Gaza" does not sound like G in Arabic. There is no equivalent to this sound in English, the "ghayn." It is a voiced velar fricative, and involves a tightening and narrowing of the upper palate, a vocalized breathing through that tightening.

Gaza, whose name is written in the military records of Thutmose III, fifteenth-century B.C., from the word meaning fierce or strong, also meant "prized city."

"When It Rains in Gaza"[1] (a poem in *Shrapnel Maps*) began when I saw photos of a girl in a green hoodie pulling books out of the rubble, her malnourished arms like oversized pencils. Her eyes caught the camera's eye as she piled the books in the crook of her arm. Not corpses half buried in dust, but this girl living after the apocalypse—that is what haunted me. Not the dead, but the living who had to pick up after the destruction, to get back to the business of daily life.

As Wislawa Szymborska's "The End and the Beginning" depicts, that girl reminded me of what I could not see, that after every bombing,

> Someone, broom in hand,
> still recalls the way it was.
> Someone else listens
> and nods with unsevered head.
> But already there are those nearby
> starting to mill about
> who will find it dull.[2]

No matter the stark image she left, I knew she would not be covered in our American media, addicted as it is to bleeding ledes and the next conflagration. She would be left, gathering books, as her family picked themselves up to rebuild.

But I'm thinking about her, how that girl "recalls the way it was." How, as Simone Weil puts it, "at the bottom of the heart of every human being, from earliest infancy to the tomb, there is something that goes on expecting, in the teeth of all experience of crimes committed, suffered and witnessed, that good and not evil will be done to him. It is this above all that is sacred in every human being."[3]

I look outside my window in Cleveland and see dawn begin to arrive. The houses across the street are all intact, secure, and still unlit. I look down at my screen and see her again, looking back at me.

Our screens and cells are at once portals and prisons. We believe them to be portals, but the portals often bring us further into the prison. Screens, cells. They hide and confine as they reveal.

We tend to think of poetry and technology as antinomian categories—poetry being a high art of the mind or spirit, technology with the mechanisms of the world of objects. More broadly, it refers to knowledge employed for practical or instrumental ends. Yet technology comes from two words: *tekhnē* (art or craft) and *logos* (the word, or the study of). What if we think of poetry (*poiesis*, a making)—that art of making words—as itself a technology.

What can poetry do, with its crude technology of black marks on a flat sliver of tree, or the span of a voice fugitive in the air, in the face of such disaster?

2. Inside Her Book Is a Tunnel Dug at Night

Gaza itself is often called "the largest open air prison in the world." At 140 square miles, Gaza is home to nearly two million Palestinians, 70 percent of whom are refugees, or descendants of refugees, most of whom fled from the 1948 war. One of the most densely populated places on the planet, it has almost no access to the outside world. The Israeli blockade of Gaza began in 2007, when Hamas took control after elections and the military defeat of their Palestinian rivals. Hamas's resistance to the Jewish state led Israel to withdraw its settlements from Gaza in 2005, and then close the borders to Palestinians—many of whom were day laborers in Israel.

Beset by hard borders on all sides, Gazans resorted to building an astonishing network of tunnels. If technology is both a reflection and extension of human need, then look no further than the Gaza tunnels. From 2008 to 2013, 1,500 tunnels had been constructed to bypass the closed Rafah Crossing into Egypt. The first tunnels were built in 1982, when the city of Rafah was divided by Egypt and Israel, but the total closure of the border and the 2008–9 bombing led to a furious digging regimen. Some of the tunnels descended nearly one hundred feet into the ground; others extended nearly a mile long. In "When It Rains in Gaza,"[14] I wrote about how the tunnels made it seem

> as if people were rodents
> no walls could hinder:
>
> computers and donkeys,
> brides and coils of rebar, small
>
> arms, rockets, flour—white
> blood cells of the stateless.

I was in awe of the technology, born out of desperation and sheer force of will, that Palestinians employed to transport fuel, gas, cement, construction materials, raw materials, pesticides, seeds, agricultural tools, preservatives, packaging material, spare parts, livestock, zoo animals, food, medicines, clothes, car parts, building supplies, weapons, and luxury items.

A 2013 story in *National Geographic* even told how bride Manal Abu Shanar was transported from Egypt to Gaza to live with her husband, Emad al-Malalha. The tunnels accounted for two-thirds of consumer goods entering Gaza, and accelerated rebuilding from the devastating war. Of course, many also died constructing the tunnels, including children who, because of their height, worked in the tunnels. By 2013, though, Egypt had constructed an underground barrier so deep that even the Palestinians could not descend beneath it. Israel has been doing the same, to eliminate tunnels that Hamas had created to breach Israel's border.

The walls descend into the earth, far past the depths of graves.

3. And Inside This Bomb Is Rahed Taysir al-Hom

If technology is an extension of the human capacities to perceive and to act in the world, then perhaps Donna Haraway was right, that humans are rapidly becoming cyborgs, "a hybrid of machine and organism,"[5] with our pacemakers, Lasix, iPhones, and Google Glass. But that doesn't make it any easier to be human. We are not a TED Talk away from total fulfillment. Technology may extend some capacities, but our hearts lag behind, caged behind our ribs.

Too often, the fever of technological advancement overwhelms the ethical urge to consider, to brake. This is nowhere as clear in the human capacity to create weaponry. Yet how much easier it is to make a bomb than to stitch a body back together.

Rahed Taysir al-Hom, who for years took apart bombs and missiles in Gaza, is one of those patient "makers" whose job it was to unmake. According to an article in the *Guardian*, "He had some training from international experts but gained most of his skills 'on the job.' . . . He had no protective clothing and used basic tools—screwdrivers, pliers and cutters—as he worked to make everything safe, be it Hamas rockets which had fallen short of their mark or bombs dropped by Israeli warplanes."[6]

Poetry is also a technology—but can it be a technology that dilates our hearts, returns us to a compassion that heals us from our fear and defuses our explosive wounds? In my imaginary genealogy of poetry, I place shamans and midwives—the healers whose words opened doors to the spirit world and closed wounds—at the foundation, alongside bards, griots, prophets, and scribes.

4. When It Rains in Gaza, the Tin Roofs Clatter

Sometimes it rains in Gaza, but not enough to mitigate the impending catastrophe. Due to a variety of factors including the blockade, 98 percent of the water is undrinkable. There isn't enough electrical power for more than a couple hours per day, and desalination plants can't produce enough drinking water. By 2020, the UN predicts that Gaza will be unliveable.

Pro-Israeli critics say, why doesn't Hamas use its money to build hospitals instead of rockets? Why don't they build water filtration plants instead of tunnels?

Pro-Palestinian critics say every people has a right to resist its own oppression, a right to freedom and self-determination.

In 2014, according to Mohammed Omer, Israel targeted water and sewage infrastructure, crippling an already-underdeveloped system.[7]

Israel blames Hamas, Hamas blames Israel. If war is a technology of child sacrifice, then blame is one of its principal fuel sources.

5. Inside the Slurry Is Anger

How strange that the resistance groups in Gaza build makeshift rockets out of metal, farm fertilizer, and melted sugar. It is a frighteningly simple technology.

Those rockets fall into the land where the fighters' families once came from. The technology of return is fueled by grief, grief transmogrified to anger.

Seamus Heaney has argued that poetry "does not propose to be instrumental or effective. Instead, in the rift between what is going to happen and whatever we wish to happen, poetry holds attention for a space, not as distraction but as pure concentration, a focus where our power to concentrate is concentrated back on ourselves."[8]

I would like Heaney to be right. After all, living in Northern Ireland, he knew the damage that instrumentalized ideologies of liberation can do. What can be rationalized for "The Cause." And there is beauty and possibility in creating that space of attention, in a world of distraction and oppression.

I'm just not sure that's enough.

6. Al-Awda Means Return

In 2014, Israel bombed an ice cream and sweets factory called Al-Awda. Al-Awda means "return," the fundamental longing of Palestinian refugees languishing in Gaza.

Rami Almeghari interviewed the owner, Iyad al-Tilbani, who said, "It was such a horrible and rather shocking moment for me—I stood helpless in the face of what was happening."[9]

Almeghari notes that "[al-Tibani] pointed to the place where modern, western-made machines were buzzing just a few days ago, but which have been replaced by silence and destruction."

I wanted to hold a space for al-Tibani's voice, his grief, and the only way it came to me was in lines:

> It smells of burning plastic and butter.
> How would it taste, the sweetness of return?
>
> Because there was no room in morgues, babies
> curled in ice cream freezers. And every day,
>
> the sea churned a white froth, salting the air,
> lapping the sand as if there were no war.[10]

Why bomb an ice cream factory? Why store dead children in ice cream freezers, except that the morgues were too full, and one needs time for burial?

7. Above the Tub, Salem Saoody Leans

One of my favorite photos after the 2014 bombing was of Salem Saoody bathing his daughter and niece in a tub. I love the joy in their faces.

> Above the tub, Salem Saoody leans,
> grinning and palming the frothing water
>
> over niece and daughter, their hair slicked
> with soap, their bodies gleaming in the brisk

delight of being bubble-wet and clean. Pull
back. Around the tub, the ceiling in piles—

the walls just a few columns and open.
The whole neighborhood a roofless ruin,

a movie set for apocalypse. After.
Welcome to the desert of the real.

Just the tub survives this Operation
Protective Edge. So focus in: laughter

and water, froth and a father's smile.
The heart will break what the eye can't swallow.[11]

I love the joy in their faces, even as I can also see the ruined building that houses the tub, and the whole neighborhood of ruins around them. Even as I know that 60 percent of Gaza's children are anemic, 50 percent have PTSD, and 7 percent have stunted growth from malnutrition.

8. When it Rains in Gaza, Children Run Out

It rains in Gaza, but not enough.

9. A Jellyfish of Smoke

During the 2009 bombings of Gaza, Israel employed white phosphorus weaponry. From the photos I saw online, it sometimes looks like a jellyfish of smoke. The photographs of exploding white phosphorus shells are almost universally beautiful, like sprays of white fireworks.

It's a technology used to identify enemy targets and hide troop movements, but it has been banned for use in civilian areas.

If it comes into contact with flesh, it burns right to the bone. The photos of flesh burrowed through with white phosphorus are not beautiful. From a distance, war looks beautiful.

How to write a poem of war that does not blind with beauty, but opens our eyes to what is beneath its inhuman force?

10. A Sky's Eye, Tracking by Heat of Body

Israel's military blockade extends in every dimension, especially in the sky, where drones monitor every movement, and occasionally engage in targeted killings. Every new technology promises greater accuracy, to reduce civilian casualties, but they always fall well short of perfection. Whether it's technological or human error, it doesn't matter to the families who bear the loss. There is a difference between the seen and unseen, the seeable and the unseeable. The drones, it is said, buzz like lawnmowers. Israel calls its strategy of counterterrorism "mowing the grass."

What does it mean to write poetry in a world where metaphors are weaponized, and people erased in them?

A week into Operation Protective Edge, on July 16, 2014, Israeli drone strikes killed four Palestinian boys (between the ages of nine and eleven) on a beach in Gaza. They had been playing soccer at the time. In his *New York Times* article, Tyler Hicks writes:

> There is no safe place in Gaza right now. Bombs can land at any time, anywhere. A small metal shack with no electricity or running water on a jetty in the blazing seaside sun does not seem like the kind of place frequented by Hamas militants, the Israel Defense Forces' intended targets. Children, maybe four feet tall, dressed in summer clothes, running from an explosion, don't fit the description of Hamas fighters, either.[12]

Their names were Muhammad, Zakaria, Ismail, and Ahed Bakr.

Salwa Bakr, the mother of Muhammad and Ismail, can't forgive herself for waking up Muhammad to do an errand for her.

"I woke him up to get him killed," she said to Naomi Zeveloff, covering the story for *The Forward*.[13]

11. Operation Summer Rains Tomorrow

Israel called the 2014 campaign "Operation Protective Edge." According to one Palestinian Ministry of Religious Endowments, sixty-four mosques were destroyed in that campaign. Another says the number is seventy-three, with two Christian churches also damaged.

Israel accused Palestinian militants of launching attacks from mosques, schools, and hospitals, making them legitimate targets.

I write: "You can read all the statistics online. / The heroic couplet cosigns to a lie."

Prayer comes from *precaria*, entreaty—and shares the same root as the word "precarious." What's the old phrase: there are no atheists in foxholes?

And what can poetry do, when sheer numbers numb us to the human dimension?

12. Over the Wall, Other People Stroll

After enduring the brunt of thousands of primitive rockets fired from Gaza over the years, Sderot now finds itself protected with the Iron Dome missile intercept system. During the 2014 war, Iron Dome shot down hundreds of rockets. The Israeli citizens of Sderot still live in fear of what can rain from the sky. Like Reagan's Star Wars, Iron Dome is not perfect.

The technology of security constantly butts up against the impossibility of total safety and imperils basic human freedom.

Everyone has the right to security. Everyone has the right to be safe.

13. Deema, I Want to Soften the Gnaw of Loss

What I know of Gaza is partly from reading Deema Shehabi's *Thirteen Departures from the Moon*. Her poems don't depict a lunar, bomb-cratered landscape, but a place complexly beautiful, unknowable even to her:

> My mother is from Gaza, but what do I know of the migrant earth,
> As I enter a Gazan rooftop and perform ablutions in the ashen forehead
>   of sky? As my soul journeys and wrinkles with homeland?
> I could tell you that I parted with my mother at the country
>   of skin.[14]

I love her enigmatic phrases that cut two ways at once. In her phrase the "migrant earth," she calls forth an image of the earth and its migrants and at the same time gives rise to the notion that the earth itself is a migrant in the sky. The earth itself is a body in her poem, with an "ashen forehead of sky," and her mother's body is also a country. Poetry is a technology of reseeing what we thought were the dimensions of countries and bodies, a telescope and a microscope all at once.

Deema's grandfather was the mayor of Gaza, but that was long ago now. I wish I could capture the sadness in her eyes and voice when Deema talks of غزة .

Whatever Gaza I think I know, it is a Gaza of the mind. Not Gaza.

14. Amal, I Pray You Have Not Folded

The girl in the photo, gathering the books? Her name is Maram. It means Wish.

I learned her name while reading Marcello Di Cintio's *Pay No Heed to the Rockets*. After traveling to Palestine to meet with poets and writers, he'd gone to Gaza to search for the girl in green. Using the technology of talking to Palestinians face to face, he found her.

He'd contacted the photographer, Mo'men Faiz, who, in 2008, lost his legs to an Israeli rocket attack. Six years later, Mo'men employed the technology of a wheelchair to pull himself through Gaza's bombed streets, to discover Maram cleaning up. A few years after that, he and Mo'men were able to locate her.

In my poem, I called her "Amal," meaning Hope. She'd seen pages from the Quran blowing on the street, and followed the pages into the rubble.

This is how the poem ends:

Amal, I pray you
have not folded

inside phosphorus,
or nestled beside

uneaten ice cream.
There is no us.

There is no them.
That by late light

this night, you read
until you believe

the wall will fall
the siege will end

and missing walls
will rise again.[15]

At the end of his book, Di Cintio writes that the Nakba—the catastrophe of Palestinian dispossession—"is a poem that never ends, persisting and pressing forward."[16] May this poem, "When It Rains in Gaza"—for all its limits in seeing, its failures to account for what it cannot see—be a technology that slows, or even unwrites, a little of the seemingly endless poem of erasure.

2018

CHAPTER ELEVEN

"To Be the Poet of Troy"

An Interview with Mosab Abu Toha

Mosab Abu Toha is a Palestinian writer and founder of the Edward Said Library in Gaza. He taught English language at the United Nations Relief and Work Agency (UNRWA) for three years, before he traveled to the U.S. as a Scholar-at-Risk fellow at Harvard University. This interview was conducted first via Facebook Messenger, and then via email in April 2020, during the COVID pandemic's first "shelter in place" quarantine.

PHILIP METRES (PM): What stoked your passion for English literature, and how did it inspire you to found the Edward Said library in Gaza? I understand it began with a book found under rubble.

MOSAB ABU TOHA (MAT): English is a subject in Palestine at schools from first until twelfth grade. I found myself very good at this particular subject and decided to major in it at university in 2010. Due to the imposed siege on Gaza since 2007, my only way to practice the language was by chatting with Facebook friends during the few hours of electricity. The siege means that no one can easily leave Gaza or enter it. The only time I could spend some days with foreigners and where I could speak English was in the summer of 2014, where I volunteered to translate for a couple of journalists. A terrifying experience for someone who wanted to focus on his language improvement.

Aside from the university library, there was not a single library that I could access in my city. The only English books that I possessed were books some of my online friends sent to me. However, it was in 2014 that the idea of establishing a public library flashed into my mind. Because of the fifty-one-day aggression on Gaza, not only did my graduation ceremony get postponed, but also the English Department was turned into rubble. During the few hours of ceasefire, I could make a quick visit and see the ruins and the many English books buried there. One book that I was able to rescue was *The Norton Anthology of American Literature*, a book, I discovered later, one of the instructors had used in his lectures.

Our house was also badly damaged and the few English books I had collected were critically ruined. For about a month we stayed away from our house. Even one of the places we stayed in was targeted by Israeli barbarity. It was an UNRWA school. Fifteen people were killed along with ninety casualties.

Therefore, I thought of establishing a safe haven for books in the form of a public library that aspires to find good readers, writers who would make use of its books and the place. My definition of a public library is that place where people can find books and participate in cultural, social, and intellectual activities.

PM: If I may ask, where does one go when one's house is being bombed? You stayed in a school that was targeted as well! Was there any safe place in Gaza at that time?

MAT: In fact, at the time of aggression, when the Israeli army declared ground invasion, many Gazans left their houses, especially those who live near the border, to schools. We have no shelters in Gaza.

In our case, during the 2008–9 aggression, we had to evacuate our house to our aunt's house. It was there that I was wounded while going to buy some food for my little siblings. I was sixteen at the time. Then we moved to our other aunt's before we returned home and found our house slightly damaged. Upon returning, I saw part of some white phosphorus shell remains. When I tried to rub it with a stick, it started to burn again.

In the 2014 aggression, lasting for fifty-one days (the longest in decades), we evacuated our house just one day before our neighbor's house was completely destroyed with an F-16 missile. Our house was severely damaged and my small library turned into ruins. Our beds and closets were destroyed, the water barrels were damaged, and the hens and ducks my father had raised all died.

My family spent some days in the Abu-Hussein UNRWA School in Jabalia Camp. At the dawn of July 30, 2014, several shells slammed into the crowded school, which was used as shelter for the displaced, killing at least fifteen people and wounding ninety. My then-wife, along with her family, was sleeping in the room right next to that which was bombed. It was miraculous they were safe. Because of the summer heat and the overcrowded classrooms, some of the families had been sleeping in the school playground. A dozen of those men, women, and children, who thought they would be safe in the schoolyard, all died or were wounded that morning.

A terrifying day with many funerals.

Luckily, my family had left the school for my aunt's house just hours before the bombing.

I think we were fortunate to have some space to live temporarily in another house with relatives.

PM: I've read of the astonishing levels of PTSD experienced by Palestinians in Gaza. How do you deal with that level of precarity, that daily uncertainty? What helps you survive your conditions? What brings you peace, joy, and beauty?

MAT: You're right. The levels of PTSD in Gaza, especially during and after every Israeli assault, are unbelievable.

Whenever Israel bombarded Gaza or when rockets were fired from Gaza, two neighbors of mine used to shake in fear. No matter how small or "unserious" the explosion was, these two would demand that they leave their house either to their grandparents' house or to a school. Ibrahim, especially, would cry and visibly go pale. I learnt from his parents that he got bad grades in his school exams whenever there was a raid.

It is noteworthy that nearly half of the Gaza residents are under the age of fifteen, which means that about one million children are vulnerable and susceptible to traumatic experiences, not to mention the many women and the elderly.

On a personal level, whenever there was an attack or rumors of an impending war, I would absorb myself in reading and writing or in following the news. Sometimes I thought of myself as a piece of breaking news on TV or the radio.

In 2018, a big explosion very close to our house shook the whole area. Some of my books on the shelf fell off and a small vase broke next to me while I was writing. This incident inspired me to write a poem. This is an excerpt:

Edward Said is out of place
again:
His books on my shelf
fall off on the broken glass.

[Palestine is also out of place:
Its map
falls off my wall.]

The books' exile bleeds
of wars,
of continued estrangement.

Whenever there was a chance, I used to go to the seashore before sunset. I would take photos of the waves and the setting sun. I think that had a great effect on my psychological well-being.

PM: In your poem, "Blockade," published in *Banipal*, you have a metaphor that alludes to the strangeness we feel in another language, subtly: "I see a new poem / in a foreign alphabet."

BLOCKADE

Sleeping,
I discover my own theory
of existence.

I write my new poem.
A new Kubla Khan.
I get up and look
at myself in the mirror.
It tells me that I still exist.

On my face,
I see a new poem,
written in a foreign alphabet.
I smash the mirror.

The glass falling down
creates a word that probably
could become the title of my final piece:
"Loss"—
a word that describes perfectly
my Palestinian current
reality.[1]

It must be strange to express yourself in English, knowing the legacy of the British Empire and the current role of the U.S. in the situation. Doubly strange, because when we speak another language, we are not quite ourselves. We become someone slightly other. Could you talk about this poem and being Palestinian, writing in English?

MAT: It is true that I feel strange finding myself writing poetry in English. I first started to share my thoughts and creative writing in English on my Facebook page, especially during and after the 2014 aggression. I felt it necessary to address the English-speaking world. Not necessarily the governments but the people who stand in solidarity with our just cause, and who are doing their best to affect their governments.

When I write in English, I feel like being free from the confinements of my existence in Gaza, even if briefly.

We are trapped in Gaza, we are attacked from time to time by Israel, and we experience the ramifications of the political rift between Hamas and Fatah since 2007, Fatah being the Palestinian Authority in the West Bank.

It is still ironic that I feel more free in English when it is the language of the Balfour Declaration of 1917, the notorious declaration that promised the mainly Arab-populated Palestine to Jewish immigrants, and the declaration why I find myself unsafe in my home with my kids and wife, why I find myself sometimes writing about melancholy dreams and thoughts.

The poem that I found written in a foreign alphabet on my face represents the tragedy incurred on us Palestinians by foreign agents, government, probably the infamous Balfour Declaration.

PM: That's fascinating and very poignant—that the language both produced alienation (on the level of political structures, the support of the Zionist movement, etc.) and freedom for you as an individual. In order to speak to empire, you must use its language, literally. I'd love to know more about your family roots. Where is your family originally from? Did they become refugees during the 1948 Nakba? What stories did you hear from your elders (grandparents, parents) about their original villages?

MAT: My family originally comes from Yaffa, a beautiful Palestinian city on the seashore of the Mediterranean Sea. We call it "The Bride of the Sea." My grandfather, his four brothers, and their father had to walk to Gaza under the gunfire and airstrikes of 1948. They all lived in Al-Shati Refugee Camp, or Beach Camp, where I was born in 1992. Due to the 1967 war, three of my grandfather's brothers fled to Jordan, Egypt, and Saudi Arabia, never to come again to Gaza.

My grandfather, Hassan, died in 1986, just before my father got married. It breaks my heart that I never had the chance to sit with him and listen to his stories and adventures in Yaffa. In Yaffa, my grandfather and his brothers worked as farriers and fishermen before the Nakba, my father tells us.

Hassan also worked in orange and grape orchards in Yaffa. Oranges had been Palestine's trademark, especially Yaffa's oranges. (Just like falafel and hummus, many people have been misguided to think that "Jaffa" oranges are Israeli.)

In the camp, my grandfather worked for UNRWA, United Nations Relief and Work Agency, founded in 1949, as a porter, carrying large amounts of frying oil, wheat flour, and vegetable boxes from trucks to stores. He had great muscles.

In one of my latest poems I ended:

> My grandfather was a terrorist—
> My grandfather was a man,
> was a breadwinner for ten,

whose luxury was to have a tent,
with a blue UNRWA flag set on a rusting pole,
on a beach next to a cemetery.

PM: Thank you for sharing this background. Some of my dear Palestinian friends are from Yaffa. In *Shrapnel Maps* (see the section called "Returning to Jaffa"), I try to tell the story of Nahida Halaby, whose family fled in April 1948.[2] In the process of learning about her family, I couldn't help but be entranced by the story of Yaffa itself. I found out that Yaffa was supposed to be part of the Palestinian state for the 1947 UN Partition Plan—but as an island surrounded by the Israeli state. It was absolutely untenable. The arguments about the plan often focus on the percentages of land "given" to each side, but they don't talk about the fact that the biggest Arab Palestinian city had no geographical connection to the offered Palestinian state. I also learned about the disappearance of the municipal archive, which meant that no one could settle their claims to property and land. The erasure was not just of Palestinians and their rights, but also their archives. The outpouring of Palestinian literature has really been to stanch the loss of history due to destruction, dispossession, and diaspora. What do you recommend among Palestinian literature that speaks best to your sense of the Palestinian predicament?

MAT: Since the Partition Plan in itself was unjustifiable in the first place, what would ensue after its implementation would not strike me hard. The Jews, who were a minority in Palestine, were given the larger part of it. The Zionist project relied on expansion rather than on security or coexistence with their Palestinian neighbors, who of course had the right to be furious about the plan and its results.

Mahmoud Darwish expressed it best when he said, "We haven't heard Troy's account. I'm sure there were poets there. The voice of Homer, the victor, vanquished even the Trojan's right to complain. I try to be the poet of Troy. Is it painful? I love the vanquished."[3]

I think the issue with the Palestinians is that, as you rightly said, not only their lands and properties were stolen, but also looted were their archive, historical documents, land deeds, etc., which one can find at Israeli universities, libraries, and the military archives.

What the Palestinians so far have been doing is documenting their stories in the form of history and academic books (important and encyclopedic works written by Walid Khalidi, Aref Al-Aref, and Mustafa Al-Dabbagh, especially the latter's eleven-volume encyclopedia *Biladuna Filastin*) and literary works, specially by novelist and short story writer Ghassan Kanafani, poet Mahmoud Darwish, and Jabra Ibrahim Jabra, among others.

The works of Edward Said have helped draw the attention of many people worldwide to the Palestinian story, when the word "Palestine" was either unknown or seen as a term equal to terrorism and inferiority. Said urged every Palestinian to "tell their story." His books *After the Last Sky* and *Out of Place* are excellent examples. Kanafani's *Returning to Haifa* is particularly rich in its sense and agony of homecoming and the feeling of guilt. Saeed and Safiya, the two main characters, not only left their house but also their child, Khaldoun, who they failed to find while leaving. When the couple returned in 1967 to visit, they found their house occupied by an old Jewish woman, an immigrant, and met their son, now David, serving in the Israeli army. One of Darwish's poetry volumes is titled *Why Did You Leave the Horse Alone?* and this again talks to me about probably the same question of guilt.

PM: I'd love to ask you about your move to the U.S. What induced your desire to leave, and would you talk a bit about your being sponsored by Noam Chomsky?

MAT: Noam Chomsky is one of the first people whom I reached when I began collecting books for the library. In October 2012, Chomsky visited Gaza for the first time. He was the guest speaker at a conference at my university. I was a sophomore then. Chomsky was surrounded by many people after the event, and I was lucky to talk to him for a few minutes. I even asked for his email address and signature and took a photo with him.

A few months after my alma mater was targeted by the Israeli warplanes in the 2014 aggression, I sent Chomsky an email along with our photos and a photo of the targeted university building. I told him about the situation. He sent me four of his books with his signature. In April 2016, he sent another big parcel with some of his books. However, the

Israeli authorities had decided that all mail to Gaza should be stopped. They claimed that the military groups in Gaza were getting materials that could be used for military ends.

Apparently, the situation in Gaza had not worn me down completely. I still did not think that the draconian Israeli ban would apply to books for children, linguists, and anyone interested in British and American literature, but I was wrong. Chomsky's books were held up by the Israelis from May 2016 until January 2017.

When I started the fundraising campaign in early 2017, Chomsky endorsed the campaign, donated some money, and invited his fans on Facebook to support the initiative.

In early 2018, I was recommended for a fellowship at Harvard University to be a visiting poet and a visiting librarian-in-residence. I arrived with my wife and two kids in the U.S. two months late for the fellowship, after a long and tortuous journey. I was denied the permit twice to attend my visa interview at the U.S. embassy in Jerusalem and denied again from crossing "Israel" on a shuttle bus to Jordan. I had to go to Egypt and then fly to Jordan. Instead of a four-hour journey from Gaza to Jordan through "Israel," it took me two days until I arrived in Jordan, having paid a lot of money for crossing fees to Egypt and for the flight.

That was the first time for me to leave Gaza, at the age of twenty-seven. It was the first time for me to board a plane. We don't have an airport in Gaza, not even in the West Bank, or a seaport. Can you imagine?

PM: A 2012 UN Report predicted that Gaza would be unlivable by 2020, yet somehow people in Gaza continue to survive. It seems like a stunning testament to the will of people to overcome their circumstances. How have they done it?

MAT: Well, it is true the people of Gaza are still surviving. However, survival has been their only option. If surviving is about continuing to be alive, then trees, stones, and the sea are surviving, right?

The people in Gaza have been trying to shout out loud to the whole world. They have tried to protest against the political rift between Hamas in Gaza and Fatah-PA in the West Bank.

Nonetheless, those who took to the streets in Gaza were violently suppressed by Hamas. They were treated as agents of the PA who were trying to oust Hamas from power. But those people in reality were protesting the electricity cuts, taxes, and unemployment.

On the other hand, some people took to the streets in the West Bank in support of Gaza, especially in 2018 after the PA president, Mahmoud Abbas, cut the salaries of almost all of the PA's Gaza staff, while those in the West Bank went unaffected. Those protesters were also suppressed by the PA forces.

So people in Gaza survive only because they clutch at the straws of hope, which most of the time keep flying away in the gusty winds in Gaza's sky.

In the past few years and months, the reports about suicide in Gaza have been alarming. The siege, having surpassed its thirteenth year, has produced new challenges to Gazans. They not only face occupation and wars, not only the rift and siege, not only unemployment and ban on movement, but now they are facing themselves, people who almost have nothing to do but to question their mere existence on earth.

PM: What has life been like since coming to the United States?

MAT: I arrived in the U.S. with my wife and two kids last October. Unlike life in Gaza, life here is very busy but calm. In Gaza, the only sound that came from the sky was that of the drones, F-16, or helicopter. Here, it is either the airplane, or birds singing. This is not to say that we do not have birds. We do. But their singing is drowned by the chaos coming from all sides, especially from above.

Since I arrived here, I have found people really interested in listening to my voice. There are many literary events, especially poetry readings. This is something you rarely find in Gaza. One reason is that Gaza's cultural societies and groups are not sufficiently funded, if at all. Again, a result from the political rift.

PM: I understand that you were not only dealing with the privations of living in Gaza because of Israeli control, but also because of threats by Hamas? Why would your library be a threat?

MAT: Not only were my endeavors to found a public library in Gaza discouraged by getting zero support from the Gaza government or its Ministry of Culture, but also I was summoned for an investigation. I thought they wanted to learn about how I started such a promising project. The office that summoned me deals with people who are suspected of being spies.

Although many reports in Arabic, English, Italian, and French were written about me and the library from day one, the Intelligence office dealt with me as a spy. They took my phone and ID away, not respecting that I was an English teacher at UNRWA schools or that I was planning to organize a reading club at the library that same day. A month later and after my father contacted some people, they returned the phone and ID without revealing the result of their investigation. One guard threatened to jail me for six months, because when they attacked me, I pushed him in defense. Their suspicion was irrational and extreme. Maybe my being independent and not affiliated with them helped worsen my treatment.

PM: So you've become a Scholar-at-Risk at Harvard University this academic year, and you're a librarian at the Widener and Houghton libraries. Have you been able to work in the library at all, given the COVID crisis?

MAT: A group of writer friends recommended me for a fellowship at Harvard University. I was appointed as a visiting poet at the Department of Comparative Literature and a visiting Librarian-in-Residence at Houghton Library. During the first semester, I met with many librarians and directors with whom I shared my experience and from whom I learnt much. Unfortunately, due to COVID-19, I have been unable to go to the libraries and meet with staff. But I remain in touch with many people.

PM: What has it been like, to be here in a new kind of confinement?

MAT: The title of a recent column I published on Arrowsmith Press was "We Are All Gazans. Sort Of."

I wrote that the new reality for me and for my American friends "has been the norm for all Gazans for a long time, except that in Gaza the internet runs at a snail's pace for a Zoom call, with electricity available for only eight and sometimes four hours a day."

PM: What are you working on now?

MAT: Aside from continuing to write poetry, I am doing some research on exile and its meaning in Palestinian poetry, especially Darwish's. Other work can be found at Arrowsmith Press and We Are Not Numbers. Three of my poems appeared in *Banipal* last month. I have many other poems that are not yet published and which I hope I can publish in different places or in a chapbook or a poetry collection. I would love to see them published.

PM: What do you want all Americans to know about life in Gaza?

MAT: Simply two things: that people in Gaza are just as human and intelligent as all people on earth are, and that people in Gaza long for their freedom, for a life based on equality, democracy, love, and mutual recognition.

Not all people in Gaza are Hamas or Fatah. Most of them wish to live a simple life, raise their families, build their dream house, have a job, write books, go to the seashore and watch the sunset, and visit their relatives in neighboring countries.

I myself was able to see my aunt Alia last year when I visited Jordan. As I mentioned, I went there for a visa interview. I suspect the Jordanian authorities would have allowed me to go to Jordan for a mere visit to her. Going to the U.S. embassy in Amman was strong enough.

The last time we saw her was in late 1999 when she visited Gaza for the last time. For twenty years now, neither she nor her family in Gaza could meet. It is only four hours by car between Gaza and Amman. All of this is a result of the Israeli occupation. Not only that, the Israeli authorities did not allow me to accompany my wife and two kids on our way out of Gaza to Jordan on a shuttle bus. Let's imagine that while you are in Boston, you cannot visit your sister in New York. I know this might be the case these days. But in Gaza, it has been for over twenty years now.

I was told by a Palestinian American friend of mine that when she usually goes to visit her family in the West Bank, she gets treated badly by the Israeli authorities. She gets stranded for long hours. However, when she goes with her husband, a European, and their two children, she faces almost no trouble. That is shameful.

PM: Tell me about the decision to put Israel in quotation marks. It seems to speak to the level of pain that you feel about its erasure of Palestinian life. Is that correct?

MAT: To be honest, I just recently started to put "Israeli" in quotation marks, not only because it does not recognize us, distort history, deny our rights, and dehumanize us, but also because they claim the right to the small part of Palestine that is left for us, especially the West Bank. I am sure you heard about the Israeli government's plan to annex large portions of the West Bank. It has not been enough for them to build illegal settlements but now they want to steal those lands and claim rights over them.

It is now my right as a Palestinian to be recognized as the victim and not the Israelis. Sadly, as Edward Said once said, "We became the Jews of the Jews." And I am sure what is meant by Jews here are those who ethnically cleansed our parents and grandparents from our Palestine and continue to oppress and kill us.

But ironically enough, if I may say and as Mahmoud Darwish once told his Israeli interviewer in 1996, "We are lucky because you are our enemy. You have given us . . . publicity."[4]

On my part, I am, like Darwish, "busy with my own right to return. I cannot defend the Israeli's right to return."[5]

PM: Do you have any hope that something could change. What would a viable and just peace look like, from your perspective?

MAT: A viable peace, I believe, should be between equals. My hope that in this world people will start to see the Palestinians as brothers and sisters and not as inferiors or as victims who are craving others' sympathy. The only hope, I think, for all is to live in a place where being this or that (X or Y, US or THEM) would not affect how we look at each other.

My only concern is that the Palestinians continue to be perhaps the only nation in the world to feel that today is better than what the future holds for them.

2020

CHAPTER TWELVE

Dispatches from the Land of Erasure During a Genocide

> *I wish children didn't die. I wish they would be temporarily elevated to the skies until the wars end. Then they would return home safe, and when their parents ask them; where were you? They'd say "We were playing with the clouds."*
>
> —GHASSAN KANAFANI

1.

On October 9, 2023, Israeli defense minister Yoav Gallant in an Israeli army situation update advised that Israel was "imposing a complete siege on Gaza. No electricity, no food, no water, no fuel. Everything is closed. We are fighting human animals and we are acting accordingly."

2.

On October 31, when asked why he was not fleeing the north of Gaza, Dr. Hammam Alloh responded: "If I go, who would treat my patients? We are not animals, we have the right to receive proper health care."

Two weeks later, he was killed in an Israeli air strike.

3.

By the end of October, it was estimated that 6,000 bombs per week had been dropped on Gaza.

By December, Israel's military attacks had "wreaked more destruction than the razing of Syria's Aleppo between 2012 and 2016, Ukraine's Mariupol, or proportionally, the Allied bombing of Germany in World War II."

4.
The destruction wrought by Israel is so extreme that "Gaza is now a different color from space . . . a different texture" (Corey Sher).

5.
Gauze, in one etymological positing, is connected to Gaza. A center of weaving in the so-called Middle Ages, Gaza was known for its fine silk (*qazz* in Arabic) that was imported into Europe. The delicate covering is now used to stimulate wound healing.

6.
Well over 1,000 children have had at least one leg amputated since the bombings began.

7.
Did I take the time to walk a little outside during the genocide?

Did I phone an old friend, remember the old days and catch up on the new, during the genocide?

Did I share a kind smile with strangers on my way to and from work during the genocide?

Did I see Amina Ghanem, thirteen-year-old girl, her black irises seeming to crowd out the white, in her gray Adidas hoodie and blue surgical mask, the blue star clip in her black hair?

She told the journalist, "We were sleeping and we heard the sound of tanks when they came and walked [drove] over the caravan in which I, my father, and my brothers lived. The tank squeezed us inside the tin all night until the morning, and when they took us out, I found that my father and my little sister had been killed."

Did I take a deep breath and count to ten when I became angry during the genocide?

Did I keep watching those black eyes, whose Blackness beyond the iris was not iris but blood vessels broken, and those dancing hands, as they gestured the flattening of the tanks over her family in their tin hovel, during the genocide?

Did she remind me of my daughter?

Did I text my daughter at school to check in on her when she was struggling, during the genocide?

8.
Did I remember that the genocider was also once genocided, and what preceded the genocide was an attack that brought back memories of the genocide, during the genocide?

9.
How could I forget?

10.
Why did it take attacks by Hamas for people to pay attention? Is it possible that we only understand the logic of violence?

In the wake of Hamas's attacks, some critics like Judith Butler noted that critique itself—at least in official, corporate media—was suddenly suspended, even forbidden. And in some sense, the ongoing disinformation and censorship campaigns have created their own no-speak zones. Social media—despite its own measures of social control and the matrix of the information war—has been a space where once marginalized voices and perspectives have suddenly gained purchase, even popularity.

11.
In early November, my daughter Leila tried to mobilize the Diversity Council she cofounded at her high school to do a walkout and day of mourning for Palestine. To stand with the other Arab American students, for the first time, as a group.

The school said no, it's not a good time.

That month, I received an email from the DEIB (Diversity, Equity, Inclusion, and Belonging) office at my university, stating that I was the subject of a Bias Report. Because of my social media posts, one of which stated, "From the River to the Sea, let every precious life be free," this student asserted that I was wishing for the death of Jewish students.

Let every precious life. Every precious life. Precious life.

12.
With the murders of Palestinian journalists and poets, what can poetry do? Poetry's durability is sometimes in proportion to its belatedness. Poetry is often a practice where first thought is usually not the best thought, nor even the final word. Poetry's belatedness hauntingly echoes international law's belatedness when it comes to defining genocide.

Calling any event a genocide, particularly when unmoored from legal definitions of genocide, has become one of the go-to politicized moves of attention-grabbers. And yet, what if calling an event a genocide can prevent the further unfolding of a genocide?

13.
The documentary/investigative poetry impulse spans historical and contemporary and ought to create a thread between them, but the present constantly recedes like the angel of history blown into the future. In a situation where genocide may be unfolding, is there not a need for other kinds of poetry, more transient, fugitive, and truthful to the moment?

In "Notes on Craft: Writing in the Hour of Genocide," Fargo Tbakhi writes: "We must be engaged in this kind of writing, which calls others into mobilization, generating feelings within our audiences that cannot be dispersed through the act of reading, but must be carried out into collective action."

What if the best poem of the Association of Writers & Writing Programs (AWP) convention of 2024 is the Radius of Arab American Writers (RAWI) email encouraging all panels to begin with a land acknowledgment that recognizes that we are living in a time of genocide?

14.
Pastry chef Masoud Muhammad al-Qatati was killed in an Israeli airstrike on his house on November 3, 2023. His shop's motto "let the poor eat"—and reputation for giving away the popular Palestinian treat *knafeh* to indigent customers—had earned him the nickname "Father of the Poor."

The Israeli minister of security Itamar Ben-Gvir clarified the government's position in a televised address, stating "to be clear, when we say that Hamas should be destroyed, it also means those who celebrate, those who support, and those who hand out candy—they're all terrorists, and they should also be destroyed."

On November 10, the U.S. vetoed the first U.N. resolution for an immediate ceasefire.

15.
In early November, my daughter Leila tried to get her school to do a day of mourning for Israel and Palestine. The school said no, it's not a good time. She resigned from the Diversity Council.

Now she knows, I thought suddenly, what it's like to be Arab American.

16.
In December, I learned a new term: shadowban. When a social media platform mutes a user without informing them.

On December 8, only one rescue vehicle was reportedly operational in the whole of Gaza, with survivors forced to try to dig for survivors with their bare hands.

On December 8, the U.S. vetoed the second U.N. resolution for an immediate ceasefire.

17.
In January, when I printed out the names of the dead children of Gaza, each name a line, it came out to one hundred pages. I flipped through them, looking for names I knew. The first four names:

Abd al-Jawad Mizar Jamal Hoso (0 years old)
Abdel Khaleq Fadi Khaled Al Baba (0 years old)
Abdel Rahim Ahmed Abdel Rahim Awad (0 years old)
Abdel Rahman Ahmed Essam Salah (0 years old) . . .
On the final page, it read: this is half of the dead children.

18.
It's not enough to share the poetry of Hida Abu Nada or Refaat Alareer, two recent poets killed in Gaza. It's not enough to publish Palestinians, though they should also be published.

Palestinians want to go home. We, the citizens of this empire, are funding the Israeli effort to make that impossible.

In the five months since October 7, the U.S. has made over 100 arms deliveries amounting to billions of dollars of military aid to Israel, including "thousands of precision-guided munitions, small-diameter bombs, bunker busters, small arms and other lethal aid."

19.
Perhaps no poet has been more tireless in his writing—and his widening reach—than Mosab Abu Toha. His work, and indeed the work of Gaza journalists like Motaz Azaiza, Bisan Owda, Wael Al-Dahdouh, and many others, invite us to think about a criticism that could treat a social media curation as a form of live documentary poetry.

Once we release the page as our only source and look to new media, we might find how poets deploy language and narrative to fit the nebulous, changing story of an ongoing, massive traumatic event.

20.
Already in January, many people in Gaza had resorted to eating animal feed, mixing it into flour to make a bitter bread.

In February, Abu Toha wrote:

Humans!! My family are telling me they don't have wheat flour or rice. There is not enough food.

Please help!!!

21.
Did I savor each bite, or did I scroll through my phone and fog-eat, during the genocide?

Did I remember to floss my teeth each night, despite my fatigue, during the genocide?

22.
On February 7, Abu Toha wrote, from Egypt: It's shocking. I feel utterly outraged to watch a video of a child from Gaza drinking from a pool of polluted water in the street today.

23.
Did I stay hydrated during the genocide?

24.
On February 20, the U.S. vetoed the third U.N. resolution for a ceasefire.

Did I tire of reading posts about the genocide, during the genocide?

I did.

Was I watching my weight during the genocide?

I tried.

Did I say, when I saw the girl in Gaza who made Cinnabon to raise funds during the genocide, see how resilient they are, they will survive, during the genocide?

I did.

25.
There are now over 120 mass grave sites. Not 120 graves. 120 mass grave sites. All the cemeteries are full, one headline reads. A trench in the earth, bulldozed open. They are covered in white cloth. When white cloth runs out, they are wrapped in bright blue tarp, zip-tied at the top and bottom and laid on top of each other.

26.
Did my bald spot grow wider during the genocide?

Did I worry about the shadow on my father's CT scan during the genocide?

Did I see the bodies wrapped in white lowered into the hole during the genocide?

27.
Gaza's healthcare system has all but collapsed, with reports of operations, including amputations and caesarean sections, taking place without anesthetic.

Contagious and epidemic diseases are rife among the displaced Palestinian population, with experts warning of the risk of meningitis, cholera, and other outbreaks.

Did I bathe enough, and wash my hands enough, during the genocide?

28.
In March, a senior Israeli official stated that "the food shortage and use of the word 'hunger' have been exaggerated. There is no hunger in Gaza," he said, explaining that most of the food that Israel has been sending into the Strip has "immediately been taken by Hamas terrorists, who then sell some of the supplies for ten times more than what it's worth."

29.
The entire population in Gaza is at imminent risk of famine, whereas the proportion of households affected by acute food insecurity is the largest ever recorded according to the Integrated Food Security Phase Classification ("IPC"). Experts warn that silent, slow deaths caused by hunger and thirst risk surpassing those violent deaths already caused by Israeli bombs and missiles.

30.
Was I too tired to make the call when the Congress was voting to continue to fund the genocide during the genocide?

31.
Can I say how much I love Students for Justice in Palestine?

Can I say how much I love Jewish Voice for Peace?

Can I say how much I love Sumud?

Can I say how much I love We Are Not Numbers, Jewish Currents, Writers Against the War on Gaza, the Palestine Youth Movement?

Can I say how much I love RAWI?

Can I say how much I love the students at Brown University who went on hunger strike, trying to get their university to divest?

Can I say how much I love Aaron Bushnell, who could not bear the brutality he was asked to bear, who became a pyre of flame crying Free Palestine?

32.
In mid-October, Israeli President Isaac Herzog made clear that Israel was not distinguishing between militants and civilians in Gaza, stating in a press conference to foreign media—in relation to Palestinians in Gaza, over one million of whom are children: "It's an entire nation out there that is responsible. It's not true this rhetoric about civilians not aware not involved. It's absolutely not true. . . . and we will fight until we break their backbone."

The Israeli president is one of many Israelis to have handwritten messages on bombs to be dropped on Gaza. He wrote "I rely on you."

33.
Israel is said to be dropping "dumb" (i.e., unguided) bombs on Gaza, as well as heavy bombs weighing up to 2,000 pounds, which have a predicted lethal radius "of up to 360 meters," and are "expected to cause severe injury and damage as far as 800 meters from the point of impact."

One in every 100 people in Gaza has now been killed.

34.
Did I learn to accept what I cannot change during the genocide?

Did I come to understand that poetry that does not clog the arteries of the empire with its fury is a species of obscenity, during a genocide?

35.
An estimated 1,779 Palestinian families in Gaza have lost multiple family members, and hundreds of multigenerational families have been killed in their entirety, with no remaining survivors—mothers, fathers, children, siblings, grandparents, aunts, cousins—often all killed together.

One month into the genocide, 312 Palestinian families in Gaza had lost over 10 members each. Many Palestinian families have lost 70 members each.

Did I imagine losing 70 members of my family tree, during the genocide?

The level of mortality in Palestinian families is such that medics in Gaza have had to coin a new acronym: "WCNSF," meaning "wounded child, no surviving family."

36.
Have you called your congressperson?

Have you retweeted, reposted, storied out, the content, or did you wonder how you would look, retweeting this thing that made you uncomfortable, during the genocide?

But I prayed during the genocide. I prayed for the hostages. I prayed for the prisoners. I prayed for the living and the dead, and those in the middle.

But I fasted during the genocide. I chalked sidewalks. I called Congress. But I led peace walks. But I awoke in the middle of the night from uneasy dreams.

I kept going to work during the genocide. I graded poems about paradise during the genocide. I asked the students not to forget to write their paradise haunted by the knowledge that there is suffering in the elsewhere, even if it seems to be a distant dream.

That even in paradise it will be remembered.

37.
What has been lost?

Gaza's Central Archives
Great Omari Mosque
Over one hundred mosques and churches
Thirteen libraries
80 percent of all schools
All of the universities

There is a history of such erasure of history. In 1982, when Israel invaded Lebanon, the first thing they did was seize the Palestine Liberation Organization (PLO) archive, the world's largest collection of manuscripts on Palestine.

38.
Can I say how much I love you, who overcame your fear. Who overcame the trauma. Who defied the rules. Who spoke up. Who pestered your reps. Who shamed city halls. Who walked out. Who disrupted the ugly peace of empire, because others could not, or do not.

39.
In February, at her high school, my daughter is reported to have written in chalk on the sidewalk, "Save Gaza" and "Ceasefire Now" and "Free Palestine."

We receive an email from the principal that states, "We are planning to connect with her tomorrow about this to let her know that that's not an action that is permissible on campus right now."

40.
What is permissible, right now?

Did I wake up rested during the genocide?
Did I remember my dreams during the genocide?
Did it even happen, the genocide?

In March, Susan Abulhawa reported:

> People first resorted to eating horse and donkey feed but that's gone. Now they're eating the donkeys and horses. Some are eating stray cats and dogs, which are themselves starving and sometimes feeding on human remains.

41.

She wrote: Save Gaza. Ceasefire Now. Free Palestine. Not an action permissible right now.

On Instagram: a child in Gaza
floats in the wide blue sky—

between two nearly invisible
and dead electric wires—

he untangles the blue
and purple tail of his kite.

42.

Am I dreaming
Right now
I am waking up.
Save Gaza.
Are you waking up
Right now.
Good morning.
Ceasefire now.
Right now.
We're dreaming.
Let's get to work.
Free the captives.

Free Palestine.

Many lines are drawn, sometimes nearly verbatim, from South Africa's Application for Proceedings on Genocide against Israel submitted to the International Court of Justice in January 2024.

February-April 2024

III.
The Poetics of Justice

CHAPTER THIRTEEN

Poetics/Documents/Justice

A Conversation

with Susan Briante, Philip Metres, M. NourbeSe Philip, and Craig Santos Perez

May–July 2020

PHILIP METRES (PM): In their call, *Synthesis* writes, "In their form and content, these different currents of documentary aesthetics all accord a privileged place to the judicial system, interacting with its regime of proof, the frameworks of the enquiry and the trial, and its mission to administer justice. . . . However, though such works structurally undermine claims to aesthetic autonomy and voluntarily confine themselves to the historical particular, they circulate in extra-judicial spheres and invite forms of judgment that differ from those administered by the legal system. What motivates this recourse to art, and what effects might this aesthetic supplement seek to engender? Do such works act to shore up the judicial system in place? Do they seek rather to complement it or palliate its shortcomings? Or do they sometimes turn the tables and put the law itself on trial? To what ends? What, if any, alternative conceptions of the just do they generate? And what, if any, changes do such works aspire to effect on the course of the history they engage with?"

Rereading these questions, I woke up this morning (May 29?) and read more about the murder of George Floyd and the rebellions in protest against the police in Minneapolis and elsewhere. I wondered at my own silence on social media. My first thought was, shouldn't I have immediately taken to Twitter and registered my outrage? My second thought was, what would another post on Twitter do for George Floyd, for justice, for reparations? What I wrote instead was, "If I were elected President of the United States, on day one in office, I would call for two Truth, Reparations, and Reconciliation Commissions (TRRC): on the U.S. responsibility to the indigenous peoples of the Americas, and on the U.S. responsibility to African-Americans." (I added reparations because of the failure of the South African TRC to address the economic dimension of colonialism and apartheid.)

The gesture itself is as empty as any other virtue signaling, but I began thinking again about truth commissions. Truth commissions are transitional justice mechanisms for societies attempting to confront the past, reestablish the rule of law and governance, and move into the future. The problem in the U.S. is that these problems are ongoing and systemic, and to address the past alone fails to account for the past's persistence in the present. A TRRC on slavery would be one thing, but what about Jim Crow? What about mass incarceration? What about voter suppression? So our political and economic systems hauntingly perpetuate inequities shared with slavery's hundreds of years.

Then I started thinking about the peacebuilding and conflict transformation process in Northern Ireland—how, despite a radically successful twenty-plus year peace process (which has included an astonishing reform of policing, powerful economic investment, and shared governance), the parties have never agreed to a truth process, dealing with what they call "the legacy of the past." With the exception of the U.K.'s Saville Inquiry on Bloody Sunday (itself a model), governments have stayed out of the truth trouble. But what has happened are smaller initiatives and endeavors, by grassroots organizations, cultural and educational institutions, and the arts, that have amounted to something like a truth process. What has not happened on the level of law and government still gets told. It's not lost in the erasure of History. Of course, it doesn't carry the weight of official, state-sponsored speech, as when the Prime Minister David Cameron apologized to the families of the killed during Bloody Sunday, of course. I would much prefer that. But to get the Saville Inquiry at all took the work of dozens of activists (often victims and their families), thousands of hours of their own gathering of testimonies, and constant political pressure—for many years—before Tony Blair would call for a reopening of the U.K. government's official understanding of what happened on Bloody Sunday, published in the terrible Widgery Report, a hack job that absolved the British army for the murders.

What connects our various projects as poets is that they are doing the work of truth commissions—not only by gathering testimonies that haven't been aired widely, but also by examining, working with, and critiquing the political, legal, economic, and cultural systems that engineer oppression and injustice. That's why I'm so grateful to have us together to talk about our recent poetry projects—which are more than books of poems, but cultural interventions with historical and political implications. I'm not interested particularly or ultimately in *documentary poetry* as an aesthetic genre, but, as I write elsewhere, "to transform and be transformed by the radical possibilities of creating spaces for poems to happen, by widening the idea of authorship beyond the academy, finding poetry where it always existed: in the mouths of those who have been shut up and shut down, from the pens of those whose lives have been written out of history and must make their own."[1] And not only for poems to happen, I want to say now, but also for spaces and histories and futures to be reclaimed.

SUSAN BRIANTE: I'm interested in the documentary project (I have a degree in journalism), the materiality of documents, and the archive itself. As someone who lives in southern Arizona and who has witnessed the immigration crisis created by our government, the relationship between the state and the document becomes evident in a myriad of ways: What information is included in or omitted from the documents created by the state? Who possesses the document deemed necessary, legible, or acceptable by the state? What kinds of documents are not "legible" or "acceptable"? What stories do they tell? The answers to these questions can change lives as well as the narratives created around those lives. And these are questions that any of us who work with legal documents have to keep in mind.

I started writing *Defacing the Monument*[2] as an attempt to document some of what I witnessed of the immigration crisis. (I live in Tucson just seventy-two miles from the U.S.-Mexico border.) But looking at the court calendar for an Operation Streamline hearing, a process by which migrants are prosecuted in groups of up to seventy-five at a time for the crime of illegal entry, I realized how fraught the documents and the documentary project can be. The Operation Streamline calendar provided so little information about the migrants themselves, the conditions that lead them to immigrate, the involvement of the United States in the reasons for their migration, the brutality they often faced on their journey or at the hands of the Border Patrol, my own complicity as a citizen. Absence haunted the document and the court proceedings that turned these migrants into criminals. So the book became an interrogation of the documentary project itself, an attempt to discern the limits of that project as well as to chronicle and suggest possibilities for alternative methods to approach documentary work.

For example, in the book, I consider the documents, as well as the knowledges, that exist beyond the legal system, that remain beyond the official records or histories of empire. These documents and the information (gossip, dream, folk tale, remedy, oral history, etc.) that remain outside the archive are as important and often more important than what appears within the archives of the state. In fact, they often subvert the power and knowledge of the state.

As I write this, we enter our third week of uprisings sparked by the murder of George Floyd at the hands of Minneapolis police. Floyd is one of the latest in a too-long list of Black men and women killed by police in the United States, whose murders we've seen because of cell phone videos shared by witnesses. And as protests have spread across the United States calling for police accountability and abolition, continued examples of police brutality captured on video circulate. The documentary work done by such videos is invaluable. But we should not need a cell phone video to believe the decades of testimony from Black men and women. Who gets to tell the stories that are archived? Whose stories are believed? These are also vital questions for the documentarian.

CRAIG SANTOS PEREZ: I currently live in Hawai'i, and the waves of viral images and videos of police brutality and civil protest have reached our shores and have reverberated across the Pacific. I have tried to document the ongoing solidarity and antiracist movements in the Pacific Islands and the diaspora in a blog post titled "Black Lives Matter in the Pacific."[3] As an activist writer and public scholar, I believe it is important to document this profound time for my Pacific Islander community to learn from and remember.

This documentary impulse is also present in my ongoing, serial book project *from unincorporated territory*, which I have been working on since 2006 and now includes four volumes. The title refers to the colonial, political status of my home, the Pacific Island of Guåhan (Guam), which has been a territory of the United States since 1898. Beyond depriving my people of self-determination and sovereignty, the U.S. military also occupied 30 percent of the island's landmass, having displaced us from our ancestral lands while also contaminating the land with military waste.

I consider my work to be at the intersection of documentary, indigenous, and decolonial poetics. Similar to others, I find poetry a powerful space to document injustice, especially colonial injustice. I also believe that poetry has the power to expose, critique, and even subvert the documents of empire, whether those be colonial law, history, or political documents. I often work with collage to unsettle documents in my work. Lastly, I think poetry is a profound space to archive indigenous documents that may have been buried or erased. These decolonial documents could be official archives or they can be more informal, such as oral stories, memories, family genealogies, and more. At least for me, poetry has become an important space to document (verb) and to more deeply understand documents (noun).

PHILIP METRES: Craig, how has your approach in the work *from unincorporated territory*—a massive, multidecade project, truly a life work—changed over time? How do you balance the confrontation of history and the imagination of a recovered future? Do you imagine an end point to the project? And, relatedly, how do you imagine this work as related to the political project of justice and liberation?

CRAIG SANTOS PEREZ: My general approach has not changed much in the sense that each book centers indigenous Pacific culture, history, and stories. The poems have remained documentary, avant-garde, and decolonial. With each new book, I have tried to experiment with new forms from earlier books. For example, my first two[4] books explore a kind of lyric, abstract expressionism, whereas in books three[5] and four[6] I worked more with fragmented, narrative prose poems. Since the series is autobiographical, the books have captured changes in my life. Two of my grandparents who I write about in my first book have since passed away, so I have eulogy poems for them in the forthcoming volume. Another grandparent that I wrote about in my second book has since been diagnosed with dementia, so I have been writing about her memory loss in subsequent books. I also got married and had two children, so those life changes are major themes in my fourth book.

In my culture, and many Pacific cultures, we view time as a spiral so that the past, present, and future are all entwined. My fourth book, [lukao], explores this more deeply in terms of turning to history to help guide us into the future, especially as we confront climate change. To be more specific, I believe that indigenous ecological knowledge has a lot to teach us about how to live sustainably on the planet.

I will continue to write this series until my homeland and people are free and independent, so that may be my whole life. This is related to how I imagine the work as a project of justice and liberation. As a decolonial writer, it is my responsibility to continue to recover my people's histories, to articulate a liberatory politics, and to imagine a sovereign future.

PHILIP METRES: Susan, in *Defacing the Monument*,[7] you advocate for a poetics of hauntology (as in NourbeSe Philip's *Zong!*),[8] a poetics of entanglement (as in James Agee's *Let Us Now Praise Famous Men*)[9]—rather than the sort of static liberalism of representation and inclusion. Could you talk a bit about the ethos of these approaches, as well as address the question of the project of justice? How does this provide a path to justice?

SUSAN BRIANTE: The idea of "hauntology" comes from Derrida's reference to the persistence of elements of the past. But I am also thinking of Avery Gordon's book, *Ghostly Matters*, in which she writes about finding "shapes" defined by absence or "the paradox of tracking through time and across all those forces that which makes its mark by being there and not there at the same time."[10] In my reading that process of "tracking" allows Philip to tell a story untold in her beautiful, essential, and innovative work *Zong!* That tracking becomes an act of conjuring the names that have been forgotten and channeling the voices that are absent from the legal document *Gregson v. Gilbert*. It's important to note the care with which Philip resurrects this narrative. She works to create the conditions necessary to listen through the silence and discern the absence left in the wake of the massacre of enslaved Africans on the *Zong*: she visits a "traditional shrine close to one of the slave ports in the homeland of the Ewe people,"[11] to meet and speak with elders and the priest of the shrine; she visits the port of Liverpool from which the *Zong* set sail. Part of that work involves research, part of that work involves asking permission from the living. That is what makes *Zong!* so different from the kind of ventriloquism that some writers resort to when working with documentary evidence.

Entanglement, for me, represents an extension of the necessary "research" in that it involves an investigation of the histories, legacies, processes, systems, and conditions that produce the events about which we write. But beyond archival research and the searching for what has been excluded from the archive, beyond the contextual research that helps us to understand the systems and conditions about which we write—we need to do the research on ourselves to map our relations and entanglements with the people and events that become the subject of our writing. In his 1975 chapbook *Investigative Poetry*, the poet Ed Sanders outlines an expansive methodology for the documentary or investigative poet that includes such tools as data grids, case files, investigative glyphs, mortality lists, and garbage grids.[12] The latter refers to lists of a subject's moral failings or the injustices attributable to certain actors. (He describes making a garbage grid for Henry Kissinger for example.) But then Sanders proposes something very important: "One useful method, if you find yourself preparing garbage grids, and you want to MAINTAIN ACCURACY, is to prepare some garbage grids on YOURSELF . . . that justice pulse along your grids of others."[13] As writers, it's imperative that we note how we might be complicit with the very systems we critique. We need to be willing to understand our place within oppressive systems because ultimately understanding our relation allows us to learn how to fight for change.

Both of these models offer something more than what you very aptly call "the static liberalism of representation and inclusion." "Representation and inclusion" have all sorts of institutional connotations for me in relation to failed attempts to counter white supremacy. Or perhaps they are not failed attempts but rather attempts that do exactly what they were supposed to do, which has nothing to do with countering white supremacy. I am thinking of the universities where I have studied or worked, of the departments that hired faculty of color without making any changes in practices, policies, or attitudes and then wondered why none of these faculty stayed.

I want to be careful when thinking about documentary poetics and justice, or writing and justice, in general. I think it has been too easy for too long for too many writers—especially white writers—to rely on documentary forms as their only method to engage with injustice. It's not enough to represent injustice in our writing. In fact, simple representation of violence can produce its own kind of violence. We are at a moment now in which there are a million ways to do the work to counter injustice as teachers, students, listeners, organizers, protestors, donors, volunteers, etc. Our writing does not have to be our only activism.

PHILIP METRES: When I read the work of fellow poets like Susan Briante, Craig Santos Perez, M. NourbeSe Philip, and many others, I'm in awe at the variety of poetic approaches and the tender tenacity, the ways in which they hold and explore and also interrogate and lament the depredations of the powerful, and the traces they leave in the archives. That old cliche about history being told by the victors, in this information and digital age, is less true, but not entirely untrue either.

Reflecting on my practice and poetry in *Sand Opera* and *Shrapnel Maps*, I see that I'm not interested merely in plundering archives of declassified government documents, for interrogation or deconstruction. I'm interested in undoing erasure, often about particular people that I know or whose lives have become proximate to mine. My friendship with Nahida Halaby Gordon, learning her story, inviting her to present at my Israeli and Palestinian Literatures course over the years, meant that I was responsible. I was also a witness. Sometimes it's the reverse order—research begins the journey, and relationship clarifies it. Nahida, a Palestinian refugee from 1948, became the lens through which I understood the unique place of Jaffa in Palestine, and also the hints of what's been called Plan Dalet—the Zionist plan to remove Palestinians from the land. The Haganah leaflet that Nahida's father had in his papers burned in my mind for months. It seemed to be a door into understanding why Palestinian Arabs fled their homes in 1948. They have long argued that they were expelled by force and by fear. Israelis and those who support the Jewish state argue that they left of their own accord. The Haganah leaflet indicated a level of coordination that suggests otherwise—gathering the men in the center of the city, asking for the Jaffa municipal archives to be secured for purposes of further land claims, etc. That Jaffa archive has "disappeared." Archives—at least as material repositories—are never complete, and are often curated and withheld by the powerful.

Another anecdote. The first place the Israeli Defense Force headed, upon invading Beirut in 1982, was to the PLO Research Center, in order to abscond with their archive. Archives—not only state-run archives, but the archives of any people or community—are powerful and potentially dangerous. They contain the evidence.

So perhaps poetry, particularly poetry with the range and capacity for including masses of material evidence, can be a sort of counterarchive—part of what could be summoned in a truth process in the future, as well as a marker for the present. As Briante and Perez both argue in their own way, the informal and human archives of stories, artifacts, songs, and other informal material create another history. The term "documentary poetics" seems too small a term for what we're trying to do, fixating on a formal procedure—working with documents—rather than on a poetic-political vision of what's possible. Documentary poetry seems to then fall into an elegiac relationship with time and its materials. We need elegy, we need grief, but not being frozen in grief. What can the future look like?

When I say that I'm trying to situate *Shrapnel Maps* as a dream of a new past, I mean that neither the past nor the future are fixed, and in this apocalyptic age, we need to go further back to find a way out of the nightmare of the present-future. It's about witnessing the palimpsest, not selecting a single history, but the many histories of that place, of that being-in-place. As the Palestinian poet Ghassan Zaqtan notes, "if you want to belong to this place, you have to belong to all of its history and respect 10,000 years of civilization."[14] And in an age of climate change, we should go even farther than respecting civilization to respecting the persistence of creatures situated in ecosystems.

M. NOURBESE PHILIP: Notes towards Sealing Forensic Landscapes

!

When I first visited the continent of Africa, invited as a guest of the Pan African conference, I took with me a small machine, a metal seal embosser that lawyers use to emboss their seal on affidavits after swearing a document. I had stopped practicing law but had kept mine. I carried that machine with me because I wanted to prove that something had happened. That my ancestors had been kidnapped and sold away from this continent I was about to visit, a place which had lived so large in the minds and hearts of the people of the cari[bbean] basin. What document was I going to seal? Its nonexistence was irrelevant. There was an urge to make the (un)memory matter—literally; to document and verify that something had happened and the affidavit seal would do that.

!!

As a law student I experienced a profound psychic disturbance as we were being coached and trained in the centrality of the law and the need, as future lawyers, to uphold it always. How could I? Why should I? When this very hallowed system once enshrined in its codes that I was a thing. Not a being who was always. Being. Human. How could anyone respect a system that generated such a belief? Against being. Could I be judge of that system. Find it, despite the trumpeted reliance on justice and precedent, severely lacking. It was that fundamental distrust, even as I acknowledge the universality of law—be it customary or traditional, or laws imposed through colonial systems—that underwrote my challenging the legal document, *Gregson v. Gilbert*.

(Question to myself: Are there any societies without laws?)

(Observation: The universe itself is governed by laws of physics that over time we have been discovering. The law of gravity pins us to the earth) Engaging with law is essential to being the being that is Is. Being human.

!!!

We in the Americas live in forensic landscapes[1]—arenas where great crimes have been perpetrated, but which have never been acknowledged as crimes. Theft of the land from the indigenous would constitute the original crime; theft and enslavement of African peoples would constitute the second and twinned crime. Could we argue—I want to argue—that since the commission of the crime, the perpetrators have been attempting, through a variety of means, to erase and destroy the evidence of the crime—the continued survival of the very people who were trafficked—Africans. From discrimination of various sorts resulting in poverty, incarceration, and in general shortened lifespans up to and including actual murder and lynching in the case of the U.S., the law has spawned a network of ways in which to destroy the evidence. Remember that even Lincoln had not intended that liberated African Americans would remain in the country. Indeed, the refusal to see what has happened as a crime—a crime against humanity—results in yet another layer of erasure of acknowledgment of the crime. Perhaps this refusal to acknowledge these founding crimes haunts American life and culture (I'm speaking here particularly of the U.S.); perhaps this explains the country's cultural and societal obsession with crime—law and order—in its myriad forms, evidenced by the plethora of crime shows the public consumes.

The U.S. is not unique in being founded in crime or wrongful action: after killing his twin brother Remus, Romulus founds Rome, which would later become the center of a world empire. The Old Testament recounts that Jacob deceived his twin brother Esau, received his father's blessing, and became the progenitor of the twelve tribes of Israel. Twinning, empire, and crime—motifs that haunt the forensic landscape so many call Home.

!v

the logic of law vs the logic of the heart

Perhaps as a poet working in a forensic landscape where the laws function to erase and destroy evidence, where evidence of crime is continually discounted, documenting then assumes a different and perhaps greater significance. I am thinking of "documenting" here in a sense different from the way we usually think of it—as using the archive or preexisting documents. I'm thinking of the poet as documentarian, documenting the Silence of the archive, because that Silence is where we, from whom so much has been taken, to whom so much harm has been done, reside. This Silence is akin to the virtual, digital world, which appears suspended in time but which has a mattered, matted, material aspect—the undersea cables, the mining projects that exploit people, the sweatshops employing low wage workers all creating this algorithmic landscape. That too is a forensic landscape of sorts. Special tools are necessary to read the Silence of the archive, and these tools, to quote Audre Lorde, cannot be the master's.[15] How do we write poetry within forensic landscapes—does it change the way we think about what we're doing? Do we become advocates, as I felt I had become when writing *Zong!*, on behalf of all those silenced voices on board the *Zong*? "Suppose the law / a lie." Do those ex-aquaed voices become judge and jury? What's the verdict? I think it important to understand that the work we're doing at present is being done within forensic landscapes—we are the living, breathing evidence of the crime; we also inhabit the scene of the crime, simultaneously as we document for the purposes of evidence, for the purposes of the Ancestors, simultaneously as we sift the evidence for truth. In pursuit of another system of justice.

To be (dis)continued.

The idea of forensic landscapes was sparked by reading about the work of Forensic Architecture, particularly the events surrounding the Ayotzinapa Case: A Cartography of Violence.

Facebook post dated May 30, 2020

Several weeks ago I wrote about the need to stoke our anger and nurture it for a time in the future, post pandemic, when we would need to draw on it to ensure that politicians did not claw back positive changes, or to force them to make necessary improvements. Think of the shambolic way in which long term care homes have been managed leading to the death of far too many of our older generation. Little did I expect that my anger would explode during the pandemic, as I heard myself wishing for retribution and vengeance in the wake of George Floyd's murder. Audre Lorde's essay, "The Uses of Anger," directed primarily to Black women, but relevant to all who care to listen to her wisdom helped to ground those feelings. It is distressing but also remarkable how applicable her words continue to be. Excerpts from that essay follow:

> Anger expressed and translated into action in the service of our vision and our future is a liberating and strengthening act of clarification, for it is in the painful process of this translation that we identify who are our allies with whom we have grave differences, and who are our genuine enemies. . . .

> Anger is loaded with information and energy. . . . We operate in the teeth of a system for whom racism and sexism are primary, established, and necessary props of profit. . . .
>
> Mainstream communication . . . wants racism to be accepted as an immutable given in the fabric of existence, like evening time or the common cold. . . .
>
> We cannot allow our fear of anger to deflect us nor to seduce us into anything less than the hard work of excavating honesty . . . because, rest assured, our opponents are quite serious about their hatred of us and of what we are trying to do here. . . .
>
> This hatred and our anger are very different. Hatred is the fury of those who do not share our goals, and its object is death and destruction. Anger is the grief of distortions between peers, and its object is change. . . .
>
> Anger is an appropriate reaction to racist attitudes, as is fury when the actions arising from those attitudes do not change. . . .
>
> For it is not the anger of Black women which is dripping down over this globe like a diseased liquid. It is not my anger that launches rockets, spends over sixty thousand dollars a second on missiles and other agents of war and death, pushes opera singers off rooftops, slaughters children in cities, stockpiles nerve gas and chemical bombs, sodomizes our daughters and our earth. It is not the anger of Black women which corrodes into blind, dehumanizing power, bent upon the annihilation of us all unless we meet it with what we have, our power to examine and to redefine the terms upon which we will live and work; our power to envision and to reconstruct, anger by painful anger, stone upon heavy stone, a future of pollinating difference and the earth to support our choices.[16]

This morning I listened to Sweet Honey in the Rock singing "Ella's Song" (in memory of the civil rights leader and activist Ella Baker): "Those who believe in justice cannot rest . . ."[17] and all I could do was cover my face and weep, for so much that I find inexpressible. I'm particularly grieved by the fact that we've all been made unwilling accomplices in becoming voyeurs to the murder and lynching of Black people, even as we are grateful that through digital technology we now have the evidence of what Black and African descended folX have always known. Can we, perhaps, console ourselves that we are witnesses, not voyeurs, in a system that has always fed on the trauma and death of Black bodies? I don't know, but what I do know is that Black folX, supported by white allies, dragged the US, kicking, screaming and murdering, to a better form of democracy, imperfect as it remains. Same with South Africa—not to mention the improvements we've been instrumental in making to Canadian society in areas such as policing and human rights. Oh, but how we long to rest, how we long to rest . . . And breathe.[18]

Facebook post dated June 19, 2020

> I want to thank all who have received my posts over the last several weeks in generosity. I am not very adept at social media, but FB [Facebook] has provided me a space to manage the range of emotions I have had, beginning with the pandemic and morphing into the uprising in the aftermath of the lynching of George Floyd. It wouldn't be FB, however, if it hasn't also contributed to my own disturbance, but on balance it has helped to post. Am not sure why I write this—now. I've come to a place of rockstone silence that is more times than not filled with rage as I witness the mea culpas of companies and people acknowledging that they should have done otherwise regarding Black and African-descended folX. Anna Wintour of Vogue comes to mind here, as well as the awful b&w images of white celebrities "confessing their racial sins."

Why rage when the expected response should be joy at the revelation of what Black folX have always known and lived with—exclusion and rejection, from the subtle to the aggressive, from the emotional to the rational? Because those who were and are doing the exclusion, be it the individual or the individual on behalf of the system, knew and know what they were/are doing (witness the current Peel Board of Ed. and Parliament excluding Jagmeet Singh) and their current, often tepid, acknowledgment owes everything to the uprising and the fear and consternation it has generated. And yes, I do believe the burning and looting has had an impact. As it did in '68. Unfortunately the language of the system we live in and with is violence and that is the one language it best understands, MLK and nonviolent resistance notwithstanding. I also know that systems change the better to remain the same, so I remain skeptical.

Earlier this week I saw myself as a landmine on which someone had just stepped and we were both going to explode when whoever it was lifted their foot; a grenade with a loose pin ready to explode at any moment. I did not want to see another Black man crying on TV or social media (pace(peace) John Boyega): I wanted them to take up arms. Alongside women. I wanted neither understanding nor pity—I wanted—the I standing in for the collectivity—to be feared and respected. This rage is mediated by an anguished grief as I read, or am told by friends, about experiences of racism, some going back many years. As I think of my own experiences with racism. We, humans, all carry wounds but I'm reminded of Thomas Merton who wrote: "There are things the Negro knows that the white man can never know. Things which belong to the pure, unique, spiritual destiny of America, and which have been denied to the white man, will be denied to him forever because of his brutality to the Negro and to the Indian. So, too, there are things the Jew alone can know, things closed forever to the gentile, even to the best of Christians."[19] I would add that the "pure, unique, spiritual destiny" has everything to do with who we, Black and African-descended people, are. The evidence is there in all the beauty we have wrought out of the evil directed at us and given to the world. "They [Black people] know this evil," Merton wrote. "They have seen it, kept silent about it, borne it for generations." But we have been speaking out about it, working to change it, marching, rioting and looting—I claim it all, will not eschew any aspect of the struggle—yet it has to take a Black man being lynched in public for the great awakening to happen? (Aided, no doubt, by all the various spin-offs from COVID-19.) And by struggle I mean the worldwide struggle on the part of Black, African, and African-descended people against white supremacy and its systems for equal rights and respect. Yet the murders by police continue and Billie sighs and begins to sing softly about "strange fruit . . . Black bodies swingin' (again) in the Southern breeze."[20] To the white man who said "it takes time," this is what Fannie Lou Hamer replied: "For three hundred and more years they have had 'time,' and now it is time for them to listen."[21] And act, I would add.

The experiences and emotions described above have been akin to removing a bandage from a wound, only to find that the wound is septic, suppurating, has developed gangrene and the rotten, rotting substance has to be cut out, excised, removed somehow.

Today is Juneteenth and I extend my best wishes for the safety and wellness to the African American tribe/family of the Afrospora as I turn once more to Fannie Lou Hamer whose words are as relevant today as they were decades ago when she uttered them: "Nobody's free until everybody's free." This week saw how the bloody struggle for civil and human rights for African Americans continues to redound to the benefit of others, in this case LGBTQ Americans. To repeat a statement I've made in an earlier posting—as imperfect a democracy as America is, it was Black folX and allies who brought it kicking, screaming and murdering closer to the ideals of what a true democracy should be. As also happened in South Africa, long heralded as a democracy even as it held millions of its Black citizens hostage in a brutal apartheid system. "Nobody's free until everybody's free" and once again I see Black folX, with some allies, straining and pulling the entire world to a higher and better system of free.

Happy Juneteenth![22]

2021

CHAPTER FOURTEEN

"A Story That Can't Be Told, Yet Must Be Told"

Interview with M. NourbeSe Phillip

PHILIP METRES (PM): First, congratulations on having *Zong!* voted as the reader's choice for most influential book in our twenty-first century! This is what I'd written about why I selected it: "I discovered M. NourbeSe Philip's *Zong!*[1] only after I'd written *abu ghraib arias* (which became *Sand Opera*) when critics saw parallels in the work. *Zong!* is at once a brilliant documentary long poem and a sort of ritual exorcism of the demons of the slave trade. Built out of the language of the legal document of *Gregson vs. Gilbert*, *Zong!* brings to light the murder of Africans on board a slave ship in 1781 for financial gain. The kidnapped and enslaved Africans had been purposely thrown overboard so that the owner of the *Zong* could benefit from his insurance policy. Philip's visionary use of the burying language of law to recover the shreds of the voices of the lost is stark, elemental, and electrifying. It is poetry raised to the level of a truth commission. This work has launched a thousand poetic justice projects in the mode of documentary recovery."

What does it mean for you to have *Zong!* recognized as such a pivotal work, one that has resonated with both readers and writers, and given birth to many other books interested in the parallel ongoing work of documentary poetics, archival unearthing, and attending to the trauma of those subject to the slave trade and other imperial and colonial depredations?

M. NOURBESE PHILIP (MNP): I do get a sense every so often of the work that *Zong!* has been doing. For instance, a professor shared with me that they were doing a job search and every job applicant had mentioned *Zong!* in their application. As writers and poets we all want our work to be read, noticed, and cherished, so when I become aware that others have found something of value in what I've written, it's not so much that I'm happy, but I feel myself more settled—I can exhale. And this allows me to take another deep breath. That the work I've done has made some small contribution to expanding our understanding of what poetry can do in our ongoing attempts to correct the awful legacy of, and ongoing practices linked to, empire, race, class, gender, and sexuality is heartening; it shores me up when I grow tired and question whether we can actually extricate ourselves from our present position on the brink of environmental and human disaster.

PM: You write extensively about the process of creating the work in "Notanda," toward the end of *Zong!*, including a journey to Ghana to get a blessing to do this work. But I'd also love to know more about your relationship to Setaey Adamu Boateng—listed on the title page as "as told to the author by . . ."—and the process of collaborating with the ancestors while creating this work. Do you have advice for other writers about this practice?

MNP: I abdicated my role as author of *Zong!* in the sense we think of authorship and I explore this in "Notanda." Indeed, I describe myself as the unauthor of the work. I was following gut feelings when I felt the need to ask permission to bring these voices forward, and I would say that the most important aspect of the process of working with those energies, which are larger than us, is humility—a putting aside of the ego to be able to allow what needs to come through to manifest.

The names of the Ancestors on the cover of *Zong!* represent at least three different legacies, which it wouldn't be appropriate to go into. Having said that, however, I should say that I didn't see myself as collaborating with the Ancestors so much as listening to what seemed needed or necessary. These are all comments that run athwart how we talk about poetry today, although as poets we more often than not occupy that place in our thoughts, psyches, and emotions that as often remain unnamed, or when identified, as Keats attempted, bear names like "negative capability." Living with uncertainty, accepting opacity, welcoming mystery, and, most importantly, humility or learning to put the ego out of commission (a difficult task for us as Westerners so used to wielding the ego), these are all necessary for poets interested in this type of work. As poets, language is our medium—language used with great care—and in caring for language and the wonderfully difficult work it does, we learn to care for others, for the least among us; we care for their lives, filled with wonder, heartache, tragedy, and trauma. In caring for this thing—language—that makes us beings who are human, in caring for the lowly comma, or period, for the syllable or phoneme, for where they're placed, we begin, I think—I hope—to care for others. Care and attention—take care and pay attention is what I believe the craft of poetry to be about—paying attention and taking care. This would be my contribution to trying to find a way to work with that which might appear past, or to working with the Ancestors or howsoever we choose to describe this particular kind of work. For instance, as part of our annual performances of *Zong!*, I developed the Protocols of Care, which are essentially directions to help readers and participants feel cared for, at ease, and at home for the evening. The process also creates a space that allows for the presence of the Ancestors throughout the performance.

PM: In our conversation for *Synthesis* magazine, you talk about the fact that in the Americas, we are living in forensic landscapes: "arenas where great crimes have been perpetrated, but which have never been acknowledged as crimes. Theft of the land from the indigenous would constitute the original crime; theft and enslavement of African peoples would constitute the second and twinned crime. Could we argue—I want to argue—that since the commission of the crime, the perpetrators have been attempting through a variety of means, to erase and destroy the evidence of the crime—the continued survival of the very people who were trafficked—Africans."[2] *Zong!* is an example of how a poem might work to be part of truth processes that might unerase those crimes. How does your other work participate in this project of truth-recovery, or marking the impossibility of truth-recovery? For you right now, what is the task of the poet and of poetry?

MNP: I enjoy writing essays—it's an area in which I draw on my training in law to make argument. It's an important activity for me because I don't wish to make argument in poetry—I want to inhabit the contradictions—"english is my mother tongue / is my father tongue."[3] Essay writing also allows me space to explore ideas and issues in a more logical, left-brain way, and, in a sense, to discharge that impulse and energy. Having said that, however, for the last several years I have been experimenting with bringing into essays some of the resources of poetry, such as repetition and fragmentation.

What you describe as the "impossibility of truth-recovery" aptly describes my view of the "project of truth-recovery," particularly as it applies to poetry. It explains the refrain throughout "Notanda," that this is a story that can't be told, yet must be told, and it can only be told by untelling or not-telling and all the inherent contradictions that accompany that statement.

Regarding the task of the poet and poetry—I think that each poet has to decide how s/he views their own work and the work they want it to do. For myself, the inestimable value of poetry lies in what I call its necessary uselessness. It is because poetry will not save us that we need it; it is because poetry cannot save us that it is more necessary than ever before. This may sound like a contradiction of what I've said in answer to your first question in which I talk about enlarging the space of possibility for poetry, but I don't think it is—at least no more than the realization and understanding that we are all end-stopped rather than run-on lines. We all come to an end, but that in no way prevents us from creating the marvelous—we continue to make art, music, poetry, startlingly beautiful buildings, bridges, electric cars, rockets, and novels in the face of what could be said to be the futility of life, which ends in death. Always.

PM: Are there any questions that you would like to be asked and to answer?

MNP: Living with *Zong!* has been a learning practice and I confess that sometimes I do feel the weight of it, which I try to carry lightly—not always successfully. A weight in the sense that I am presently facing two instances of people wanting to use the work, but treating it as fungible. In one case the curator wanted to use pages of *Zong!* in a public outdoor art display, but attempted to sanitize the text by not wanting to use any pages with the word "negro" in it because of current "increased sensitivity of the word negro." In another case the work was translated unbeknownst to me, although they had acquired the rights from the publishers who failed to let me know. The result is a "translation" that completely destroys the conceptual and formal underpinnings of the work, resulting in a facsimile or a transcription rather than a translation that respects the work and the event it marks. Most importantly, in not allowing the words to breathe as they must, in ignoring or destroying the form, which is so integrally linked to breath and reparation, as limited as it might be, the "translation" fails to honour the dead and the Ancestors. This grieves me deeply. People appear ineluctably drawn to the work, yet often aren't able to accept it on its own terms. Or, as happened a couple of years ago, they appropriate the ideas and the underlying theoretical and conceptual constructs without acknowledging the source, or, more importantly, the restorative work it is doing. As I say, it becomes weighty and demands a lot of energy to deal with these kinds of issues. I am trying to find a way to put in place a system to shore me up. Underlying it all is a kind of sedimented racism and sexism that is so much a part of the colonial or what I call the we-own-the world project, because these people are all well meaning and see themselves as wanting to help—to make a change. Too often, however, the same currents of white supremacy continue to swirl around these issues. As they say: Plus ça change, plus c'est la même chose.

2021

CHAPTER FIFTEEN

Black Lives Matter and the Poetics of Racial Justice[1]

At a speech for Black writers in 1976, June Jordan said, "As I think about anyone or anything—whether history or literature or my father or political organizations or a poem or a film—as I seek to evaluate the potentiality, the life-supportive commitment/possibilities of anyone or any thing, the decisive question is, always, *where is the love*?"[2]

Jordan's words offer a clarion call, in times of necessary and rightful rage, to locate where love pulses at the heart of our practice of art and activism. It rhymes with Cornel West's notion that "justice is what love looks like in public."[3] What if we aim as writers to create works that make love public—that is to say, that honor the fundamental dignity of all people, and name and dismantle the oppressive systems of power?

To explore how writers and writing can contribute to the struggle for justice and liberation necessitates flipping the (white) script that limits the purpose of writing to making something beautiful and pointless. This chapter performs a thought experiment that unwrites some of my academic training in an aesthetic regime of white taste and writes toward the vibrant tradition of literature as a key cultural contributor to movements for social change.

In particular, I want to create space here for a range of poetry particularly by Black poets that contribute to the Movement for Black Lives. I highlight how poets participate in the visionary aspects, as well as the struggles, of social movements. Poets are both challenged by and can challenge the pieties of social movements. Finally, I write this as an invitation for those who share a passion for both writing and social justice, but have not quite found a way to bring them together.

Background and the Question of Audience

I'd like to begin my sharing about myself as a way of self-positioning. Because I was born to an Arab American father, a veteran of the Vietnam War, I knew the impact of war. My father held in his body and psyche its mysteries, and I never knew if his bouts of depression and anger were related to that experience. I never knew where the war ended and my father began. When I was a college student, the 1991 Persian Gulf War broke my heart and blew up my worldview. My fellow citizens cheered a killing spree that was depicted like a video game, censoring and erasing the bloodshed. The liberal illusions I had about my country were could not bear what I learned about U.S. empire at home and abroad—of its indigenous genocide, of the enslavement and oppression of Black people.

As a writer, I wanted to resist those forces of empire and white supremacy, to take part in efforts to make the world a more just and peaceful place. My writing and activism focused on war resistance—through my graduate work and my critical book, *Behind the Lines: War Resistance Poetry on the American Homefront*—as well as my own poetry. In *Behind the Lines*, I sought to track the interactions between poets and the peace movement, seeking models for how a poet can contribute to the work of resistance and making change. Looking back, I was swimming upstream against not only a society thirsty for war but also a poetry world that spurned political poems.

In creative writing workshops, whether in undergrad or grad school, I found my work occasionally greeted with puzzlement. The very idea that poems could be political was outside of the mainstream workshop view.[4] I wrestled with the resistance to my own poems that were trying to do something other than confess or ironize or lament. Ideology, of course, is not just a province of politics, but pervades our educational system—even in the liberal bastions of literary study and creative writing. Poets whose work announced itself as partisan or political were often dismissed as being unlyrical, unnuanced, self-righteous, rhetorically clumsy.

To be sure, my study of war resistance poetry did involve reading quite a bit of "bad" poetry—that is to say, poems that did not feel much like the poetry I was reading in literature courses. But there were also other poems that suggested another way. In *Behind the Lines*, I wrote about the astonishing work of war resistance poetry—not only as poems but also as elegant dancers between the claims of art and the claims of conscience, between the nation and the peace movement.

What I argued about war resistance poetry may apply, tentatively, to poetries invested in social movements like Black Lives Matter. The secret of American poetry was the "presumption that poetry should be bounded by, limited to, or produced for the nation. War resistance poetry thus requires us to pay attention to the ways in which poetry constructs, addresses, and negotiates its nation(s). The dangers of employing that 'we' are obvious: it can produce a lyric subjectivity that refuses to acknowledge its own epistemological limits while speaking to the already-converted in a language that fails to challenge the writer or her audience."[5]

Poetry in conversation with movements for social change necessarily invites questions of audience, and how we define the nation. In *Behind the Lines*, I centered poetry that was able to address both its intimate audience and imagine the wider national audience. When we look at how poets have contributed to racial justice movements, the question of audience emerges with particular intensity. *Who am I addressing* is not an abstract rhetorical question for the writer of social justice poetry, but one that is marked and scarred by ideological and generational wars.

During the Black Writers Conference at Fisk University in 1966, poet Robert Hayden made the argument that he didn't want to write for a Black audience alone, and found himself in the crosshairs of Amiri Baraka and others who represented a separatist nationalism in Black poetry.[6] In 1965 Baraka had changed his name after the assassination of Malcolm X and ushered in what would be called the Black Arts Movement. It might be too provocative to say that the fifty-three-year-old Hayden was canceled. But not by much. It was a devastating blow to the elder poet, and he didn't even show up to the next year's Black Writers Conference, even though it was at his home university.

Phillip Brian Harper has argued that the rhetorical address of Black nationalist poetry relied not only upon a split between Black and white nations but also within the Black nation itself. "The other within" for Black nationalism, according to Harper, was the Black person who sought assimilation with whites, who "sold out" his race.[7] That was Hayden, who found himself metaphorically thrown "out the window," as Baraka's poem "Poem for Half White College Students" imagines.[8] On the continuum of poetries, the Black Arts Movement chose a separatist view in the intergenerational and political battle about the future of both the movement and of poetry.

Such arguments within excluded communities are not only inevitable, they can demonstrate a productive vitality. They are crucial to sustain and grow social movements. But there is a difference between lighting a fire beneath someone who is complacent and burning their house down. What if disagreeing with love could look more like a "calling in" rather than a calling out? In the age of Twitter, it is far easier to call someone out on social media than engage in the more difficult work of wrestling with each other over tactics in a movement.

The Art(s) of Social Justice

The goals of what's now termed "social justice art" could not be more different from the aims that attended my graduate poetry workshops in the late 1990s. That our art could primarily seek to raise critical consciousness about systemic oppression; share stories that have been suppressed, denigrated, or erased by the dominant culture; build community; and motivate individuals to promote social change and catalyze action to alter systems of oppression—I wonder how my work would have changed if these aims were at the heart of our collective workshop practice.[9] But they weren't. And it's not as if the poets and professors in workshops would have necessarily militated against them. We believed we were inside a brutal, competitive system that could not be changed, and that whatever justice or change we sought had to be done elliptically, evasively, a poetic subterfuge. Many of us, inducted into this selective service system of the arts, were trained out of thinking about a community and audience that did not involve a panel of unforgiving, elitist, powerful judges. It's not that we couldn't imagine the communities to which we belonged, and the communities that we joined intentionally to make change in the world—but that poetry world did not care.

It's hard to remember now that, just a decade ago, the twin doyennes of elite white poetry criticism, Helen Vendler and Marjorie Perloff—who probably would never agree about anything regarding poetry—both lambasted Rita Dove for using "multicultural inclusiveness" as a principal editorial criterion for her 2011 *Penguin Anthology of 20th Century American Poetry*.[10] Like Hayden, Dove herself is no radical, in poetry or in politics, but her selections made serious waves. Now, it's as if the paradigm has so completely shifted, that Harmony Holiday could, in a recent Tweet, create a meme of Dove's wonderfully annoyed expression after being asked by an interviewer: "You're an African American poet but not a Black poet in the movement type of way . . ."[11]

Dove's place in poetry is, of course, well established. Today, thanks to new liberatory models of education and social media democratization, young poets have a new place of possibility where the aesthetic and the political, where beauty and justice are not polarities but interconnected and overlapping fields. We will not resolve the old tensions between poetry and power, but a new generation of poets and writers have access to learning about and participating in the struggle for liberation and against white supremacy and empire.

Poets like June Jordan and Mark Nowak have been exemplars in this work, reclaiming and resituating poetry in contexts where people from excluded and oppressed groups could work with poetry as a means of survival and transforming society. Literary organizations like Cave Canem, Kundiman, and RAWI (Radius of Arab American Writers) foster community and mentor young writers of color, utterly changing the face of contemporary poetry. More recently, Felicia Rose Chavez's popular *The Anti-Racist Writing Workshop: How to Decolonize the Creative Classroom* (2021) also offers an alternative to the Iowa workshop model, one that creates spaces designed for the thriving of writers of color. Finally, Split This Rock, an exemplary Washington, D.C. nonprofit, founded to promote social justice poetry, "celebrates poetry that bears witness to injustice and provokes social change."[12] Split This Rock aims not only to uplift social justice poetry but also to overcome the alienation of poets and the individualism associated with the art. In the words of their mission, "The work of writing the poems that split open the injustices in society is in some ways a solitary act, but it is also an act that requires community."[13] Their activities have included a biannual festival, youth engagement, readings, workshops, community collaborations, and hosting an online archive, The Quarry, that offers an alternative canon of social justice poems that "help us name injustices and grieve losses both personal and communal. They speak our rage and our resistance. And they imagine another world, one built on justice and with the power of love."[14]

But poetry's role in social justice movements is not self-evident. Tensions abound. To enter into the fray for justice, particularly if you want to be an ally, we may need to set aside our desire to be right, and our need to be seen as good. *Virtue signaling, performative allyship, clout chasing*—these recent terms describe public actions that center the person doing the action rather than the movement for change; they're taking credit, not helping to transform oppressive social structures.

Finding productive ways to participate in a social justice movement is not easy. People will disagree about both strategies and tactics. You may get criticized. Take Tamika Mallory. Her unforgettable 2020 "State of Emergency" speech after the death of George Floyd captured widespread attention.[15] But after her 2021 Grammy performance with Lil Baby and Killer Mike, Samaria Rice, the mother of the murdered Tamir Rice, called her a clout chaser. She said: "You're not going to continue to benefit on the blood of these families. If you're fighting for justice of the families, make sure you've got the families on the front line. Don't make a career out of this, when your loved ones aren't the ones who were killed."[16] Responding to a now-deleted response from Tamika Mallory on YouTube, one commenter wrote: "She needs you to stop commodifying Black death. You can ask Ms. Rice what you should do with the money you made off of that Grammy performance." This anonymous commenter has struck to the heart of the matter for any poet or writer interested in contributing to racial justice: How do you write in a way that doesn't benefit from Black labor and Black suffering?

During the Black Lives Matter protests of 2020, racial justice activist Deepa Iyer shared a helpful visual called "Mapping Our Roles in a Social Change Ecosystem."[17] While it's not complete, it does offer us ways for thinking about how we might play a role in movements for social justice, not just as writers.

Iyer's visual map offers us pathways to participate depending on our strengths and possibilities. Rather than seeing activism as merely the province of courageous, confrontational youth, Iyer reconceptualizes and widens the very idea of social justice work to include those working beyond the street protester. Caregivers and storytellers and healers and weavers, for example, can play a crucial role, not just disrupters and visionaries. Quite simply, everyone has a role to play.

So how do poets fit in? In *What Is Found There: Notebooks on Poetry and Politics*, Adrienne Rich argued that the problem with most political poetry is not its politics, but its lack of engagement with political struggle: it is "bad. . . . not because it is engaged, but because it is not engaged enough: when it tries to express what has been logically understood but not yet organically assimilated."[18] If you want to write engaged or justice poetry, know the struggle in your bones completely. Enter the struggle yourself. Otherwise, we are mere tourists among landscapes of pain—extractors, not creators of justice.

In the months after the murder of George Floyd, I started to reread Black poets' responses to that death and the countless deaths that preceded it. I began to see a general taxonomy of racial justice poems emerge: Declarations of Self and Community, Elegies/Antielegies to Martyrs, Exposing Systemic Oppression, Calls to Action, Subversions of Order, Joyful Celebrations/Visions of Hope/Alternative and Utopian Futures, and Documentary Poetics: recovery projects/speaking truth to power. In what follows, I center Black poets across generations, but at the end, I also address the role of non-Black writers in the struggle for racial justice. This is just a tiny glimpse of the abundant field that is Black poetry, and my readings of the poems cannot do them the full justice they deserve. This is only a start. My hope is what I share here can be adapted (provisionally, of course) for other social movements.

Declarations of Self and Community, Advocacy, Solidarity

By speaking for oneself in a way that responds to community conditions, the poet speaks in relation to collective struggle. In a society that has systematically denigrated or commodified Black subjectivity, poems that claim subjective space offer a powerful resistance. Among many powerful poetic declarations of self-advocacy, Jericho Brown's "Bullet Points" (2019) is particularly devastating:

I will not shoot myself
In the head, and I will not shoot myself
In the back, and I will not hang myself
With a trashbag, and if I do,

I promise you, I will not do it
In a police car while handcuffed
Or in the jail cell of a town
I only know the name of
Because I have to drive through it
To get home. Yes, I may be at risk,
But I promise you, I trust the maggots
Who live beneath the floorboards
Of my house to do what they must
To any carcass more than I trust
An officer of the law of the land
To shut my eyes like a man
Of God might, or to cover me with a sheet
So clean my mother could have used it
To tuck me in. When I kill me, I will
Do it the same way most Americans do,
I promise you: cigarette smoke
Or a piece of meat on which I choke
Or so broke I freeze
In one of these winters we keep
Calling worst. I promise if you hear
Of me dead anywhere near
A cop, then that cop killed me. He took
Me from us and left my body, which is,
No matter what we've been taught,
Greater than the settlement
A city can pay a mother to stop crying,
And more beautiful than the new bullet
Fished from the folds of my brain.[19]

The poem functions as an advance argument for the prosecution against the police, a series of "bullet points" about the facts of his future case—in case of sudden death, Brown assures us, know that it was not suicide. I love the poem because it also seems to function as a life insurance policy. You (the city, the state) will pay, he seems to say, but whatever you pay will never be enough. The fact that he put this in writing tells you the level of terror that Black people live with every day.

Elegies and Anti-elegies to Martyrs

I recently came across an article in which a poet talked about a wonderful poem "inspired" by the death of George Floyd, and a shiver went through my body—"inspired," of course, coming from the Latin words meaning to gather breath in. If we want to write a poetry of justice, it's a good idea to not require Black pain to be inspired. The elegy, of course, is a powerful mode of mourning the dead, and when that death is political, the elegy also becomes more than a personal loss; it becomes a collective one. However, poems like "Why I Don't Write About George Floyd" (2020) by Toi Derricotte work in that discomfiting space between feeling the need to speak out, to elegize another Black man murdered, but also being aware of the dangers of such an elegy:

> Because there is too much to say
> Because I have nothing to say
> Because I don't know what to say
> Because everything has been said
> Because it hurts too much to say
> What can I say what can I say
> Something is stuck in my throat
> Something is stuck like an apple
> Something is stuck like a knife
> Something is stuffed like a foot
> Something is stuffed like a body[20]

This anti-elegy shows by not showing, by refusing to depict the dead—thus opening a space for the uncertainty and grief about a poet's role in the face of such unjust killing by the state. Derricotte explores language's insufficiency and the feeling of suffocation—a moment of profound identification with the deceased and also a sense of complicity in writing a poem about his death.

Ross Gay's "A Small Needful Fact" (2015), relatedly, wants to center something of the life of the murdered Eric Garner. And that thing, it turns out, is central to Gay's own life—working in gardens.

Is that Eric Garner worked
for some time for the Parks and Rec.
Horticultural Department, which means,
perhaps, that with his very large hands,
perhaps, in all likelihood,
he put gently into the earth
some plants which, most likely,
some of them, in all likelihood,
continue to grow, continue
to do what such plants do, like house
and feed small and necessary creatures,
like being pleasant to touch and smell,
like converting sunlight
into food, like making it easier
for us to breathe.[21]

Gay imaginatively finds his way into what is for him and for us another person's life, as a way to push against all the demonization and martyrology of Garner. Both demonization and martyrology, in the end, diminish human dignity and mystery. Gay's poem also contains a rhetorical tentativeness that feels bracingly humble. The "perhapses" and "in all likelihoods" act as counterweights but suggest the longing to see how Garner's life was more than the death he suffered.

Exposing Systemic Oppression

Poems that expose systemic oppression invite readers into seeing the acts of police violence in a wider context of white supremacy, legal discrimination, and mass incarceration. Audre Lorde's "Power" (1978) meditates on how violent policing takes place in a wider context of legal discrimination, exonerating white officers from killing. Lorde begins the poem by riffing on W. B. Yeats's notion of the divide between poetry and rhetoric. While Yeats articulates the separation as between the argument with self (poetry) and the argument with others (rhetoric), Lorde's poem begins by suggesting that for Black people, that separation is more fraught, with dangerous consequences:

The difference between poetry and rhetoric
is being ready to kill
yourself
instead of your children.[22]

The enjambments enact the ways in which violence pervades the subjective experience of being Black in America. The first enjambed line foregrounds the idea of threat—"being ready to kill"—that Black people live in a situation where the threat of death is omnipresent, and killing almost seems necessary as a mode of defense. But Lorde's next enjambment reverses that, turning the killing inward, against the self. It takes Yeats's notion and shows its potential damage—that one might countenance self-murder to protect the lives of one's children.

Further in the poem, Lorde explores how a jury of eleven white men and one Black woman did not convict a white police officer for a killing. She understands, but laments, the woman's inability to push back against a system that does not value Black lives. The poem concludes by reflecting on how her lack of power (the title of the poem) incites a rage for revenge in her that cannot but lead to more death:

I have not been able to touch the destruction
within me.
But unless I learn to use
the difference between poetry and rhetoric
my power too will run corrupt as poisonous mold
or lie limp and useless as an unconnected wire
and one day I will take my teenaged plug
and connect it to the nearest socket
raping an 85 year old white woman
who is somebody's mother
and as I beat her senseless and set a torch to her bed
a greek chorus will be singing in 3/4 time
"Poor thing. She never hurt a soul. What beasts they are."[23]

Calls to Action

Claude McKay's electrifying "If We Must Die," published in 1919 during the widespread attacks on Black people during Red Summer, is nothing short of a call to arms. Employing the classic poetic form of the sonnet, that great traditional form of love poetry, McKay calls Black people to fight back in a language that must have astonished its readers:

> If we must die, let it not be like hogs
> Hunted and penned in an inglorious spot,
> While round us bark the mad and hungry dogs,
> Making their mock at our accursèd lot.
> If we must die, O let us nobly die,
> So that our precious blood may not be shed
> In vain; then even the monsters we defy
> Shall be constrained to honor us though dead!
> O kinsmen! we must meet the common foe!
> Though far outnumbered let us show us brave,
> And for their thousand blows deal one death-blow!
> What though before us lies the open grave?
> Like men we'll face the murderous, cowardly pack,
> Pressed to the wall, dying, but fighting back!

McKay uses the sonnet—a traditional mode often suited to declarations of love—for this political end, inviting us to consider how this is, indeed, itself a love poem. Perhaps this is not the nonviolent love that Martin Luther King and Cornel West call for, but a love based on self-preservation in the face of a social order that is calling for their death.

Subversions of Order

Experimental poets like Harryette Mullen and Douglas Kearney, employing aesthetics of subversion and discomfort, compel readers to confront the deeply damaged nature of a social order that seems to require Black subjection. Mullen's "Elliptical" (2002) plays with and skewers conventional syntax and thinking, as each sentence-start contains an othering of some "they" the poem elliptically gestures toward:

> They just can't seem to . . . They should try harder to . . . They ought to be more . . . We all wish they weren't so . . . They never . . . They always . . . Sometimes they . . . Once in a while they . . . However it is obvious that they . . . Their overall tendency has been . . . The consequences of which have been . . . They don't appear to understand that . . . If only they would make an effort to . . . But we know how difficult it is for them to . . . Many of them remain unaware of . . . Some who should know better simply refuse to . . . Of course, their perspective has been limited by . . . On the other hand, they obviously feel entitled to . . . Certainly we can't forget that they . . . Nor can it be denied that they . . . We know that this has had an enormous impact on their . . . Nevertheless their behavior strikes us as . . . Our interactions unfortunately have been . . .[24]

The binary thinking that underlies the (racist) stereotyping alluded to in her poem underscores the implicatedness of ideology and systems of oppression and control; the other is X, and therefore we must Y. What is revealed is the speaker's own dehumanization.

Joyful Celebrations (Visions of Hope/Alternative and Utopian Futures)

Given what Black people have faced, poems that embrace joy and offer visions of hope resonate with a significant countercultural power. Poet lucille clifton, in poem after poem, invited readers to celebrate:

> won't you celebrate with me
> what i have shaped into
> a kind of life? i had no model.
> born in babylon
> both nonwhite and woman
> what did i see to be except myself?
> i made it up
> here on this bridge between
> starshine and clay,
> my one hand holding tight
> my other hand; come celebrate
> with me that everyday
> something has tried to kill me
> and has failed.[25]

Clifton's poem is an invitation to joyfully mark a (somewhat tentative) "kind of life" in the face of the murderous environment, the Babylon of white patriarchy. Over and over, clifton's poems are odes to survival, a sometimes-lonely survival in which the speaker must hold her own hand. But she's not asking for pity, just recognition.

Similarly, Maya Angelou's "Still I Rise" (1978) has at its center an irrepressible, ever-resurrecting subjectivity. It feels like a counterpart to Langston Hughes's transhistorical Black subject of "The Negro Speaks of Rivers," a voice that contains both itself and a whole people. It begins:

> You may write me down in history
> With your bitter, twisted lies,
> You may trod me in the very dirt
> But still, like dust, I'll rise.
>
> Does my sassiness upset you?
> Why are you beset with gloom?
> 'Cause I walk like I've got oil wells
> Pumping in my living room.[26]

Angelou's speaker refuses to be tromped down by the boots of oppression. She rises, and sasses, and will not be denied. Her direct rhymes have no shame in them. They glory in their own glory.

One final example. In their stunning "summer, somewhere" (2016), Danez Smith creates in this moment of the poem a sanctuary, an alternate heaven for Black boys (the original title of the piece):

> no need for geography
> now that we're safe everywhere.
>
> point to whatever you please
> & call it church, home, or sweet love.
>
> paradise is a world where everything
> is a sanctuary & nothing is a gun.
>
> here, if it grows it knows its place
> in history. yesterday, a poplar

told me of old forest
heavy with fruits I'd call uncle

bursting red pulp & set afire,
harvest of dark wind chimes.

after I fell from its limb
it kissed sap into my wound.

do you know what it's like to live
someplace that loves you back?[27]

In the space of the astonishing poem's utterance, the "here" of its reading/speaking, a heaven comes into being—a place where love is justice and justice is love. Where Black children are safe. Where trees have fruit that is not strange. Even if it's just for the span of the poem, Smith has created a visionary site where Black people are in a place "that loves you back."

Documentary Poetry, Social Poetics, and the Role of Non-Black Poets in the Struggle for Justice

Documentary poetry has become a powerful recovery method for making visible both lost voices and lives and the systems of erasure and oppression that have destroyed them. M. NourbeSe Philip's *Zong!* (2009) and Claudia Rankine's *Citizen* (2014)—among many other incredible books—stand out for their ability to engage with official documents and oral narratives in order to render visible the systemic violence of white supremacy.

White poets have done brave work at exploring their own racism, family history, complicity, or privilege. It's a strange irony of literary history that the failure of Tony Hoagland's poem "The Change" led to the profound rejoinder that is *Citizen*, one of the most celebrated books of poems in the twenty-first century.[28] Martha Collins (in *Blue Front*, *White Papers*, and *Admit One*), Ailish Hopper (*Dark Sky Society*), and Ilya Kaminsky (*Deaf Republic*) have all shown diverse ways that white poets can explore white supremacy and its racial violence.[29] Collins, in particular, employs documentary methods to unpack her own racial privilege in ways that are bracing and necessary. This work by white poets to confront systemic racism is so important, even if it is difficult and uncomfortable. After all, racism in America is a white people's problem to solve.

Mark Nowak provides an intriguing case for how a white writer has shifted his practice to align better with a social movement. While his books have done incredible work in the class struggle, Nowak found himself dissatisfied with the limited use of his poems to workers. Nowak's solution was to pivot from being a producer of poems to becoming a producer of poets—starting the Worker Writers School and hosting workshops for workers directly. His response to the question, Is your poetry ultimately really for other poets, and thus parasitic to or extractive in its relationship to the movement for social change?, was to stop writing poems and center other poets.

For those of us non-Black writers interested in being allies, advocates, or activists, the work to support, amplify, and act to make systemic change can take many forms. It begins with our listening, and listening again, to what Black people have been saying for centuries about their experience. The ongoing process of educating ourselves without relying on Black labor is essential. Center the voices at the heart of the struggle. Host readings that feature Black writers. We need to leverage whatever privilege we have to stand up and make change for those without that privilege and power.

It may well be that the last thing Black Lives Matter needs is poets who write poems that pretend to do the work that they are not doing—like voting, marching, boycotting, and divesting. But poetry's gift can also be its ability to refuse to fit neatly into the narrative that a social movement might ask of it. One of the things I love most about poetry is how it often dramatizes so well the Yeatsian "struggle with ourselves." A poem's work may also be to resist the demands of a movement for simplistic binaries, for othering those whose tactics may differ. Keeping love at the center, a poetry of justice may also not only stretch what has seemed possible in poetry but also sustain and widen a movement, through its bracing visions, its necessary outrage, its keen intelligence, its hope.

2022

CHAPTER SIXTEEN

Revolution in the First Person Plural

Mark Nowak's *Social Poetics*

During one of his eight-hour days facilitating poetry workshops with the National Union of Metalworkers of South Africa (NUMSA) in 2006, poet Mark Nowak found himself among Ford workers inspired to respond to Denny Dickhausen, an auto line worker from St. Paul, who'd lost his job when the Ford plant closed. The South African workers had watched a video of Dickhausen standing outside the fence that surrounded the Minnesota plant, reading a poem he'd written about his forty-year job with Ford and how he'd felt when he lost it: "thrown away like an old shoe."[1] Now, the NUMSA workers composed their own poem to answer Dickhausen's. Their stanzas, individually composed and then brought together by a chorus—"Oh! What a Life!"[2]—inaugurated both a collective poem written in what Nowak calls the "first person plural" and a transnational poetry dialogue between workers resisting the conditions of their work in the same transnational corporation. Later that day, Nowak wrote in a notebook, "I don't ever know if I've felt what I do as a poet more vital than this afternoon, this opening of a dialogue."[3]

Nowak recounts this story in *Social Poetics*, his compelling exploration of radical working-class poetry, which crystallizes a project begun in his own poetry twenty years earlier. Even at their most complexly modernist—often collaging from multiple texts, including workers' first-person accounts and news reports—Nowak's poems have always centered the voices of workers, struggling for dignity amid economic exploitation. In his first book, *Revenants*,[4] Nowak sings where he comes from: the

Polish American working class of western New York. The early poems in this book are personal, lyrical, mythic, and ethnographic, stewed in the sultry kitchens and factories of the eastern Rust Belt. But toward the end of that book—and in the two that followed, *Shut Up Shut Down*[5] and *Coal Mountain Elementary*[6]—Nowak eschewed autobiographical lyric and began to work in a chorale form. The poem "Capitalization," for example, braids the voices of workers, news reports of the 1981 air traffic controllers' (PATCO) strike, and grammatical rules for capitalization. While *Shut Up Shut Down* focuses on the labor struggles of American workers, *Coal Mountain Elementary* summons an internationalist vision of coal mining disasters, from the Sago Mine in West Virginia to the brutal mines of China.

But even as Nowak's poetry pressed further into explicitly radical forms and content, he grew increasingly suspicious that his work—despite exposing neoliberal structural violence, class warfare, and the fight for social justice—was not reaching working-class audiences or contributing to the labor movement as he hoped it would. When I spoke with Nowak in 2010—a conversation that became "Poetry as Social Practice in the First Person Plural: A Dialogue on Documentary Poetics," published in the *Iowa Journal of Cultural Studies*—Nowak described "having a personal crisis with poetry and [being] at the cusp of abandoning it completely [in 2006]." This crisis, he told me, was part of what led him to write his crucial essay "Neoliberalism, Collective Action, and the American MFA Industry," in which, he says, he "suggest[s] a historical model of radical writers workshops (the John Reed clubs of the CPUSA [Communist Party USA], Ernesto Cardenal's *talleres de poesia*, etc.) as more tenable models for writing praxis and pedagogy than the neoliberal MFA industry."[7] Yet he felt that even this practical turn was too theoretical, too disconnected from action. He told me, "I began asking myself . . . *well, what are you doing about it other than writing this essay?*"[8]

Over the past decade (and since 2011, under the moniker of the Worker Writers School), Nowak has spent much of his creative energies conducting workshops with workers across a wide variety of industries—especially domestic workers, whose poems and testimonies have brought particular power to the international campaign to create a domestic worker bill of rights. As a result, Nowak has emerged as the closest thing we have to a Wobbly poet. Nowak, like those early twentieth-century activists who organized with the Industrial Workers of the World, is a true radical culture worker who aims to create solidarity among low-wage workers and leverage that power for justice.

Drawing from this work, *Social Poetics* stakes a claim for a radical working-class poetics. In particular, Nowak seeks to reclaim the poetry workshop, "that often degraded and disdained centerpiece of the neoliberal writing culture—a largely untapped radical potential for social transformation."[9] Nowak's idea of "social poetics" draws inspiration from Langston Hughes's 1947 essay "My Adventures as a Social Poet,"[10] written when he had begun shifting the focus of his poems from his individual plight to the struggle of ordinary people. Hughes observed that there must be power in this radical practice, because "when poems stop talking about the moon and begin to mention poverty, trade unions, color lines, and colonies, somebody tells the police."[11]

Nowak's notion of poetry as a potentially radical technology for social change echoes Barbara Harlow's 1987 book *Resistance Literature*, in which she argues that resistance poetry functions as "a force for mobilizing a collective response to occupation and domination and as a repository for popular memory and consciousness."[12] Capturing collective response and retaining collective memory have been two of the greatest challenges for the working classes; divided by owners and politicians and laboring under the hegemony of capitalism, people of the working class rarely have the time, energy, capital, or access to participate in literary production. Poetry—in its succinctness and its cheapness to produce—may indeed be an ideal form to capture the gritty detail and dreams of working people. In the words of the South African poet Es'kia Mphahlele, poetry is a "fugitive means of expression."[13]

The first half of *Social Poetics* offers a genealogy of radical poetry workshops—first in the United States, and then in Kenya, Nicaragua, South Africa, and elsewhere. In the chapter on American workshops, Nowak moves deftly through an exploration of youth workshops beginning in the 1960s—laboratories for young chroniclers of what radical historian and activist E. P. Thompson has called "history from below." But Nowak never labors under the illusion that all such projects succeed. By beginning with writer and television producer Budd Schulberg's workshops and docudrama, *The Angry Voices of Watts*, organized in the wake of the 1965 uprising over racial injustice in Los Angeles, Nowak unearths how those motivated by well-intentioned but paternalistic liberalism often erase the very voices that they purport to highlight—in particular, in this case, that of the young radical Quincy Troupe, who was left out of the anthology altogether because of differences with Schulberg. Nowak argues that Schulberg failed to provide an adequate class and race analysis of the uprising, perpetuated stereotypes about Black resistance as "anger," and excluded poetry he perceived as too radical (aesthetically as well as politically) for a white readership. (Troupe would go on to create his own samizdat-quality anthology, *Watts Poets*.)

By contrast, Nowak glowingly describes the work of the now-legendary Black poet June Jordan and teacher Terri Bush's 1967–68 workshop, which led to the 1970 anthology *The Voice of the Children*.[14] At the very moment that Jordan and Bush were providing space for youth poets in Harlem and Brooklyn "to critique their everyday lives in their schools and in their communities as both poets and 'people's historians,'"[15] New York City teachers were engaging in that city's longest strike, often battling Black and Brown local families advocating for "community control" of schools. Jordan and Bush's work faced all manner of challenges, ultimately folding due to lack of long-term funding. Nowak trains his ire on the creative writing and publishing industries for directing its funds elsewhere. He writes that "we have lost a crucial half century of theories, impressions, and critiques from the poetry of young people by not following Jordan's pedagogical lead much earlier. . . . Our poetic culture and history have been significantly weakened."

In the second chapter, Nowak broadens his study to key postcolonial workshops, highlighting the work of writers such as Ngũgĩ wa Thiong'o in Kenya, Ernesto Cardenal in Nicaragua, and the members of the Durban Workers' Cultural Local in South Africa, which Nowak calls "one of the foremost manifestations of anti-apartheid worker control of cultural production."[16] While the work of each poet manifests differently, their work holds in common what Nowak identifies as the four areas central to social poetics. The first is *imaginative militancy*: a temperament of resistance to conditions of oppression, understood as an insistence on one's innate dignity, humanity, and capacity to dream of something better. The second is *migration*, meaning that social poetics is often marked by the condition of forced migration, often because of economic necessity; so many workers find themselves dislocated, part of what poet and trade unionist Alfred Temba Qabula called the "moving forest of Africa."[17] The third area is *social reproduction*: social poetics is attentive to the ways in which so much human labor is often excised from a vision of the working class. The work of Durban Workers' Cultural Local poet Nise Malange proves particularly useful for Nowak's exploration of the way that traditional accounts of labor have tended to exclude women's unpaid and unrecognized work. In "Nightshift Mother," for example, Malange writes:

> Left with a double load
> At home
> My children left uncared
> Anxiety
> At work
> My boss insists we should
> Be grateful for the opportunities
> He gives women to be exploited.[18]

Finally, for Nowak, social poetics involves and activates *collaborative cultural production*; in contrast to the neoliberal romantic model of the solitary poet, social poets write alongside and with each other, creating collective statements and harnessing them to make change.

The second half of *Social Poetics* concerns Nowak's own efforts to create communities of collaboration, first with the Union of Radical Workers and Writers (URWW) in the early 2000s, founded to help unionize a Borders bookstore in Minneapolis, and later with the Worker Writers School, to practice social poetics as he conceives it. It's a story as filled with false starts and failures as it is by moments of triumph. For example, Nowak describes how, though the URWW's union drive succeeded, he felt that the URWW never truly integrated workers and writers—and never saw workers as possible writers at all. In the end, Borders shut down the store. Such moments lead him to wonder whether social poetics is "also a poetics of abject failure and muteness."[19]

Still, Nowak highlights the way that social poetics can become a conduit for what writer Nick Montgomery and filmmaker carla bergman call "joyful militancy" in their book of the same name, an approach that emphasizes "the connections between fierceness and love, resistance and care, combativeness and nurturance."[20] Nowak sees joy come alive in his workshops in South Africa, where a "first person plural" becomes embodied and activated, an experience he has found ways to replicate all over the world.

Nowak's explicit linking of various kinds of labor—of work, of writing, of community organizing—offers a model for poets to create something beyond feel-good consciousness-raising. And while I often found myself longing for an epilogue, a "how-to" chapter for starting one's own "school," Nowak's thick descriptions of his workshops—from how they came into being to what they inspired—do offer a blueprint by way of example. We read, for instance, about how Nowak, using a Japanese tanka by Kunio Tsukamoto as a model, walks a group of nascent writers through the process of creating a poem based on their hands. "I want you to imagine you are six years old. Where are you? What are you doing with your hands?," he asks them. "This morning before class, what did you do with your hands?"[21] Question by question, Nowak creates a space for Nasim, a man from Iraq, to write his first poem in English:

hands hold phone
hands cook rice
hands touch door
hands point to the home in Iraq
hands write sentences[22]

As Nowak points out, "the evocative final line of Nasim's tanka can be read in many ways: an Iraqi refugee who sees and is proud of his own hands writing sentences of a poem in English, [and] his experience in the United States during this time of Trump's presidency feel like a sentence (i.e., a punishment)."[23] Nowak's attentiveness to Nasim's work—and to the indignities of the political context in which Nasim finds himself—exemplifies the practice of social poetics.

As a poet and tenured professor, I felt a mix of awe and regret reading *Social Poetics*, thinking back to the years that I could have better leveraged my position of privilege on behalf of those who have been denied platforms and power. While Nowak's work implicates those of us who replicate the very conditions we should want to reform or even overthrow, it also invites us down a path where solidarity through poetic community can lead to radical social transformation. It was Nowak's work that inspired me, in 2017, to become the faculty advisor for a group of students who formed Writers In Residence, a program that facilitates creative writing workshops with young people in juvenile detention. (This student group has now expanded into a nonprofit organization operating throughout the state of Ohio.)

These efforts have a history. But because the stories of incarcerated people—and of workers, immigrants, and refugees—are often unwritten or erased, that history tends to remain buried. *Social Poetics* uncovers the past as a guide to the future. Early in the book, Nowak alludes to workshops with incarcerated writers led by Native poet Joseph Bruchac in the early 1970s. Nowak includes part of the transcript of a discussion with Bruchac, in which Bruchac recalls: "I was told many times that when [the participants] were in the workshop they did not feel as if they were in prison."[24] Imagine: what if the writing workshop were widely understood as a site not of taste-making or star cultivation, but of collective liberation?

2020

IV.
The Poetics of Peacebuilding

CHAPTER SEVENTEEN

I Never Saw Him Drowning

Great-Uncle Charlie, the Great War, and the Peace Show

Leaning over my desk in January 1991, news coverage of the Gulf War droning in the background, I read for first time the opening lines of Wilfred Owen's "Dulce et Decorum Est": "Bent double, like old beggars under sacks, / Knock-kneed, coughing like hags, / we cursed through sludge."[1] I felt transported, imagining the weight these young soldiers bore in the strange hellscapes of the front. I was a junior at Holy Cross College. All semester, my English professor, Mike True, guided our class through "The Nonviolent Tradition in Literature," while on television, military leaders touted missile-eye images of "smart bombs" and "surgical strikes." It was terribly surreal to encounter such polar views of war, knowing that each was only a partial picture. Yet Owen's garish images and his fierce rhetorical conclusion confirmed something that I felt deep in my gut—war was an ugly thing, destroying bodies and haunting minds. On the other side of the world, even though the news coverage would not show it, people were dying under our bombs; it would take poets and artists to slip beneath the media's redactions and censorship to imagine the horror.

Even then, I found myself drawn most not to the lurid language and angry retort of "Dulce" but to its dreamlike center, when the soldiers find themselves attacked by chemical gas, and one man fails to adjust his mask in time:

Dim through the misty panes and thick green light,
As under a green sea, I saw him drowning.
In all my dreams before my helpless sight,
He plunges at me, guttering, choking, drowning.[2]

In contrast to much of the poem, the language here is starkly plain and subtly recursive, filled with internal rhyme and assonance. Words flicker and return: green and green, drowning and drowning, and the piling on of gerunds creates the effect of a flashback, of a past imposing itself on—even devouring—the present. Each night, the speaker drowns in the memory of his comrade's drowning. In World War I, after Owen's dear friend was killed in a bomb attack, the poet suffered from acute mental distress and wound up at Craiglockhart Hospital in 1917 for treatment. They called it "shell shock" then, what we might diagnose now as Post-Traumatic Stress Disorder. Though some treatments included electric shock therapy, Owen's doctor recommended writing.

It was no surprise that I linked Owen's depiction of the Great War to the Gulf War; my father is a veteran and my mother a pacifist. After joining the U.S. Navy through the ROTC program in college, my father served during the Vietnam War, an advisor on a Vietnamese patrol gunboat who survived Tet. Upon return home, he taught counterinsurgency and later produced a dissertation on the emotional impact on families of soldiers who were prisoners of war or missing in action (POW/MIA), and later became a clinical psychotherapist.

In recent years, it has been his great passion to work with veterans making the long emotional return from all of our wars, but back then, when I was young, he may have been making the long return himself. I want to say that he still carried the war with him, but it's probably more accurate to say that I didn't know where the war ended and my father began. A deeply loving and powerful man, he was nonetheless prone to suddenly foul moods that would descend upon our whole house, causing us to scurry around for whatever mask might protect us. Was this the war, I wondered, or something else? I never could be sure.

My mother abhorred violence—both real and represented—and forbade guns (real and play) in the house. She was chagrined when my father pointed outside one day, where I had picked up a stick in our yard and pretended to shoot my friend with it. Part of her pacifism grew out of a story that she'd been carrying for years, one that goes all the way back to the First World War.

Her mother, Grandma Sheila, was just six years old when her big brother Charlie, age twenty-two, went off to fight in the Great War. It was 1917, the same year that Owen was convalescing at Craiglockhart. My grandmother must have looked up to him, literally and figuratively, as he stood in the doorway in his trim wool uniform and its gleaming bronze buttons, saying his goodbyes.

About a year later, when the war was supposed to be ending, her parents sat her down and gave her the news. Charlie would not be coming home. He had died in the war. It must have shaken her to the core. How could this strong and beautiful man be gone? She would always look up to him, and imagine him in heaven, looking down at her, protecting her.

Fifty years later, precisely the same year that my father was in Vietnam, Sheila opened a curious letter from the Veterans Administration. It was a notice that her brother Charlie had recently passed away in a VA hospital.

I imagine her falling into a chair, rereading the letter. Her brother had been alive and she had not known. She must have been beside herself with grief, because everyone had pretended he was dead. Since her parents had passed away, she could never ask them why. Why had they hidden the truth? Had anyone from the family gone to visit him? If so, why was she robbed of the chance to do the same thing?

The reasons have been lost to the great silence of time.

My mother has carried my grandmother's story with her for longer than I've been alive. In the years after, she married a Vietnam veteran and would not allow toy guns in our house.

Uncle Charlie's story is one reason why I spent many Labor Days in the shadow of the jets, talking to veterans and civilian survivors of war at the Peace Show, a celebration of nonviolence that took place for about a decade during the War on Terror years, held as an alternative to the Air Show and its cozy relationship with the U.S. military.

In 2011, the Peace Show resembled a street fair, set downtown near the famous Free Stamp in Willard Park, overlooking Lake Erie. Many people who came to the park to view the planes flying overhead also used the Peace Show port-a-potty and ended up getting their kids free face-painting or folded paper cranes. Along the sidewalk, they passed progressive groups presiding over tchotchke-packed tables and heard, from a main stage, speakers, local bands, and poets. An obstacle course featuring hay bales and information stations taught kids about nonviolence. Some years, single boots stood in rows along the lawn, each boot with a little sign that carried the name of a soldier killed in war.

In fact, though the Peace Show once gathered over 2,000 people during the height of the Iraq War, it gradually disappeared due to the cost and labor of putting it on. While the Air Show attracts 70,000 paying spectators a year, the Peace Show's organizers had trouble coming up with $3,000 for permits, porta-potties, and the soundstage.

In the years I've talked to and interviewed participants in the Peace Show, I've discovered that many of the strongest opponents of war are its military and civilian survivors. I think of Lou Pumphrey, who witnesses for peace by wearing his U.S. Army uniform from his service in Vietnam and carrying his peace flag on his shoulder. He talks to anyone who will listen about seeing his lieutenant killed and learning of the lies that mire wars.

I think of Yoshiko Ikuta, who worked in an orphanage during the Second World War in Japan and had to comfort the orphans who'd waken from bad dreams. In Kyoto, later in the war, she would see "children who were skin and bones because of malnutrition, not knowing where their parents are, and begging for food." She remembers flies sucking at the sores on their skin.

"This is the reality of war," she says. "I don't want to see it ever again. That's why I don't watch any war movies, because I don't want flashbacks."[3]

And I think of Leonard Shelton, an African American veteran of multiple wars, who wasn't ready to tell his story. "I'm sure you'll want to hear what I have to say," he said, "but my head just isn't straight enough to submit to an interview yet."[4]

T. S. Eliot once wrote: "Human kind cannot bear very much reality." We don't like to hear that war undoes so many, but if we don't listen to what its military and civilian veterans tell us, we risk repeating the same mistakes.

Of course, dear reader, I share some of your skepticism. Nonviolence is a harder path than war-making. It requires great discipline and spiritual resolve, and its adherents are ill-funded.

One Labor Day, a friend of mine, looking up at the jets, confided that he always loved air shows. There is something truly awesome about flight, the gravity-defying displays of technological mastery.

But something in us seems to crave the awe of domination. We forget that these jets kill from a distance that reduces people to targets and collateral damage—not human beings. Can any small act of demonstration compete with the terrifying power of jets and their eardrum-blistering screams? We go mute when they pass over.

The people who organized and attended the Peace Show remind us that we must be wary of our own awe of power, that military might is often misused and that people who suffer our wars in their countries run in terror when our jets pass over.

Because we never know whether the stories we're told are true, I recently looked in an ancestry database to find out what I could about Uncle Charlie. I found his registration card for World War I and census records from 1920 and 1930, in which he was listed, in careful cursive, as a "patient" in two different hospitals.

There were many, many names alongside Charlie's. Like those empty boots, they had disappeared from their prewar lives. How many Charlies were pronounced dead before their time, silenced out of family shame, confusion, or despair?

Great-Uncle Charlie is one of the many reasons that I've devoted a good deal of my life work—my poetry, essays, and scholarship, not to mention my teaching—to resisting the glamor of war and promoting peacebuilding and conflict transformation. From *Sand Opera* to *Shrapnel Maps* to my translations of poets from enemy countries, from my book on poets and the peace movement to my courses on Israel-Palestine and Northern Ireland, I've tried to find ways of understanding the geography of violence and pointing out the paths of peace, justice, and reconciliation.

This is all I know about Charlie. According to his military registration card, he was 5-foot-7 and slender. His eyes were blue and his hair was brown. Prior to his service, he'd worked at Western Union. He'd tried to claim exemption from the draft because he had nasal trouble, though its cause is not listed. He must have had trouble breathing, a physical weakness I may have inherited. I suddenly cast back to Owen's "Dulce et Decorum Est" and the images of a man drowning, sputtering in the green sea of a chemical attack. After fifty years in a Veterans Administration hospital, Charlie died in 1967, just as images of my father's war had begun to flood the nightly news.

2012, 2022

CHAPTER EIGHTEEN

Poetry, Precarity, and Israel/Palestine

A Pandemic Lockdown Dialogue (with Mosab Abu Toha, Conor Bracken, Erika Meitner, Rachel Neve-Midbar, and Naomi Shihab Nye)

Before we started the dialogue, we met via Zoom, some of us for the first time. Rachel sent this note afterward, on September 29, 2020:

RACHEL NEVE-MIDBAR:

All,

It was an honor to meet all of you this early morning "face-to-face," to hear your stories and to begin to imagine how this conversation will unfold. Thank you again Philip for setting us all on this path, especially as (at least Erika and I) embark on a new year. There is a lot of magic here.

Someone shared a Hayden Carruth poem on Facebook just now that I want to share with all of you.

I COULD TAKE

I could take
two leaves
    and give you one.
Would that not be
a kind of perfection?

But I prefer
one leaf
    torn to give you half
    showing

(after these years, simply)
love's complexity in an act,
    the tearing and
    the unique edges—

one leaf (one word) from the two
imperfections that match.[1]

One word or many—I'm looking forward with great hope and an ever-expanding heart.

Rachel
October 2020

PHILIP METRES: *For our first question, let's start off somewhat broadly: How have you been engaging with poetry these days? How has it helped you to negotiate the tricky complexity of the current moment (or tricky complex moments of the recent or distant past)?*

PHILIP METRES: My friend E. J. McAdams is an avid birder and a poet. Once, when his son was a child, little Joe pointed to his father's birding kit (which contained binoculars, his bird book, etc.) and called it his "poetry." Do you have your poetry with you, he would ask. Perhaps he'd seen a bird, and wanted to take a closer look. I love Joe's story because I think it carries the notion of poetry as a technology of observing closely, of ritual documentation—attention being a form of prayer, a door to love. Something that we carry with us, even when we're not always using it.

We're living in the year of vision, 2020, 20/20, when things suddenly have become all too clear, even when the future feels more uncertain than ever—a global pandemic, an uprising against police violence and white supremacy, massive forest fires in the American West, ongoing global climate change, and a presidential election. This was also the year that a 2015 UN Report predicted that Gaza would become uninhabitable. Everything feels precarious.

It was also a terrible time to release a book. When *Shrapnel Maps* came out in April, most of us were in complete physical lockdown, not to mention emotional shock. I doubted that people would have the bandwidth to navigate this complicated book and its wrestling with the conflict in Israel and Palestine that has riven people to the core. I had hoped the book would be a bridge to conversation, a door to an opening, where people could gather and sit with each other's stories, our pain and our joy, and our hopes for a future where all could belong.

So our gathering together to talk last night via Zoom and here to write to each other now feels like a fulfillment of that dream of Rumi's field. I don't know what we'll discover, but I'm looking forward to listening, to seeing each of you and your stories. More than ever, I see how we are both authors of our own story and characters caught in stories and systems that we did not make.

During the early months of the pandemic, I found myself reading and working with the Psalms—I called them Plague Psalms, employing n+7 Oulipian procedures to try to find my way into a psalmic engagement with the pandemic. I don't know if any of them are worth keeping, but they were a way of wrestling with my sense of anger at a God who would let this happen, the sort of wild swing of emotions that are part of the Psalms. I feel as if I need a whole new set of prayers, mantras, and spells to hold off this great despair.

I've been trying to do a lot of reading for my next book, called *Fugitive/Refuge*, dealing with human migration and the precarity of our planetary future. But I've needed many breaks from the relentlessness of the (bad) news—both online and in books—so I've taken to reading the neighborhood around me, on walks with my wife every day, as we watched spring yield to summer and now to fall. That's the book I've been enjoying most. Just yesterday, I saw many neighbors from my office window heading to synagogue, the men wearing white robes, on Yom Kippur. I feel that need to atone so much right now, to repair, for reparation.

MOSAB ABU TOHA:

> *"What is poetry which does not save*
> *Nations or people?"—Czesław Miłosz*[2]

A very big question that haunts me has been "Why should I write poetry?"

How can poetry rescue me, the people I write about, the places from which my vocabulary is pulled? I really don't have an answer.

The only thing that consoles me when I think about that occurs when people who read what I write find it worthy of reading and listening to. If I can make people feel what my people and I experience, if I can make them see through my eyes places they cannot reach (which I, too, cannot easily reach because of the occupation and blockade), if I can erect houses from under the rubble with my words, then there is a reason why I should poetry.

I first started to write poems, even though simple when I look back at them now, during the 2014 assault on Gaza. I wrote them not in Arabic, but in English, the language of my oppressor (that of the Balfour Declaration) but also that of my online friends who gave me their ears when I most needed them.

It is strange to me that after I moved to the U.S. to attend a fellowship at Harvard last year, my heart and mind wanted me to write in Arabic. And so, I did.

I'm not sure what happens when I write in Arabic and then in English. I fear that my pen would think I'm crazy to write in totally different languages. A few months ago, I wrote a poem about "mirror" in Arabic. A few days later, I convinced myself to write a poem in English about the same thing, "mirror." It was a completely different poem.

I feel that when I write in Arabic, I address my very inner self. When I write in English, I'm talking to someone else, someone who would attentively listen to me and grab my hand to cross to the other side of the river.

Poetry can give us a transient feeling of pain or enthusiasm, just like songs. During times of Israeli military escalation against Gaza, the many radio stations would play patriotic, sad, or consoling songs. "But what if a bomb falls on your house? You and your radio exist no more," I ask myself.

Politicians and military readers talk about numbers: how many they killed, how much suffering they incurred on "them," how much infrastructure was wiped off the map.

But when poets speak, they speak about the mother who weeps over her killed children, about students rummaging through the rubble for their coloring books and crayons, about a child watering a plant near an unexploded bomb, about a teacher writing on a shattered board at his school.

I would like to have that kind of conversation where military maps, orders to soldiers to kill, and reports about how many "enemies" were targeted are all absent.

I would want soldiers' and leaders' wireless devices to sound not "the target is moving in that direction!" but to sound poetry about the sea, the flowers, the blossoming trees, and the rain.

CONOR BRACKEN: Poetry as a technology of attention, as a kind of telescope that redirects our vision away from military maps and ordnance toward the child watering a plant beside an unexploded bomb—what Phil and Mosab have said has really resonated. Often when I'm sitting with poems, I think of this Simone Weil quote: "Two prisoners whose cells adjoin communicate with each other by knocking on the wall. The wall is the thing which separates them but it is also their means of communication."

There are many ways to think of how a poem operates, or what makes a poem successful, but for me, when I hear someone else on the other side tapping or banging, rhythmically and/or frantically, that's when it clicks. This happened the first time a poem had a real effect upon me (Countee Cullen's "Incident," which recounts a childhood visit to Baltimore that turns on a racial slur directed at the speaker) and recently, when I read *Shrapnel Maps*, as well as Mosab's stunning images. These operate in ways similar to Eavan Boland's work, I think, which distinguishes between history as a written (often white, patriarchal) bird's-eye enterprise and the past, as a lived, experienced, sensory phenomenon that is, due to its richness and counterfactual nature, excluded from the annals.

In my own writing I'm interested in this distinction, too, though from the vantage not of the suppressed, but the suppressor. Why? I'm of Irish and Lebanese descent, but my family has been stateside long enough for us to be fully assimilated, to the degree that my identity, if it ever comes up, is a curiosity at most. (So American are we that we have repped the U.S. in various diplomatic posts—mostly sub-Saharan Africa—due to my father's job with the government.) Wherever I am or have been, I've always been aware of what my father called luck, and what I now know to call privilege.

Poetry is a means of perceiving and tracing connections among seemingly disparate nodes, and I find myself most interested in limning the webs of cruelty and complicity on the part of people whom I look and sound like. Not to humanize them, but to see the small selfishnesses that add up to dehumanization. In this current moment, of climate catastrophe, public health disaster, and renewed attention to the violent criminalization of Black and marginalized lives by precarious whiteness, I have been listening, reading, and amplifying (and arguing with family members who are less inclined to see how we benefit from the current order and to what degree). There is enough cruelty and complicity for us to suss out and contend with as it is; my ration of it doesn't need to be added to the heap at the moment.

But to answer the question a bit more directly, how has poetry served me recently? One of the things that it has been consistently good about trying to teach me is silence. When to use it, when to listen to it, when and when not to trust it. I still have much to learn in terms of when my silence is powerful and when my silence is complicit, but I am trying, these days, to be quiet when truth is speaking, and loud in the ears of those who want history to talk over the knocking that when we hear it, reminds us that history is written not on paper but on bodies.

RACHEL NEVE-MIDBAR: For me the pandemic has been a time of waiting. What I am waiting for I'm no longer sure, but I continue to wait: For the end? Some sort of resolution? Perhaps all of life is waiting for what comes next and learning how to observe the world around us in the meantime. These days we observe the four corners of our living spaces, the intricate lines on the faces of our partners, our children, the way the clouds move along the window and how they change day to day.

I rushed to Israel in early March because my daughter, who is turning thirty-two this week and has cerebral palsy, was getting kicked out of the assisted living situation I had found for her before I left for USC. As I boarded the plane the airline told us we would be in quarantine in Israel. Crazy as it sounds, I imagined I would get over my jet lag in my partner Joe's apartment in Haifa while all of my kids (I have six and three grandchildren) would gather around me. I had no idea what quarantine even meant. In the end my daughter went to her sister and I went to Haifa as the entire country of Israel shut down completely.

Those early weeks are a blur to me now. I was jet-lagged, but needed to be up (as I do now) for classes that were taking place in L.A. and went on all night. Between classes and not being allowed outside, I lived in limbo. When I finally was allowed to leave the apartment I was scared to drive between cities, but I needed to pick up my daughter.

Here in the north there were virtually no cars, no police, nothing. But as I got further south I began to see more and more cars, each floating something black from their windows: black T-shirts, black garbage bags, anything. They began to form a long line and suddenly there were police everywhere and I realized I was in the middle of a huge anti-Netanyahu rally (and with nothing black to sail out my window!) Yes, we here are living the nightmare you in the USA are only awakening to the possibility of: a leader who has been elected out of office, who refuses to leave, and who manipulates the pandemic to stay in power. The most recent form of this antidemocratic misuse of power is the edict that all demonstrators will be arrested because they are "spreading the virus." Instead we have all added a frame today to our Facebook profiles: a black banner with the word "lech," which means "get out."

Haifa is as new to me in some ways as Los Angeles. And the pandemic and repeated government closures don't make it easy to get to know the city. We are in our second lockdown and more than 9,000 people a day are being diagnosed. I never expected to be here this long and am still living in the three dresses and two pairs of jeans I brought with me in March.

Joe made me an office on an enclosed porch where I can look out at the tops of trees and sky on three sides as I work. From the stairs outside, called the Holocaust Stairs, Arabic and Russian drift up. I barely hear any Hebrew. A guy in an apartment nearby plays his music loud in the afternoons. A kind of Backstreet Boys vibe, in Arabic with an oud.

Joe himself is collecting unemployment. He was laid off when the oil and gas industry closed down in May. He spends his days on the phone with relatives all over the world: England and Germany and Ghana. They talk for hours in a language called "Ga." They laugh long and deeply together and I can tell they are remembering childhood antics in Accra.

I spend my days reading for my field exams and once a week I manage to cough out a poem like a rough hairball from my throat. Everything feels dry and hot and over-lit. The inside of a lightbulb. A world surviving, waiting. Waiting.

Though Haifa seems a city of connection, of bridges. Erev Yom Kippur two men were spackling the walls in an apartment in the building next door. With all the windows open I could hear the familiar scrape of sand against cement making the new walls smooth, their radio playing, the sound of their banter back and forth, loud and punctuated with laughter in Arabic. Suddenly one of them caught sight of a man going down the stairs outside and quickly called out through the window "Yoseph, Yoseph! G'mar v'chatima Tova!" The Yom Kippur greeting in Hebrew, "May you be inscribed in the Book of Life." The man on the stairs, who was wearing a kippah, looked up and waved and the year opened out in front of me.

NAOMI SHIHAB NYE: I'm very moved by all your responses. Sorry to be slow but that's one thing I've really been absorbed by during the pandemic—my ingrained, essential slowness. And I've realized how slowness has always been my true home, even when I was dashing through airports, from city to city. ("Life is so short we must move very slowly," used to be my favorite proverb, from Thailand.)

As a child I loved the slowness held within lines of poetry and the spaciousness beyond—which gave plenty of time for further slow thinking. This is how poetry has served me during our time of isolation. To read a poem and carry it inside all day—to return to it—to consider it differently while not looking at it. Since I was the poetry editor for the *New York Times* magazine during half of 2019 then this weird year of 2020, till the end of November, I lived next to a mountain of new poetry books, arriving daily—and found great sustenance in pawing through them constantly—so many voices new to me, so many powerful perspectives. I felt comforted by the largeness of our family in poetry and also the stunning click inside when I would find a poem that felt just right to me, for the magazine. Selecting other people's poems for sharing has been a joy I learned first in second grade—and it has never diminished. How would the world feel different if more people carried poems inside?

I've thought a lot about empathy and our leaders who don't have it.

Mosab's comment about what poetry focuses on, in contrast to the "numbers" and horrors of war, is most meaningful to me. Phil's reference to the birding kit as "poetry" is gorgeous. That close look—at anything—which engenders care. How does poetry help us live? The great Nina Cassian once said to me (only time I ever met her, in Jerusalem, oddly) "I want to make poems that are useful as tools, that help somebody get through or do what they need to do."

I've been writing poems, but maybe less, and reading more. That feels fine to me. We're trying to figure this weird thing out. And we won't. We won't!

I had the first draft of a book sequel to finish (a novel for elementary readers, *The Turtle of Michigan*, sequel to *The Turtle of Oman*) for the first few months of lockdown, and how comforting it was to be in a different world inside a young boy's head. I'm looking forward to working on the second draft soon. And I've spent a lot of time with our now four-year-old grandson, who talks as a poet always, and gives me plenty of incredible lines to inscribe in secret little notebooks. I did this with his daddy too and unfortunately his daddy grew out of the world of metaphors as do so many people, so I know again how precious this time is.

Recently we were talking about things we miss. Connor said, "I miss riding buses!"

"I miss being in elevators and talking to the other people!"—"I miss playgrounds with lots of other kids running around!" and Connor said to me, "*I miss myself when I'm not here.*"

We miss ourselves when we're not in the best world possible. A better world that people might make together.

Poetry helps us keep believing in it.

I want to urge you all to watch the premiere of Jen Marlowe's film *There Is a Field* in memory of Asel Aslih, the Palestinian Seeds of Peace member killed in the streets as he stooped to help someone else stand up, twenty years ago last week—a film made with the greatest research and love. I posted the link on Facebook but can send it otherwise if you can't find it.

ERIKA MEITNER: Naomi, I'm so glad you reminded me about the documentary in memory of Asel Aslih. I had put aside the link to watch it, but everything has been chaos lately here—mostly because I'm trying to do a full-time job while both my kids are in school on opposite schedules for 2.5 hours, four days a week. Like Rachel (and probably Mosab and Conor too), I've been derailed from my usual work by my caregiving obligations. In the "it's a small world" department, the last time I lived in Israel was from 1996 through 1997, in Jerusalem, and my neighbor and dear friend there was Ned Lazarus, who served as the Middle East Program director for Seeds of Peace from 1996 through 2004. I did manage to watch the "Peaceful Thoughts" tribute he linked to for Asel on his Facebook page, which is heartbreaking.

To be bluntly honest, poetry right now for me has been an occupational obligation. I'm not writing—and haven't been since the pandemic began—because I have no childcare, and I'm never alone really, except in the shower or for brief stints in my car on the way to a kid's school, or when I'm teaching my university classes on Zoom. I read student poems (with a teacher's pedagogical eye), I read poetry books I'm blurbing (with an eye for praise), and I read poetry books for contests I'm judging (with a critical, winnowing eye), but I am not reading for pleasure, and I'm not writing at all.

In any of my spare time, for the past month (true story), instead of writing poems, I have been trying to figure out whether and how I'm eligible for EU citizenship. This has involved many phone calls to the Czech and Polish embassies, gathering documents via the United States Holocaust Memorial Museum's database, and calling my father repeatedly and asking him to go through boxes in my parents' attic for any papers we have from my grandparents. For the first time in my life, due to the combination of our current administration's assault on American democracy, the rise in white supremacy and antisemitism, the mental instability of our current leader and the people who surround and bolster him, and this government's total mismanagement of this pandemic, I no longer feel safe in the U.S. I no longer feel like this country is a stable place. And I'm sure I'm not the only child of refugees and immigrants—nor the only Jew or parent of a brown-skinned child—who feels similarly right now.

Documents I have found in the past few weeks include my maternal grandmother's ID cards from Auschwitz and Mauthausen, which erroneously lists her place of birth as Hannover, Germany (rather than Łódź, Poland); her ration card from 1945 and 1946 from her time in a Displaced Persons camp; and a treasure trove of documents from the Arolsen Archives (the International Center on Nazi Persecution) filled out by my maternal grandfather prepared for the International Refugee Organization.

One questionnaire he filled out says this:

(a) Do you wish to return to your country of former residence? *Nein.* (No)
If not, why? *Antisemitz. Und alle verloren.* (Antisemitism. And all is lost.)
(b) Do you wish to remain in Germany? *Nein.*
Have you any relatives, friends or resources in Germany? *Nein.*
(c) Country of first preference: *Palestine.*

German was my grandfather's third language, after Yiddish and Polish. My mother's family did not emigrate to Palestine. They remained in a Displaced Persons camp in Stuttgart, where my mother was born. American soldiers requisitioned flats in Stuttgart from former SS members, and eventually my grandparents were resettled into one of these apartments. My family was finally able to get visas in 1952—and they sailed on the USS *Harry Taylor* not to Palestine, but to America, where they landed in the South Bronx.

While I was going through all of these papers, with the four different spellings of my grandmother's name (Franciszka, Fany, Frances, and Frajda), with their clerical errors, with their redundancies and official stamps and smudged notes I couldn't decipher, I kept thinking about our conversation on Zoom the other week when Mosab told us about his travel sagas and humiliations, the roadblocks and long delays in attempting to get to America from Gaza with his family. I thought about the "Returning to Jaffa" section of Phil's book with its historical documents, with its recountings of shifting inhabitants of buildings. One of the things that I think I share with Phil is this idea that poetry has to engage the world in some way—and as a result of that, poems can be repositories or archives for conflicting narratives. And this isn't an either/or proposition—poems can obviously be lyric spaces for internal reflection, or (as Conor reminds us) a mode of shifting or focusing attention. I think of a different Simone Weil quote, too: "Attention, taken to its highest degree, is the same thing as prayer. It presupposes faith and love. Absolutely unmixed attention is prayer"—and here Weil's *prayer* could easily be swapped out for *poetry.*

My father was born in Mandatory Palestine in 1947—in Haifa. My paternal grandparents fled Czechoslovakia in 1939, right after the Nazi invasion. My grandfather's entire family was sent to Theresienstadt, and then Auschwitz. I am named after my grandfather's niece, Eva, who was eight when she was gassed to death. When I asked my father to send me photos of my grandparents' papers—their Czech passports and marriage license—he reminded me that I could always claim my Israeli citizenship. When I started to explain to him all of the reasons why this is not something I'd consider, ranging from neutral (Israel is on their second pandemic-related lockdown), to more political (the Bibi regime is deeply problematic), to my dealbreaker (my sons would be drafted into the army), he started to get angry with me; he went into what my sister (who is a therapist and a rabbi) would call his "lizard brain" and just shut down. He couldn't hear anything I was saying and wouldn't engage beyond his emotional borders. He kept saying, "you know I have a soft spot for Israel." Mosab asks the question above, *how can poetry rescue me?* The poetry I gravitate toward takes us beyond our knee-jerk reactions. It takes us out of our lizard brains and into the place where we can hold conflicting narratives together and let them create a third thing—an open space—a place for reflection and change and possibility. (And I think this is perhaps similar to Naomi's "better world" theory?)

RACHEL NEVE-MIDBAR: Erika, I am so sorry you aren't forming poems now. Everything you write here is so resonant inside me, but none more than the idea of poetry as a third rail: that vibrating chamber that holds all of our ideas, experiences, concepts, and realities that make no sense when held together in our daily lives. I am going to send you a waterproof voice recorder so you can write in the shower. You need to feed all of these thoughts into your poems.

So much of what every one of you has written here has me thinking: about poetry, about the experience of the emigrant and the refugee, about our responsibilities vis-à-vis the land in which we live, about language and what our words mean.

I have not been able to write poems, real poems from my inner voice, since I went to live in Los Angeles. I always thought, like Erika, that I need that closed door, that quiet place in order to get the poems to the page. Not easy with six semigrown kids in the house! Then I left my place, the home I had made for my children for thirty-odd years, and I went to live in a foreign land. Life in Los Angeles provided plenty of alone time as I quickly found that though I spoke English, no one understood a word I said. I found that language isn't just the words we speak. Language lives in us at the most visceral level—in that place where our eyes blink and our heart beats, where thoughts rise up and just as quickly slips away, where a deep inner music whispers in your ear. I think about you, Mosab, there in Syracuse with the leaves turning and the days getting short and cold and you forming poems in English and in Arabic. Of course those poems are different! How hard it would be for me to even talk about poetry in Hebrew, a language that I speak and understand fluently but only sometimes lives inside my bones. How do we exist inside language?

This question makes me think of the multilanguage poetics of those who were either forced or chose to live outside their motherland and first language. Last semester I spent some time translating the poetry of the poet Avot Yeshurun. Yeshurun left his home and family in Poland in the 1920s and emigrated to Palestine. There he found an affinity with the Palestinians more than with the Jews, seeing in them his ancestry and family. He learned Arabic as well as Hebrew and those languages joined the music of Yiddish in his heart. And his poetry was always born in strong music—Yeshurun's own personal music. In 1947–48 Yeshurun had the double blow of finding out that his entire family had been obliterated in the Holocaust and that his adopted family had been decimated and cast out in the Nakba. In anger he said, "a nation that has been refugees for 2,000 years doesn't make another nation into refugees," and he penned a famous poem called "Passover in the Caves" wherein he mixed all three languages together with many made-up words to express his anger and devastating loss. The poem was published in the newspaper *Davar* in 1952.

Like Erika's ancestors writing "nein" "nein" "nein" on a page in a world blown to pieces in war and catastrophe.

So here in Haifa I am trying to think of how to get back to my heartbeat chamber, my third rail of poetry. I am no longer alone. Like others in the pandemic, everyone is home all the time and I am never alone. But maybe that isn't it. Maybe the way back to my music is to find my way home.

PHILIP METRES: I'm filled with a kind of awe by your replies, aware of the psychological toll of this moment. I think I spent most of my time compartmentalizing the great grief of this time. I simply can't bear its whole weight. It is a prophetic time, and we are in need of prophets who can release that grief, to see it and speak it, and to let us weep together, as we need to weep.

I've been trying to hold all of your responses in my head together, trying to see you in your geographical and psychic spaces and places—the places you find yourselves, the places you've come from, the places you're thinking of going. Mosab trying poems in different languages, trying to reach an ear that can change his reality and the reality of Palestinians in Gaza; Conor trying to find the right side of the border between poetic silence and silencing; Rachel, living with the predicament of waiting during the pandemic, surrounded by the voices of Haifa; Naomi, extolling the virtues of poetry's slowness, the chance to inhabit a little boy's consciousness and the place of hope; Erika's feeling of entrapment by caregiving in a pandemic, and the precarity of being a Jew in our country newly inflamed with antisemitism, thinking about escape routes, and the ancestors who sought and found escape; and Rachel's longing to get back to poetry, a home.

I'm reminded of something that Sergey Gandlevsky once told me during an interview nearly thirty years ago: "My homeland is Russian literature." It gave me such relief, since I didn't feel at home in Russia, where I was living, studying Russian poetry, and I hadn't felt at home in the United States, which had just conducted a pathological display of war fever during the 1991 Persian Gulf War. The possibility of home being inside books, inside literature, was a grace I hadn't quite imagined.

So much about the political worlds we're connected to seem toxic and almost unredeemable. Yet I've never been entirely satisfied with literature as escape or final destination. It can be a refuge, or even a retreat—like the places the Desert Fathers and Mothers would go to find God again, unable to find the Infinite in the distracted, urban present. Like the vision quests of young indigenous people, seeking the way.

But when I find myself reading things like Ben Ehrenreich's *Desert Notebooks: A Road Map for the End of Time*, I'm forced to confront things that make me want to hide: mass extinction, climate change, the end of civilization. Ehrenreich is trying to find clues to how people have survived apocalypse—looking at collapsing civilizations, the persistence of indigenous ways after genocide—yet I ended up feeling suffocated, unable to deal with the fact of the collapse.

Erika's notion of poetry as a way out of our lizard brains seems exactly right. A dilation. Like that octopus in that new documentary, *My Octopus Teacher*, whose curiosity overcomes her prodigious survival instincts and begins to explore the strange pale human creature who visits her every day. The ongoing benign presence of this swimmer draws her out from the den, until one day, she attaches all her legs to his hand, trying to understand, to taste, to experience something that she had never felt before. And in the process, she beguiles this man, who finds something that he could not find in the human world. We have always been animals, but we have forgotten that we are nature too. We have built so many walls to protect us that we have forgotten our common home.

Our "Social Dilemma" (to reference the recent documentary about the perils of social media) is that we are living in smaller and smaller bubbles of reality, thanks to the unseen Code Makers behind social media, harvesting our attention, feeding back to us the reality that it appears we want to exist in—or that activates enough dopamine that it feels like need. Oh the small tyranny of wanting more LIKES on Facebook, RETWEETS on Twitter, HEARTS on Instagram! It's strange to think that the daily suffering of so many people is due to being inside systems that are designed not for our full thriving, but to keep us in thrall, in some kind of prison. What seemed like a kind of freedom turned out to be a cell.

Mosab, I've been thinking about your mirror poem—how the sides were not mirrors at all, but something different—and would love to see poems like that, poems in conversation in two languages side by side, but not precisely the same. We need poems like that, poems for bilingual readers who can see the borders of the translatable and the untranslatable.

Languages are so particular, like peoples. The question is: Can they exist side by side, without needing that pure mirror?

How can we make space for the full thriving of people, in all of our ill-fittedness? It seems as if the predicament of Israel and Palestine is embedded in the problem of precarity. The fact that the modern nation-state has been the guarantor of individual security, rights, and freedom (and here, that guarantee is hugely uneven, problematic, and accompanied by asterisks) means that stateless people are incredibly vulnerable. It's been true for Jews, it's been true for Palestinians, and of course for so many other peoples as well. In the film *Salam Neighbor*, one Syrian man reflects: "When you cross this imaginary line, you become a refugee, and your life is in the hands of others."

All of us, caught in systems not of our making, yet in which we are implicated in or oppressed by (and sometimes both). The nation-state seems like a poor answer to a complicated question—where and how can we belong in ways that offer us a space for living, or pursuing a good life, for making a future not doomed by the past?

I've been thinking about what applying an antiracist lens would look like for imagining a future for Palestinians and Israelis. That's on the national scale. On the personal scale, I wonder what I can do for you, Mosab, and you, Erika.

MOSAB ABU TOHA: It is true that through literature, especially poetry, we can communicate with others our emotions and ideas. But I like to convince myself that we can also build our own world/s, we can build a home for us and others. I like what Darwish once wrote about words: "I have learned and dismantled all the words in order to draw from them a single word: Home." (I'm happy I can build a house with both English and Arabic.)

Phil, I really like what Gandlevsky had to say about finding his home not in Russia but in Russian literature. It's so sad that one knows about their country only through what is written about it. It's good for Gandlevsky that his (and your) country has a name. Alas, my country Palestine is hardly found on official paperwork. In the past few decades, pronouncing the word Palestine was a blasphemy. And you can ask Edward Said.

When I filled in a form for my J-1 documents for Harvard's fellowship last year, I didn't find Palestine in the options. There were many countries I had never heard of. Palestine, which is mentioned in holy scriptures, in ancient history books, and stories and poems is taboo. In the options, there was either the Gaza Strip or the West Bank. I felt relieved when I found my gender in the options.

Moreover, when I filled in the form for taxes, Palestine (not even the Gaza Strip) was not there to select. I had to choose OTHER.

I'm not sure why I should look for a word. Why should I look for Palestine? What will happen after I find it? After all, I'm married, and I have children. What would I use it for? Sometimes I tell my friends that in Gaza we use our ID cards or passports to look at photos in them, how much we have changed.

Early this month, I traveled to New York City. I met Mariam Said and her daughter, Najla. Najla wrote a book/memoir about herself and her father, Edward Said. The book's title is *Looking for Palestine: Growing Up Confused in an Arab-American Family*. Najla sent me the book when I was in Gaza. When I met her in Manhattan, I wondered if she was still looking for Palestine, if Palestine was getting closer or farther from her.

For me, I have a different picture. I wrote a poem two days after our meeting. Here are some parts:

> The sun rises and moves around.
> It sets to visit other places
> And we, we are looking for Palestine.
> . . .
>
> People travel to relatives and friends.
> They book round-trip tickets, stuff their suitcases
> with gifts and books and clothes.
> And we, we are still looking for Palestine.
>
> . . .
> Sir, we don't have airports and seaports;
> no trains, no highways.
> We don't have passable roads, sir!
> We *do* have crutches and wheelchairs.
> Young men with one or no legs,
> no longer able to work, as if there was work.
>
> . . .

We don't have embassies, sir!
The one in Jerusalem is very hard to reach.
It is only 97 km away from Gaza
but is as far as the Andromeda Galaxy.
Andromeda is 2.5 million light years.
But all we have are dark years.
It should take trillions of years.

Sir, we are not welcome anywhere.
Only cemeteries don't mind our bodies.

We are no longer looking for Palestine.
We are dying.
Soon, Palestine will search for us,
for our whispers, for our footsteps,
for our fading pictures fallen off aging walls
of silence.

I'm not sure why I feel terrified whenever I look at this poem. I sometimes feel ashamed of my bleak writing. Why do I have to write this?

In one workshop, a poet left me this feedback about this poem, "I think that you have a real knack for the idea that the act of writing poetry is political, and I don't think that you should shy away from that."

I felt unhappy with him describing my appetite for poetry as "political." I found myself writing this:

ARS POETICA FROM PALESTINE

When I write about my family and friends,
some of whom I lost to barbaric assaults,
about my love for trees and flowers,
my wish to sit at the Gaza seashore, to watch
the sunset, and to drink my favorite tea with dried sage
while my kids play in the sand,
build their vulnerable houses . . .

I long for the Yaffa Sea and orange wind
though I've never been there.

My grandparents Hasan and Khadra were expelled.
He died before I was born.
I never saw Yaffa in his eyes.
Khadar means green. When I first saw her,
she was brown as earth.

When I wish to live a normal life, without worry
about finding a job, about being turned away whenever
I try to travel, about getting regular access to electricity,
or about getting drinkable water.
This worry slows the blood in my veins.

When I curse the F-16s and soldiers who shoot
and kill kids playing football near the Mina (seaport)
in Gaza, close to Al-Deera Hotel.
(I'm talking about the four Baker kids.
aged 11 and 12 on July 6, 2014.)
The bomb kicked their ball not into the goal
but into shreds.

When I tell about how the clock on our walls struggles to
move
about how three hands, like ours, get crippled in the dark.
When I shout at those on the other side, who throw their hands
in the air (our air) playing volleyball at beaches (our beaches)
dancing at parties, while we, when we smile,
we don't see our teeth in the dark.

But this is not political poetry.

What's political is a prime minister ordering soldiers
to launch attacks on our libraries, schools, and houses,
to annex lands in the borderless state,
to prevent a pregnant mother from crossing
a checkpoint to hospitals.
She died and gave birth to a dead child,
Dead as political speeches in the Holy Land.

NAOMI SHIHAB NYE: I am so moved by all your voices and questionings and poems—there are just three small things I'd like to say this morning.

You might like to read this beautiful piece of parallels by two Nathalies, our sister Nathalie Handal one of them and our other sister Natalie Diaz, called "Map of the Next World."[3]

The great writer Grace Paley said, *Politics is simply the way human beings treat one another.* So Mosab—I wouldn't shy away from that word. It doesn't diminish a poem, it enhances it. Your poems are full of care and longing and love. They are political in their very being of attention. Your desire to create a magazine for writers of Gaza, an outlet for voices, a vessel for language, is a generous act of humanity as well as a political statement of presence. Voices are ***there***, they deserve to be heard.

I'm touched by Phil's comment that he wants to know what to do to help others. Phil, if I hadn't voted already, I'd vote for you. What more important political act can there ever be?

Also, my greatest poetic encourager since I was twenty-two died last week and I just want to note him. Thinking of what the rest of my life will feel like without him in the world is very searing right now. Also, thinking of how interested he was in the work of other people makes me want to be nothing but an encourager, forever. A devoted man of letters, Italian American, reclusive but vastly generous, active for social and racial justice, who was left with a great archive of words in his care—the many, many writings of his close friend John Howard Griffin, who wrote *Black Like Me*—he spent decades bringing out at least eight more Griffin books, as well as writing his own works and encouraging what seems like an endless number of others—Roberto Bonazzi. Please hold that melodious name in your minds for just one moment as he flies. Our friends are so precious.

MOSAB ABU TOHA:

Dear Naomi,

I am so sorry for your loss of such a great human being. My family in Gaza and I are holding him in our prayers. May his soul rest in peace.

I do pray that more people like him, you, and our comrades in this group continue to encourage and care about other young writers and artists. What we need in this crazy world are more sane leaders who can illuminate the path for the blindfolded crowds.

Even if we, poets, die, our words will continue to shine, just like those stars we see at night. My only hope is that when it's our time to shine, clouds won't envelop the sky.

But at least, the moon will take notice of our shining light.

Warmest,

Mosab

CONOR BRACKEN: Oh Naomi, I'm so sorry for your loss. It's hard to overstate how lucky we are for our friends and encouragers. Those who know us and listen to us and exhort us to share with others what we share with them. There is no replacing that.

Coming back to this conversation, to see you all braiding so many things to it—Grace Paley on politics, Mosab's poems written in heart's blood and the ink of a nation that forms won't name, Avot Yeshurun's polyglossic indignation, Erika's assertion of the poem as an open space, the kinship between octopus and human found through curiosity and so much more!—I feel fortunate, especially since outside of this space, life seems made up mostly of obstacles, viral, geographic, bureaucratic, linguistic, and otherwise. So much of the world is made of barriers, but in conversations like this, and poems as well, these barriers don't have the same, if any, power. It's one of the things I love about poems: how they reach across time and space to touch someone who they never imagined (I'm thinking of *My Octopus Teacher* in a way here, two creatures formed by vastly different pressures and currents, communing, and I'm thinking of what Mosab said, about our words "continu[ing] to shine" even after we're gone). Another thing I love is the possibility inside a poem, especially during its genesis, how it makes leaping connections in wild and novel ways that in retrospect become natural, inevitable, if not essential to its being.

The world, so often, does not allow that. The language we use every day in quotidian contexts, to ask for salt or papers or a little help, doesn't either. I'm thinking here of Rachel in Los Angeles, speaking in English but not being understood, how our expectations of language and how it is used, a kind of labyrinthine basement underneath the words themselves that governs how they're used and when, is as much a part of the language as the words themselves, but one that is learned through time and use and residence.

In this way language is insidious. Or, more finely put, in this way the users of a language can put it to insidious use. Poetry, though, has an entirely different kind of basement. One that is fluid and unfixed, multidimensional and riddled with wormholes that allow the user to assemble totally different, phantasmagorically improbable constructions that stand, plumb and strange. The possibilities that poetry unlocks in language boggle my students, and terrify the powers that be, because the more you learn to make and see the connections that help poems stand, the more you see the connections outside them, too. How conflicting narratives might not be in as much conflict as we thought. How one can be both complicit in and repressed by power structures. If you can feel the fresh joy or anguish of Sappho or Hafez, someone the impregnable borders of time and death have separated you from, then you might also be able to feel the joy and anguish of someone you've been conditioned to think is different, even dangerously so. As Muriel Rukeyser said about islands, "for God's sake / they are connected / underneath."

When my chapbook—about an abusive romantic relationship with Henry Kissinger—came out, my grandfather gave a copy to a neighbor. The neighbor, after reading some of it, said that I must not love America very much. (She's the kind of person who, if she read more poetry, would use the word "political" as a dismissal, as if things are only political when they deal overtly with nonwhite, nonhegemonic subject matter. Even though every poem is political! A poem is always reaching out to someone, and politics is, fundamentally, like poems, about how we exist together.) I wish I'd been there to tell her what James Baldwin said: I love this country and for that very reason I insist on the right to criticize her perpetually.

These kinds of people scare me more than anything. They're the ones who twisted the word meritocracy against its invention (it was coined sarcastically, to describe something that didn't and couldn't exist). They're the ones who took the proverb "pull yourself up by your bootstraps" literally (it was initially used to describe something that literally couldn't be done). They don't understand or care that Monopoly's inventor wanted people to see the dangers, not revel, in capitalism's aloof cruelty. And they're the ones who need poetry more than anything, for how it can help us hold paradox in our heads without trying to solve it. That I can point out and decry the violent colonial machinations of this country but still love the possibility it extends to those in it and in its future. That we can, as Édouard Glissant notes, remain fundamentally opaque to one another, but in that difference or distance or distinction see beauty and not threat.

ERIKA MEITNER:

Hi all,

Firstly, Naomi, I am so sorry about the loss of your mentor Roberto Bonazzi. He sounds like he was a wonderful man. I don't know if it's the compounded awareness COVID and isolation has brought us, but I feel like everything is more fragile right now; more people I know are passing away, dealing with serious illnesses, or trying to cope with loss of loved ones or jobs or other very difficult things. I've taken a while to respond as my (otherwise healthy, nonretired) mother had a stroke about two weeks ago. She waited too long to be able to get some of the more immediate treatments, and the stroke impacted her ability to speak, write, and communicate.

She has slurred speech, aphasia, and can't text, write, or even sign her name right now. This makes communicating with her difficult as she's far away in New York. In non-COVID times, I would have been on the next flight up there—but we no longer have a direct flight to LaGuardia from here due to drops in air traffic; I couldn't stay with them if I went up as both my parents are high risk now; and New York still has a two-week quarantine for people coming from Virginia. Leaving my kids for that long right now is also basically impossible. I hate that what used to be simple now seems logistically unfathomable. *How do we exist inside language?* asks Rachel. And what happens when our access to language changes? My mother and I used to talk nearly every day. We still do, but now it's almost entirely me doing the talking. What happens when dialogue becomes monologue?

There are so many good questions I want to write about here—ideas around home, and grief, and reaching out across species from Phil. I am clearly the only person who hasn't yet seen *My Octopus Teacher*! I've been thinking a lot about that Gandlevsky quote from Phil—"My homeland is Russian literature." When I first studied

Israeli literature it was back in the mid-nineties with a wonderful teacher named Sidra DeKoven Ezrahi at Hebrew University in Jerusalem. We read A. B. Yehoshua, Amos Oz, David Grossman, S. Y. Agnon, and others—but we also read Edward Said and Homi Bhabha alongside these texts, and it was the very first time I encountered postcolonial theory. Sidra presented us with the idea that literature itself can change the way people think about Jewish story and territory—that writers can create a history for a place that doesn't complicate, but rather simplifies, competing claims of nationalism. What happens when what we write has real-world consequences in the political realm? What happens when the literary imaginary creates or substantiates claims to real territory?

I was thinking, too, about what Mosab had written about political poetry. I don't even categorize poetry as political or nonpolitical anymore, but more in the way Naomi does—that there is poetry that is engaged with the world, and poetry that isn't. I always prefer the former. I think to some extent we all do or we wouldn't be having this conversation with each other. And Conor, I want to respectfully disagree—I actually don't think every poem is political simply by the act of reaching out (to an other, to a reader, etc.). Right now I have such little patience for poems that seem solipsistic or are missing what I think of as a "so what?" factor. In some ways, we write what we write. I have to follow the poem, rather than the other way around. The last book I published, *Holy Moly Carry Me*, was very much engaged with the world and its politics—gun violence and gun culture, school shootings, protest, immigration, race, the American South. The one I sent off to my publisher a few months ago is the opposite—it's a quieter book about midlife female desire, and I wrote it thinking no one would ever read it. But when I gave it to my first reader (a dear friend), she called me and said it was about other things as well. "We're on a ship that's going down," she said. "We're in the end-times, we're isolated, we've destroyed our environment, but all the love and intimacy we've felt before is still tangible—we get to be made of every intimate moment we've had, and intimacy is a shout against the dying earth."

Speaking of the dying earth—Phil talked about mass extinction and climate change, and a few weeks ago I watched a terrific panel on

Zoom hosted by the Center for Fiction called "Reading and Writing the Environment" with Emily Raboteau, Kerri Arsenault, Meehan Crist, John Freeman, Bathsheba Demuth, and Meera Subramanian. Emily and I have talked before about writing on climate change (and she also has a great book called *Searching for Zion: The Quest for Home in the African Diaspora*, which has a chapter on Jerusalem that also deals with race)—but through the panel I found an essay the writers mentioned, by Kathleen Dean Moore, called "A Call to Writers." In the essay she says, "Some kinds of writing are morally impossible in a state of emergency."[4] Amitav Ghosh's book *The Great Derangement: Climate Change and the Unthinkable* takes on this topic too—the role of literary imagination in saving the planet.[5] What I'm getting at is the ethical role of literary imagination: in presenting the world back to readers, in creating new imaginaries, in creating language itself that helps readers understand crises and moves them to action.

One of the poetry projects I'm working on now is a three-year-long ongoing exploration of sea-level rise and architecture in Miami with a photographer. We've been stumped about how to present something that's long-term and large-scale dramatic, but hard to see in small bits and daily moments, and almost impossible to photograph: the sunny-day flooding, the raised roads in Miami Beach leaving sidewalks and storefronts below grade, the giant pumps that move water from the streets back into the Bay that just look like metal boxes. What language do you use to describe the impossibility and paradox of a city in a time of sea-level rise—with the lowest mean elevation in the country—that's also built on porous limestone that allows water to come up from below? A place vulnerable to regular hurricanes, where unchecked development means that multimillion dollar waterfront houses and condominiums are still going up all along the shoreline? Should we even be describing these things at all, or working to reimagine them? What are our ethical responsibilities right now, as poets, toward the subjects we choose (or that choose us), and how we present them?

RACHEL NEVE-MIDBAR: I just lit my shabbat candles here in Haifa. Joe surprised me with a set of crystal candlesticks when I came in March. I have added several small glasses (one for each child and one for all my grandchildren) that I fill each week with pure olive oil. Joe set the candlesticks on a mirror and set another behind so that the effect is of light reverberating and repeating over and over. My oldest daughter is on a spiritual quest right now on an island in northern Greece. She wrote to me yesterday that all beauty is found within the vibration of all living things down to the cell level. Everything is alive.

From those reverberations I want to send healthy blessings to your mother, Erika. It sounds like she was young and strong before the stroke and I hope that with the right therapies that she will gain back what was lost and you two will again share your lives via daily conversation.

Naomi, I too send condolences. Roberto Bonazzi. May his name be remembered in blessing and may his memory continue to sustain you as I'm sure you sustain others and all of us.

Mosab, don't take the American workshop system too seriously. Essays abound at how difficult it is for anyone even a bit "different" to feel supported or understood in a usual American MFA workshop. And how can your classmates understand the nuances, the depths, the struggles, the history—any of it—of this complicated part of the world? You write your life and they believe it is politics because their own attachment to it is via the news.

Conor, what beautiful mystical words you have written here! What a most human call to peace! In Judaism there is a belief that every word we say, every utterance, is holy. All words, the words of our entire lives: when we tell our child we love them, when we curse our boss, all are saved in heaven and played back to us after we die. From those words the sum total of our existence on earth is measured.

A poem is found to be sustainable when each one who reads it can find themselves within its folds. We are told those are the poems that will last after the poet is no longer with us. What else can we each find ourselves within, where else can we hold separate ideas, even those that work against each other, in our two hands and be OK with the ambiguity? What is vibrating, reverberating, and how do we share it?

I want to bring the conversation back around to this land, this history and future, and what I hope we can begin to think about here. The leaf. Hayden Carruth's single leaf. I will start with my own story: a love story.

I believe I told all of you at our Zoom meeting that I came to this land in 1983 at the age of twenty. The plan was that I would take a year abroad from Sarah Lawrence College and learn a bit about what it means to be a Jew. It was on my second day here that something happened to me that has never happened before or since. I fell hard, deeply and thoroughly, in love: not with a person, but with a land. I was in the backseat of a Volvo station wagon passing through the area of Beit Guvrin. I looked out at the small, August-in-the-Middle-East brown hills and I thought, "I have never seen anything so beautiful in my life." I then reprimanded myself. My father had always had a terrific travel bug and his own small, private plane. I was fairly well traveled by age twenty. I had seen some of the most beautiful mountains in the world. The Alps! The Rockies! Even the Andes!!

But this was love and had nothing to do with logic. And this love has lasted. It's not the love of a state. It's not the love of a majority. It's a visceral connection to a homeland. A land I was taught nothing about, and about which I had no preconceived notions. Just the experience that no matter what I saw, I couldn't stop looking, stop touching, stop tasting. A couple of months later I was on a hike up Nachal David to the crest of the Judean Desert above. It was a very hard hike and a very hot day. As we climbed I grew dizzy and I suddenly found I wanted to roll in the dust. To take the sand and rub it on my face. It would be years before I would find out that for millennia the pilgrims who came here did just that: rolled on the ground and rubbed the dirt into their faces. The Holy Land.

I know this is a love that I share with Mosab. Just last week the sky was so heartbreakingly exquisite that I shared a photo of it on Facebook. Right away Mosab shared one of his own that his brother had sent him from Gaza. The same sky.

It would not be until several decades later that I would find myself living in the heart of the Judean Desert, my true heart-home, in a small settlement of 200 families just past Maale Adumim off the road to the Dead Sea called Alon. The settlement is named after Yigal Allon, the designer of the Allon Plan, the first partition plan after the Six-Day War in 1967 that included a plan to partition the West Bank between Israel and Jordan, create a Druze state in the Golan Heights, and return most of the Sinai Peninsula to Arab control.

The plan got far enough that a very windy road was built through the desert between the Dead Sea road and the northern West Bank. The settlement is on this windy road just above a natural spring, a *mayam po'em*, a rhythmic spring that stops and starts, that empties and renews itself naturally in accordance with a special limestone formation from under the ground. A spring surrounded by the ruins of an ancient Christian Byzantine settlement and sporting an aqueduct from the Roman period. And on any Saturday afternoon you find the pool filled with boys: Jewish boys, Palestinian boys, all taking turns diving into the deeper end, none distinguishable from the other with their smiles and laughter, the glint of water on their skin, the drip from their hair.

In the four short years I lived in Alon I went every day to the *ma'ayan* with full understanding of my privilege to do so. That was where I wrote my poems. Every day I walked 8–10 kilometers through the desert. I was truly home.

And once I knew that I realized I had to ask myself a very hard question: If the area of Alon became part of a future Palestinian state, would I still want to live there? Immediately the answer, for me, was a resounding YES! But then I asked myself: Who would let me live here? And if some law allowed me to stay, who would let me survive to live here?

With this thought heavy in my heart I walked through my days until one Tuesday afternoon I ran into the grocery to pick up a bottle of laundry detergent. The grocery store I went into is called Rami Levy. Rami Levy started his career as a wholesaler to small groceries around Jerusalem and finally opened his own supermarkets that cut the prices and became the popular place to shop. He then opened stores in areas around the West Bank that could service and employ both the Israeli and Palestinian communities and ran them in a fully egalitarian style, which meant the best man for the job without consideration to gender, race, or religion. The stores soon became another spot of coexistence where I might find myself discussing the best brand of *techina* with a neighbor from a nearby Arab village or sharing recipes with another wearing a veil; we were allowed to be what we were, housewives, mothers of large families juggling those heavy demands.

In the Rami Levy in Mishor Adumim there is a checkout guy from Anata named Omar. Omar and I hit it off immediately. He is the spitting image of my sister's son, Shmuel, a big teddy-bear of a guy, and, when Omar heard my American-accented Hebrew, he asked if he could practice his English with me. If Omar was working I would only get on his line, no matter how long, and over the years we prickled many feathers from other customers when our chats in English would continue in a store where the minimum wait time on line could be forty-five minutes.

That Tuesday, in the morning, there had been a particularly heartbreaking terrorist incident. A seventeen-year-old boy climbed into the window of a Kiryat Arba apartment where he found a fifteen-year-old girl and stabbed her to death. Everyone was feeling the devastation of two lives lost as we went through our day. I paid for a big bottle of Tide, but when I put the bottle into a plastic bag, the bag broke, the bottle smashed against the tile floor, fluorescent blue liquid splattering everywhere. I stood there not sure of what to do next, ready to cry, when Omar came rushing over. I assumed he wanted to help me clean up the mess and get another bottle, but instead Omar ran up to me and threw his arms around me, held me tightly, his voice a deep moan as he said, "Rachel, Rachel. I am so sorry for everything my nation has done to your nation."

I am crying now, even as I write this years later. I felt this young man in my arms, his courage. I felt his words move against my hair, I felt his body alive and quivering against mine.

I thought: this is a gift. A gift from G-d. Who in their life gets to hear this? Gets to say this? I wrapped my arms tightly around Omar's big body and I said, "I am sorry for everything my nation has done to your nation too."

I wrote about this moment in a poem that is in my book *Salaam of Birds*. Colleagues in America have criticized the poem, told me it is "not enough." Of course it's not enough, what could or would possibly be enough? And yet, it is everything.

I am not surprised that in all this we turn to mirrors, to that reflection, that refraction, that reverberation. Magic, we are told, exists there, in that glance into another universe where things might be backwards, might be different. This is my mirror poem:

MEMORIAL

I watch you call the names of your dead,
    each forms deep in your throat, falls from your mouth
like chess pieces or toy soldiers, even the children
    posed with stones or guns—everyone ready for battle.

The names tumble to the lectern, perch there
  despite the hard currents of your sorrow,
your tears, my tears, splintered
  and spilling from tabletop to floor. Yes
name your dead, each who fell in grace or not,
  in innocence or not. And I will name mine.
When I name names, am I counting doves or darkness?
  Our lists swell, the dead crowding in, anger
plain on their faces, even as we clean their bodies, prepare
  the earth, all of us greedy for some further fury,
to claw at borders, dispatch these names into the void,
  blame clutched in their talons, the language of this conflict
so easy in our mouths, so easy—
  What lies on the other side
of the mirror if we choose to walk through
  to a place where the sounds of the wounded
are lost in the whispered sand
  and we can only hear water, a river,
or perhaps just the clank of dishes in the sink,
  the soft sound of water washing away
the last of a good meal shared together?
  Lay with me back to back. Don't you see
we are two sides of the same hair?
  Please, we can do this together.
You hold the amulet while I
  carry you across the divide.

MOSAB ABU TOHA, OCTOBER 27, 2020:

Dear Erika. I really pray that your mother will get better very soon and that you and your family will get to reunite in the near future.

Before I left Gaza in September 2019, I could not imagine the world very well, how big it was or how mountains and oceans looked like. I had known there were countries called Egypt, Jordan, the United States, the UK, France, etc., but my simple mind never helped me imagine how big they were.

It sometimes helped me imagine that Gaza was like a seed and the other countries were as big as leaves, twigs, branches, or trunks of differing trees. But I never checked that.

I never saw my grandfather Hasan, Hasan who was expelled from Yaffa with his parents and siblings. They were among many, many other Palestinians who were mercilessly expelled from their homes. Hasan passed away before my father married.

Unlike my seven siblings, I've been the only one who keeps asking my father, who was born in a refugee camp in Gaza, about my grandfather, what he had worked in Yaffa, about the oranges, if my grandfather watered the trees, about their exodus, whether he had enough water or food while they walked to Gaza. I know that people usually migrate to other countries on planes, on ships, in trains, etc. But even my grandfather's journey after expulsion was different.

I used to ask my father whether he ever saw Yaffa and our family house there. He said, "Yes, the house was still there when I went. There was a big tree in the front yard."

I asked my father if the tree still had leaves and whether our house's walls were still able to stand, to stand the cold of abandonment, whether it missed my grandfather's and his family's footsteps on its floor, whether the beds longed for someone to make them after dust had slept on them.

Whether the tea my grandmother made for him
was still hot. They were newly married
at the time of the Catastrophe.
Whether their fingerprints were still
on the bathtub faucet after the last shower.

When I left our home in north Gaza to Rafah in south Gaza, the trip took about 50 minutes. This is how big the Gaza strip is. When the Egyptian authorities stamped my passport, I commenced my first long journey. It took about 12 hours in the minivan to arrive in Cairo. The distance between Gaza and Cairo is 216 miles. A few weeks ago, I traveled from Syracuse to New York City. The distance was 255 miles. It took us only 4 hours.

But I must say that the twelve hours from Gaza to Cairo was really a short time. If I hadn't paid some money beforehand for coordination, it would have taken me three days, just as it took my wife's uncle a few weeks ago. Luckily, I had the money to get a VIP permit to enter Egypt and face less delay en route.

When we reached Cairo, it was so big a city. I nearly fainted. When I wanted to travel from Cairo to the airport the next day, it took us an hour. Cairo is 1,191 square miles. Gaza's land area is 141 square miles. I thought Gaza was big. But I'm sorry, Gaza! You were big only before I left you.

When I arrived in Amman, Jordan, the following day, the same thing happened. Amman is 649 square miles.

Wait, Mosab. You've seen nothing! In the U.S., when I traveled by car from Syracuse to Manhattan, NYC, for a visit, I couldn't close my mouth. The landscapes were so beautiful and enormous. New York State is 54,556 square miles. So many open fields, so many colored trees, so many bodies of water, so and so.

But in Gaza, the land's so very small; two million people are crammed into that tiny piece of paper. Moreover, people are not left to lead their own lives. There are no jobs, the borders are mostly closed, electricity is cut almost always, air raids, gunboats fire, and artillery shells kill people during the day and night, hospitals partially function, about forty-two students sit in one small classroom with no fans in summer or heating system in winter, and so many No's.

I wish that were all. A Gazan is not only unwanted to live a good life in Gaza, not to say live at all, but s/he is also unwanted outside it. Maybe a grave is the most welcoming place.

While I watched the many empty fields in the United States, I was wondering, "Why couldn't we and others come here and live in this land? Not forever, but maybe like birds, live here for some time, then travel to other places, live what this planet earth is offering us, before we die, without visas, without borders, without hate."

I believe many, if not all, Jews can migrate to the Holy Land and they also can stay where they are. But for a Palestinian it's not the case. I'm sorry. A Palestinian is not wanted to stay in what remains of Palestine nor to travel and look for an easier life.

RACHEL NEVE-MIDBAR:

> Dearest Mosab, I am sorry for everything my nation has done to your nation.

MOSAB ABU TOHA:

> Thank you, dear Rachel. I just pray that no more innocent people are killed on either side.

December 2020

PHILIP METRES: It's been a little while—the anxiety of elections, the ongoing panic of pandemic—and my head and heart swam with dizziness. I write with relief that Biden won—the country narrowly avoided voting for the meteor ready to strike the planet. But I also write with a sober sense of the great challenges he will face, and the fact that Biden's foreign policy, while less absolutely destructive than Trump's, does not promise fairness to Palestinians.

I've been thinking of you. About Rachel's poignant story of Omar's hug in the grocery store—that moment of undeniable humanity, despite nationalities. Her poem about being two sides of the same hair—what an organic image. I just finished reading Rachel's *Salaam of Birds*, thinking about the precarity she experienced, wondering about her son's closeness to death serving in the IDF and close to the Hamas attack back in 2014.

Thinking about Mosab's travel absurdities, and how his view of the size of Gaza (that little seed!) shifted so decisively by seeing other places. His persistence, his good humor, his investment in the future with that library and his writing.

Also, about each of your words of apology, the sorry of sorrow, and the desire that violence end. My heart swells to think of the power of words of apology, of prayer for the other.

Maybe we should focus on what we're looking forward to in 2021 and the Biden administration!

I write this after dealing with a painful review of a *Shrapnel Maps*, in which I'm accused of a host of sins—colonialism, imperialism, vampirism, erasure, harm—and I felt devastated by it. Even though I knew that this response was possible, and perhaps even likely, it reminded me again of the deep pain that so many Palestinians carry, and I questioned myself again—have I been too fearful about speaking out in solidarity with my Palestinian brothers and sisters? Have I failed them utterly?

It took me a number of days to see the review in some kind of context. I think it conflates a lot of things (text and paratext, author and speaker)—but its truth is a prophetic one and important for me to hear. It's an invitation. I could be more brave, more clear. I (and all Americans, our government) have failed Palestinians, over and over, by failing to hold Israel to a basic level of accountability to human rights, to justice, and ultimately to a just peace.

How can we write into solidarity, and how can we act as citizens in solidarity? For example, are there legislative initiatives that we would agree on—for example, Betty McCollum's HR 2407: Promoting Human Rights for Palestinian Children Living under Israeli Military Occupation Act?

NAOMI SHIHAB NYE:

Dearest Circle of Friends,

Though I have not written much in our roundtable lately, you have all been with me. Thank you so much for your generous words of care to me about Roberto. He would have been touched to hear you all utter his name. One of his own books of poems was called *The Scribbling Cure* and another was *The Maestro of Solitude*. If you ever have a chance to read him—he would be grateful.

Erika, how is your mother? I hope she will continue to strengthen and rebalance. So difficult not to be able to race to be with someone who is ailing! I am fascinated by your poetry project in Miami regarding sea water, rising levels, new buildings, etc. Want to know more! Do you by any chance know the amazing Palestinian poet and professor Dr. Sharif Elmusa, an expert on water issues and a terrific poet? He lives in DC and Maine and might be someone very interested in what you are doing as well.

Phil, please don't cut the above section. We will all suffer from unfair criticisms, or misunderstandings, at some point, and it is profoundly bolstering for people to describe honestly what happens when they face it. And you have done just that, so thoughtfully.

And yes, thank goodness about the election! Though President Biden and Vice-President Harris may not have a great track record regarding Palestine, Palestinians, or justice in the region, they are both smart and attentive and might still be educated. People of empathy, with compassionate worldviews, how could they exempt one group of people entirely from their care?

Mosab, I adore how you describe your senses of the map—big Gaza, little world—it's so important to put things in contexts—how our maps keep changing—your writing is so miraculous to me. Even your description of driving up to Syracuse—the wide expensive views—feels so uplifting. We forget. We forget where we are, what we have. Sometimes when I am driving out in the green and golden winter Texas countryside with my ninety-three-year-old mother, I entirely forget, thanks to the stunning beauty, that we have crazed politicians in our state legislature who recently wanted to overthrow the federal government. It is such a pleasure to forget them.

Mosab, I know I am already bugging you about the magnificent book of poems for young readers you are working on, but I can see a picture book as well—in your descriptions of time and space and place and sizes . . .

Rachel, your compassion emanates so powerfully to me in all you write—I hope your daughter is doing well and is in a stable living situation again. Thank you for describing your workspace and the black cloths people were flying out windows—probably here in the United States half of us could have shrouded our entire dwellings for the past four years to declare our feelings for our nation's hideous nonleadership. Power and greed, is that what it boiled down to? Thankfully poets don't know much about those things.

Rachel, your great heart and spirit! Thank you for sharing your life and language and profoundly moving insights and memories. Did you ever know the writers Nava Semel or Moshe Dor in Israel? They were both such powerful writers themselves and such advocates for others. I think about them often, and wonder what efforts I could make myself to echo the care they gave to others.

And I cheer for your daughter! When you wrote that she is discovering that "all beauty is found within the vibration of all living things down to the cell level. Everything is alive."—I felt reminded of the hum at the center of this whole pandemic year. There is a hum! It's that deepest quietude we are all sharing! Sometimes my grandson Connor and I just stop still and talk about it. Hear that? It's so quiet! You can't even hear a single bus or truck or car or anything! Sometimes even the birds get quiet.

Conor, thank you for telling us about the neighbor who said you must not love America very much. This carries me back to what Phil recently suffered—a lack of understanding and depth of response to his profoundly important work. Yes, let's all stand with James Baldwin who knew the truth about such responses and continued his wider devotion to questioning, puzzling out the complexities. I love his bemused, wry expression in videos.

A teacher in a Nablus, West Bank school recently invited me to speak with her students on a Saturday. They are young Palestinians living in villages around Nablus. Their ages appeared to be around twelve and they stayed with me for the entire two hours, not one of them left. Avid readers and writers, they wanted to talk about the stories and graphic novels they have been working on—in English mostly—and they had plenty of questions. They all said they missed eating meals with their "larger families" because of the pandemic and hoped there would be a day soon when they could go outside comfortably without masks again and run to visit all their relatives.

One beautiful boy is working on a graphic novel called "Bug Wars." He is illustrating it in intricate black magic marker too. His main characters at present are spiders and ants though he said he hopes to bring in some honey bees and wasps too. He said that spiders are very afraid of ants. "Sometimes a spider impersonates an ant, so it won't get attacked." This fascinated me. "How does a spider impersonate an ant?" His answer: "It's mostly a facial expression." I can't stop thinking about this.

Thank you all for letting me sit with you at your table. My facial expression is smiling.

MOSAB ABU TOHA: Thank you, Naomi. My facial expression is smiling, too, when I think about such worlds. I strongly believe that the reason why I often write about surrealistic worlds in my poetry is that I want to escape my real world. I want to see the world from a spider's or a clock's point of view.

When I fail to do something, for example traveling to visit my family in Gaza, I give my voice to a bird. This way, I don't need to pay money to leave Gaza or even need a visa.

Regarding the American elections, as a Palestinian and someone who never voted in his life (the last times elections were held were in 2005 and 2006. I was fourteen, not eligible), I think I should feel hopeful. But this is not enough. When Hamas won the parliamentary election in 2006, many of them voted for it not because it is Hamas. But because it's not Fatah. They didn't want Fatah to rule over them. They accused it of corruption. Unfortunately, Hamas, which now rules over Gaza, turned out to be just as corrupt. They employ people who are loyal to them, they are unable to support the two million people there, financially, medically, socially, etc. Many families nowadays wait from time to time for the 100 dollars that Qatar sends to Gaza.

Now, people in Palestine are happy that Biden has won. But is it because he is Biden? Mostly no. Mostly because he's not Trump. And we all know what troubles Trump put in the face of Palestinians, not the least closing the PLO office in D.C., cutting aid to UNRWA, making it difficult for Palestinians to travel to the U.S., among other things.

Now the question is: Will President Biden fix things? This is what most Palestinians are hoping for.

July 2021

PHILIP METRES: It's been a while since we've all touched base. So much has happened globally. What's changed for you since we last talked?

NAOMI SHIHAB NYE: Naomi here. What's changed for me, after the latest horrific bombing massacre in Gaza, sixty-nine children dead in all and sixty-seven of them in Gaza, and the foolish useless missiles shot into Israel by Hamas, is—more sadness and more urgency. Something has to happen *now.* These missiles did not come out of a vacuum. What is the real situation? Everyone keeps writing to me that the world is seeing a clearer picture of what's been going on all this time in the oppressions of Palestinians, their families and homes and land and lives, and something important is on the brink of changing. So change already. It's hard to absorb one more death of a mama gone off to work—the spectacularly beautiful West Bank woman with a doctorate in psychology, this past week, for mercy's sake—and carry on. What happens with all this grief? Where does it go? How does it circle back?

Think of all the possible positive energy that is being wasted. A new government of men in suits is not very inspiring. But here's hoping Netanyahu and his meanness dematerializes like the witch in *The Wizard of Oz*. And some new great people show up and make a vast leap to a better chapter for all. The children deserve it.

CONOR BRACKEN: Since we last spoke, we moved. My wife and I bought a house outside of Cleveland and over a few days (and with the help of some movers) shifted our life from a semirural county seat in central Ohio to a liberal suburb of Cleveland. It was as much geographical as it was cultural—instead of Trump signs and billboards proclaiming marriage is between a man and a woman and that hell is real, we see Black Lives Matter signs in windows and lawn and pride flags draped from second floor windows. There are so many signs and flags like this that there are surprising variations on the theme, adding variety and creativity to the way homes display their support of marginalized folks in the U.S.—scraps of slate painted instead of signs, No Justice No Peace, flags of variable sizes displaying a slate of slogans, or just smaller ones you'd know if you got out to protests. Our move more or less paralleled the ostensible move of the U.S. back toward a more liberal order, with the election of Biden and resumption of a kind of political normalcy. And I'll admit that I'm relieved—to have someone in the White House who will be boring, who won't grant every right-wing whim coming out of Jerusalem however harebrained or desperate, and to be in a place where I can talk openly about politics and the woeful state of the world.

But with normalcy we return to the regular moderate reflexes. And though I admire the creativity of my new neighbors in how they voice their support, I can't help but feel the worry that these displays are more about displays than they are about actual change. Or, maybe it's better said that it's more about responding to particular events than it is thinking about the web of oppression that links the brutal policing of Blackness to the apartheid in Israel to the coming climate catastrophe to voting rights and reproductive health and more. Yes, there are lots of sins for white supremacy and settler colonialism to account for, and yes there's only so much a human can do in response to even a couple of them, and so movement on one or some is good, but I still fear that though I and the U.S. have moved back to places that affirm the importance of treating everyone with dignity, it is a step back toward a familiar past and not toward a radical reimagining of how the state and the individual interact. How does the state protect the individual? How does it apologize to those harmed by past wrongs? The Biden administration, though domestically progressive, has retreated to familiar and dangerous statements about Israel needing to defend itself, instead of recognizing the incredibly disproportionate distribution of power this "self-defense" is predicated upon. And of course the situation on the U.S. southern border, and the lack of empathy, clarity, and dignity, is all too familiar.

Things are better, but not for everyone. And better tends to mean comfort, which tends to lead to blinders. I am glad for the respite from vitriol and hot breath fanning the flames of ethnonationalism and right-wing terror, don't get me wrong—these are important repudiations. But a return to the previous state of affairs, at least in the U.S., is not sufficient.

PHILIP METRES: In order to return to our conversation, I reread all of our letters to each other, wondering what they would sound like, feeling weary and boggled after another long virtual residency, with never-ending Zooms. The letters filled me with that strange feeling of hope, restored numbed zones to feeling, as Adrienne Rich once proposed of poetry.

Under the Biden administration, I have the general feeling that responsible people are in charge of the United States again, people who believe that the federal government has an important role to play in the lives of its citizens, and of the world. That is a relief. Yet, this administration is playing the same tune when it comes to Palestine and Israel: Israel has the right to defend itself. Perhaps there is something happening behind the scenes that I don't know, but the public display of imperial logic is deeply upsetting. It's not that I don't believe that states have the right to defend themselves. But the fact that that is the only statement that comes out is appalling. Do Palestinians have the right to defend themselves?

So when the latest bombing and rockets began to fly in May, I felt something different this time, a greater desperation, a greater anger. I don't know if it's because of my attention to social media and its direct, uncensored, and often triggering ability to share stories, or because I'd been thinking so much about Palestine after the publication of my book, hoping to make some kind of difference, and finding mostly silence, or only the smallest of echoes in the world. I did the usual things: emailed and called my congresspeople, of course. But I also went into Cleveland with one of my kids for two protest marches. I was asked to speak at one of the demonstrations. As I was making my way toward the megaphone, I saw my friend and colleague, David Shutkin, standing with a sign among the many Palestinian families that had come out in protest, and I felt for the first time that change was possible. David was part of a founding delegation for the Center for Jewish Nonviolence, whose work involves standing with Palestinians whose houses are being demolished. He's been on a long journey to get to that point, and I respect him for that so much.

I had tea with a doctor recently who was born in a displaced persons camp, like Erika's mom. He's been so upset about what's happened, and wants to do something. He reached out because he saw one of my poetry readings online, and liked how I talked about imagining my audience having both Holocaust survivors and Nakba survivors. We talked for a while about how we understood what was happening, and how we might make a difference. We shared so much—not only the tea, of course, but a desire for peace. He wanted to write an op-ed, and perhaps include our names together. But we differed enough on some key things that I said we should keep talking. He said that we can't keep talking about the past. But the issue is that foreclosing the past is precisely what the powerful always do. And by foreclosing the past, the future is already written. I told him that you're not going to like what I'm going to say, but I advocate for an ending of all unconditional military aid to Israel. After all, the reason for the outbreak of violence is not Hamas's hatred, but their response to the ongoing dispossession in Jerusalem neighborhoods like Sheikh Jarrah and Silwan, and the violence at Al-Aqsa mosque during Ramadan. Perhaps my friend will have to take his own journey. I know that he's capable of it.

At the same time, I also see friends of mine leveling their outrage at everyone who fails to agree with them, lashing out against their own pain and despair, angry for justice. Some of it feels like bullying. It's enough to make anyone go quiet, or want to flee. In the end, I don't want to shame or coerce someone into changing their heart or mind. I'm not sure it works, anyway. I know that there have been a number of news stories recently about a rise in antisemitism, and then analyses of various kinds questioning how the ADL (Anti-Defamation League) is using or misusing their data. Both, it seems to me, are real issues. Palestinians continue to be erased and brutalized and Jews throughout the world have been subject to racist attack. I'm not comparing them or creating false equivalency. Some activists think that groups think the ADL use antisemitism as a political cudgel to beat back any real change.

One of the books that I've been reading slowly is *The Drone Eats with Me*, by Atef Abu Saif, a relative of Mosab's. It's a diary of the 2014 Gaza War, called by Israel Operation Protective Edge. It's so painful to read, I can only take it in small doses.

Last night, Mosab, Naomi, and some other friends gave a reading online to raise funds for Palestinian organizations in Gaza, trying to rebuild after another bombing. Seeing you, Mosab, on the screen, at 2 a.m. Gaza time, and hearing your voice, reminded me why I wanted to begin this conversation. The present situation is impossible, but you endure it every day, with minimal electricity and water, trying to raise your children and save them from missiles.

It's not enough that my heart is broken. It's what I do, carrying the ruins of my heart, that can matter.

The thing that's given me the most joy of late is that my daughter Leila qualified for the Junior Olympics down in Houston. It has nothing to do with politics. Watching her run around the track, her purple hair flying behind her, her legs spinning so fast they seem to blur, I see the beauty and power and goodness of creation. I wish for all of us to have such freedom in our bodies and minds, a future somewhere up ahead.

2021

CHAPTER NINETEEN

Never/Enough

Afterword to *Paideuma*'s Symposium on War and Literature

There is nothing to be said about war. No, there is nothing new to be said about war, for too much has already been said, and not enough. There is never enough said. Never enough, again. Never again, enough.

I didn't want to write this. After spending most of my adult life writing about war, I don't want to study war anymore. Down by the riverside, I want to lay down my arms, enter the clear water and cross over the river. Isn't it time to study the arts of peace? Anton Chekhov once wrote to a friend, in a similar predicament, "I simply want to be a free artist and regret that God has not given me the ability to be one."[1]

As I made my way through the poetry of the states and peoples and languages—Igbo poetry in Nigeria, Yiddish poetry of the Holocaust, Yugoslavian dissident poetry, U.S. American memoir, poetry, stories, and novels—I kept coming back to the seeming-inevitable fact of it, the persistence of this nebulous and yet all-too-clear set of mechanisms and operations of mass organized violence. William James, over a century ago, in "The Moral Equivalent of War," diagnosed the modern predicament in this way: the endless preparation for war is the war. His solution? To find some "moral equivalent" of war that would serve the social function of the military and of war, without the spilling of blood, without the trauma, without being endlessly stuck in the nightmare of history.

War, from the High German *werran*, from the deep Proto-Indo-European root, *wers*, meaning to confuse, to mix up. War is a confusion. It brings us to confusion. It fuses and diffuses. It decapitates, amputates, rakes us with its fires. And yet it keeps coming back, because we keep calling.

Among the first written texts in the world is a poem by Enheduanna, a Sumerian high priestess, lamenting the spirit of war. As long as there has been writing, there has been protest against this strange ritual of mass bloodletting, as there has been valorization of the courage of those who partake. It is courageous to risk death to protect oneself and one's family, one's tribe, one's people. It is also courageous to refuse the logic of sacrifice, but that's a courage the world too often calls cowardice.

After serving as a nurse during the Civil War, Walt Whitman admonished that "the real war will never get in the books"—and carried that real war in his body for the rest of his life. There is always something new to say about war, because every war is different, and every war is the same, and every generation must relearn what the previous generation forgot or could not find a way to tell them.

Just the other day, I was preparing to send to a digitizing service my father's letter tapes recorded during his time in Vietnam. He recorded them on 3" reels, packed them in their plastic boxes, and mailed them to his family at home. For years, I've had no way to listen to them, as the technology to play the reels went into obsolescence. As I opened one of the boxes, dated February 1, 1968, a sliver of a note tumbled out.

It read: "Dear Mom and Dad, fighting is over in Saigon. Everything is quieted down. All's ok with me. Love, Phil." He'd somehow survived the Tet Offensive. The note says everything and nothing. Never enough language to describe the indescribable, to heal a trauma. He's spent his whole life trying to stanch the blood.

There are many lies, not only Wilfred Owen's "old lie" about the sweetness of blood sacrifice. One of those lies is that there has never been a time in human history when there hasn't been war. That is meant to rationalize and naturalize its presence. The vast span of human history is, rather, marked by peace. Most of the time, people are not organizing in groups to kill each other. What if we saw war, and our ceaseless preparation for it, as the illness that it is?

Of course, there are other kinds of violence both active and structural—enslavement, oppression, exploitation, threat, torture, terror. We must face that violence in us, and between us, especially since we are experts at hiding, and failing to see, what is plain as sight.

As societies have grown more and more complex, as technology has become more sophisticated, war has kept pace. The authors of war gather and dream and conduct a metal orchestra on a scale of human inhuman endeavor that would cause the fiercest geniuses of plot and rhyme to drop their narrow instruments of description and incantation.

Some of our writers have borne the brunt of refusal, of opposition, of resistance, and have paid with their livelihoods and sometimes their lives. Sometimes they simply have refused to participate. Sometimes, they have made visible our collective complicity, saying, as Balkan writer Dubravka Ugrešić did, "I am to blame."[2]

What Charles Simic said about the predicament of the lyric poet can be said about the conscientious objector, the war resister: "Here is something we can all count on. Sooner or later our tribe always comes to ask us to agree to murder. . . . . The lyric poet is almost by definition a traitor to his own people. He is the stranger who speaks the harsh truth that only individual lives are unique and therefore sacred. He may be loved by his people, but his example is also the one to be warned against."[3]

May our writing not be a language to paper over the cracks in the walls of war. May our pens widen the cracks until the walls fall. Until the house that war built no longer stands.

But every day, someone comes and fills in those cracks with liquid capital. Builds more walls with our own sweat and blood. And finds a way to profit from other people's suffering.

So may we chronicle what went wrong, to lay bare the operations of a machine that is operated by people to destroy other people.

And then, as importantly, prophesy another world inside this one. We can see that other world all around us—in the courage of refusals, in calling out the powerful, in erasing the erasures, in imagining ourselves in webs of relationships that include even our enemies, in compassion for self and other, in dreaming of the fields where we lie together without names or causes, in lying together without names or causes, in binding our words with others, in creating shared spaces, in building bridges and bridging narratives, in acts large and small—as small as Mahmoud Darwish making coffee in Beirut during another war. Somewhere, someone is making coffee right now. Somewhere, someone is dying, and someone is being born. Somewhere, someone is changing a diaper. Somewhere, someone is making love. Somewhere, someone is heading to the river to wash.

It is us. The river is ahead, shining in the afternoon sun. As we approach, hot and tired, it opens itself like it's never been entered. We can see clear down to the riverbed.

It's time to lay down our burdens and enter the water. And, if only for its eternity of now, to be cleansed.

2022

Notes

Introduction

1. Michael Herr, *Dispatches* (New York: Avon Books, 1977), 20.

2. Walter Benjamin, *Illuminations: Essays and Reflections* (New York: Schocken Books, 1968), 257.

3. Interview with Marie Howe, "On Being," July 23, 2017, https://www.dailygood.org/story/1688/the-power-of-words-to-save-us-marie-howe/

4. "Counting the Dead in Gaza: Difficult but Essential," July 5, 2024, https://www.thelancet.com/journals/lancet/article/PIIS0140-6736(24)01169-3/fulltext

5. Fady Joudah, *[. . .]* (Minneapolis: Milkweed Editions, 2024), 12.

6. Golda Meir, *A Land of Our Own: An Oral Autobiography* (New York: Putnam, 1973), 242.

7. Samih al-Qasim, *Sadder Than Water: New and Selected Poems* (Jerusalem: Ibis Editions, 2006), 5.

8. Refaat Alareer, "If I Must Die," *In These Times*, December 27, 2023, https://inthesetimes.com/article/refaat-alareer-israeli-occupation-palestine

Chapter One

1. Jack Shaheen, *Reel Bad Arabs: How Hollywood Vilifies a People* (Northampton, MA: Olive Branch Press, 2001).

2. Gilles Deleuze and Félix Guattari, *Kafka: Toward a Minor Literature*, trans. Dana Polan, vol. 30 of *Theory and History of Literature* (Minneapolis: University of Minnesota Press, 1997), 17.

3. Edward Said, *Orientalism* (New York: Vintage, 1979), 202–3.

4. Said, *Orientalism*, 108.

5. Adam Velen Levinson, "The Fine Art of Learning to Say Nothing in Arabic," *Literary Hub*, accessed May 16, 2024, https://lithub.com/the-fine-art-of-learning-to-say-nothing-in-arabic/

6. Levinson, "The Fine Art of Learning to Say Nothing."

7. Levinson, "The Fine Art of Learning to Say Nothing."

8. Levinson, "The Fine Art of Learning to Say Nothing."

9. Laura Haugen, 2018, comment on Levinson.

10. Fatima Khansahib, 2018, comment on Levinson.

11. Levinson, "The Fine Art of Learning to Say Nothing."

12. @tclim988, "Is the Price Worth It," April 19, 2013, YouTube video, :38, https://www.youtube.com/watch?v=4iFYaeoE3n4

13. Evelyn Alsultany, *Arabs and Muslims in the Media: Race and Representation after 9/11* (New York: New York University Press, 2012).

Chapter Two

1. Ilya Kaminsky, "We Lived Happily During the War," Poetry Foundation, 2013, https://www.poetryfoundation.org/poems/91413/we-lived-happily-during-the-war

2. Philip Metres, *Sand Opera* (Farmington, ME: Alice James Books, 2015), 42.

3. Associated Press, "McCain Counters Obama 'Arab' Question," YouTube video, 2:03, October 11, 2008, https://www.youtube.com/watch?v=jrnRU3ocIH4

4. Hayan Charara, "The Problem with Me (Beginning with Abu Ghraib) Is the Problem with You (Ending Where the Earth's Surface Appears to Meet the Sky)," *Rumpus*, April 23, 2016, https://therumpus.net/2016/04/22/national-poetry-month-day-22-hayan-charara/

5. Deema Shehabi, "Ghazal 1," *Thirteen Departures from the Moon* (Winston-Salem, NC: Press 53, 2011), 12–13.

6. Israel Zangwill, "The Return to Palestine," *New Liberal Review* 2 (December 1901), 627.

7. Ben Ehrenreich with Ghassan Zaqtan, "The Dead Are Everywhere." *Los Angeles Review of Books*, October 22, 2013, https://lareviewofbooks.org/article/the-dead-are-everywhere/

8. "Cuyahoga," Spotify, track #4 on REM, *Lifes Rich Pageant*, Capitol Records, 1986.

9. Hisham Matar, "Hisham Matar: International Literature Is Hugely Underrated, While English Books Are Often Overrated," *Guardian*, April 20, 2018, https://www.theguardian.com/books/2018/apr/20/hisham-matar-english-books-are-often-overrated-it-is-boring-and-dangerous

10. Fady Joudah. "Say It: I'm Arab and Beautiful," blog of the *Los Angeles Review of Books*, December 12, 2017, https://blog.lareviewofbooks.org/essays/say-im-arab-beautiful

11. Ghayath Almadoun, "Interview: Ghayath Almadhoun—Altijd Wat," YouTube video, September 30, 2014, https://www.youtube.com/watch?v=Q2X0WoRXVTM

12. "Trees of Flame Grow: Three Syrian Poets in Translation," National Transla-

tion Month, 2017. http://nationaltranslationmonth.org/trees-of-flame-grow-three-syrian-poets-in-translation/

13. Alexis de Tocqueville, *Democracy in America* (Project Gutenberg, 1997), https://www.marxists.org/reference/archive/de-tocqueville/democracy-america/.

14. www.rachelcorriefoundation.org

Chapter Three

1. Tom Masland, "Beyond the Caricatures of Hussein and His Society," *Philadelphia Inquirer*, September 1, 1991.

2. Ramsey Clark, *The Fire This Time: U.S. War Crimes in the Gulf* (New York: Thunder's Mouth Press, 1992).

3. Nuha al-Radi, *Baghdad Diaries: A Woman's Chronicle of War and Exile* (New York: Vintage, 1998), 11.

4. William James, "The Moral Equivalent of War," *Popular Science Monthly*, no. 77 (1910), accessed May 21, 2024, https://en.wikisource.org/wiki/Popular_Science_Monthly/Volume_77/October_1910/The_Moral_Equivalent_of_War

5. *Three Kings*, directed by David O. Russell (1999, Burbank, CA: Warner Bros.).

6. Hugh Martin, *In Country* (Rochester, NY: BOA Editions, 2018), 18.

7. Ella Shohat and Robert Stam, *Unthinking Eurocentrism: Multiculturalism and the Media* (London: Routledge, 1994), https://impimaginary.tripod.com/

8. al-Radi, 11–12.

9. Christopher Allen-Doucot, "Sand Opera Lenten Journey Day 14: Now I Am What I Saw + Christopher Allen-Doucot." *Behind the Lines: Poetry, War, and Peacemaking* (blog), February 23, 2016, https://behindthelinespoetry.blogspot.com/2016/02/sand-opera-lenten-journey-day-14-now-i.html

10. Zaid Mahir, *The Way to Baghdad (Day 18 of the War)* (Bloomington, IN: Trafford Publishing, 2011), 74.

11. Mahir, *The Way to Baghdad*, 75.

12. Salam Pax, *Salam Pax: The Clandestine Life of an Ordinary Iraqi* (New York: Grove, 2003), 81–83.

13. Wafaa Bilal and Kari Lydersen, *Shoot an Iraqi: Art, Life and Resistance under the Gun* (San Francisco: City Lights), 1.

14. Bilal and Lydersen, *Shoot an Iraqi*, 10.

15. Bilal and Lydersen, *Shoot an Iraqi*, 1.

16. Bilal and Lydersen, *Shoot an Iraqi*, 25.

17. Bilal and Lydersen, *Shoot an Iraqi*, 143.

18. Grégoire Chamayou, *Drone Theory* (London: Penguin), 56.

19. Helen Benedict, "The Moral Confusion of Post-War America," *Guernica*, May 28, 2014, https://www.guernicamag.com/helen-benedict-the-moral-confusion-of-post-war-america/

20. Arwa Aldoory, Email message to author, January 31, 2018.

21. Fadhil al-Azzawi, "Toasts," in *Miracle Maker* (Rochester, NY: BOA, 2003), 107.

Chapter Four

1. Audre Lorde, "The Transformation of Silence into Language and Action," essay, in *Sister Outsider: Essays and Speeches* (Berkeley, CA: Crossing Press, 1998), 40–44, at 44.

2. Lorde, "The Transformation of Silence into Language and Action," 41.

3. Ghassan Kanafani, "Men in the Sun," in *Men in the Sun and Other Palestinian Stories* (Boulder, CO: Lynne Rienner, 1998), 21–74, at 74.

4. Philip Metres, *Shrapnel Maps* (Port Townsend, WA: Copper Canyon Press, 2020), 89.

5. John Mason, "Trump's Last Stand in the Middle East—Stirring Up Trouble for Biden," Arab America, December 2, 2020, https://www.arabamerica.com/trumps-last-stand-in-the-middle-east-stirring-up-last-minute-trouble-for-the-incoming-biden-administration/

6. Metres, *Shrapnel Maps*, 145.

7. Fargo Tbakhi, "Being Listened To: On Philip Metres' SHRAPNEL MAPS, Colonialism, and the Violence of Conversation," The Poetry Project, 2020, https://www.poetryproject.org/publications/newsletter/262-fall-2020/being-listened-to-on-philip-metres-shrapnel-maps-colonialism-and-the-violence-of-conversation

8. Email to author.

9. Email to author.

10. Email to author.

11. Livestream, 2020.

12. Livestream, 2020.

13. Livestream, 2020.

Chapter Five

1. "shrapnel, n." OED Online, December 2019. Oxford University Press, accessed February 3, 2020,. https://www.oed.com/view/Entry/178797?rskey=Wfls1O&result=1

2. Elmer Kennedy-Andrews, *Ciaran Carson: Critical Essays* (Dublin: Four Courts Press, 2009), 78.

3. Mahmoud Darwish and Ibrahim Muhawi, *Journal of an Ordinary Grief* (New York: Archipelago Books, 2010).

4. "Visualizing Palestine." Visualizing Impact, accessed February 3, 2020, https://www.visualizingpalestine.org/

5. Ghassan Zaqtan, interviewed in Ben Ehrenreich, "The Dead Are Everywhere," *Los Angeles Review of Books*, October 21, 2013, https://lareviewofbooks.org

/article/the-dead-are-everywhere/

6. Emmanuel Levinas, *Totality and Infinity: An Essay on Exteriority* (Pittsburgh, PA: Duquesne University Press, 2013), 51.

7. Philip Metres, *Shrapnel Maps* (Port Townsend, WA: Copper Canyon Press, 2020), 63.

8. Chris McGreal, "Ahmed's Gift of Life," *Guardian*, November 11, 2005, https://www.theguardian.com/world/2005/nov/11/israel1

9. Muriel Rukeyser, "Poem (I Lived in the First Century of World Wars) . . . ," Poetry Foundation, accessed February 3, 2020, https://www.poetryfoundation.org/poems/47657/poem-56d22843a6a62

10. Philip Metres, *The Sound of Listening: Poetry as Refuge and Resistance* (Ann Arbor: University of Michigan Press, 2018), 7.

11. John Paul Lederach, *The Moral Imagination: The Art and Soul of Building Peace* (Oxford: Oxford University Press, 2010), 5.

Chapter Six

1. Edward Said, *Culture and Imperialism* (New York: Vintage, 1994), xiii.

2. Amos Oz, *Under This Blazing Light*, trans. Nicholas de Lange (Cambridge: Cambridge University Press, 1996), 8–9.

3. Raja Shehadeh, *The Third Way: A Journal of Life in the West Bank* (London: Quartet Books, 1982), viii.

4. Emmanuel Levinas and Richard Kearney, *Face to Face with Levinas* (Albany: State University of New York Press, 1986), 23–24, quoted in Judith Butler, *Precarious Life: The Powers of Mourning and Violence* (London: Verso, 2004).

5. Said, *Culture and Imperialism*, 51.

6. Said, *Culture and Imperialism*, 318.

7. Said, *Culture and Imperialism*, 146.

8. Said, *Culture and Imperialism*, 67.

9. Said, *Culture and Imperialism*, 32.

10. Said, *Culture and Imperialism*, xiii.

11. Barbara Harlow, *Resistance Literature* (New York: Methuen, 1987), xix.

12. Harlow, *Resistance Literature*, 78.

13. Salma Khadra Jayyusi, *Anthology of Modern Palestinian Literature* (New York: Columbia University Press, 1995), 174–75.

14. Diane Elam, "Irresistible Resistance," *NOVEL: A Forum on Fiction* 23, no. 2 (1990): 212–17, https://doi.org/10.2307/1345741

15. Harlow, *Resistance Literature*, 2.

16. Harlow, *Resistance Literature*, 34.

17. Harlow, *Resistance Literature*, 100.

18. Harlow, *Resistance Literature*, 116.

19. Sahar Khalifeh, *Wild Thorns*, trans. Trevor LeGassick and Elizabeth Fernea (1976; reissue, New York: Interlink, 2000), 11.

20. Khalifeh *Wild Thorns*.

21. Khalifeh, *Wild Thorns*, 6.

22. Khalifeh, *Wild Thorns*, 79.

23. Khalifeh, *Wild Thorns*, 85.

24. Nejd Yaziji, "Exile and Politics of (Self-) Representation: The Narrative of Bounded Space and Action in Sahar Khalifeh's *Wild Thorns*," in *Cross-Addressing: Resistance Literature and Cultural Borders* (Albany: State University of New York Press, 1996), 104.

25. Khalifeh, *Wild Thorns*, 28.

26. Khalifeh, *Wild Thorns*, 28.

27. Khalifeh, *Wild Thorns*, 29.

28. Khalifeh, *Wild Thorns*, 29.

29. Khalifeh, *Wild Thorns*, 204.

30. Khalifeh, *Wild Thorns*, 160.

31. Khalifeh, *Wild Thorns*, 147–148.

32. Khalifeh, *Wild Thorns*, 207.

33. Barbara McKean Parmenter, *Giving Voice to Stones: Place and Identity in Palestinian Literature* (Austin: University of Texas Press, 1994), 19.

34. Menakhem Perry, "The Israeli-Palestinian Conflict as a Metaphor in Recent Israeli Fiction," *Poetics Today* 7, no. 4 (1986): 603–19, at 604, https://doi.org/10.2307/1772931

35. David Grossman, *The Smile of the Lamb*, trans. Betsy Rosenberg (1983; reissue, New York: Picador, 1990), 1174–79.

36. Grossman, *The Smile of the Lamb*, 146–150.

37. Grossman, *The Smile of the Lamb*, 18–22.

38. Grossman, *The Smile of the Lamb*, 68–72.

39. Grossman, *The Smile of the Lamb*, 36.

40. Perry, "The Israeli-Palestinian Conflict as a Metaphor," 616.

41. Perry, "The Israeli-Palestinian Conflict as a Metaphor," 618.

42. David Grossman, quoted in Hillel Schenker, "Hillel Schenker: Israel Mourns the Son of David Grossman," *Guardian*, August 16, 2006, https://www.theguardian.com/world/2006/aug/16/israel

43. Rachel Feldhay Brenner, *Inextricably Bonded: Israeli, Arab, and Jewish Writers Re-Visioning Culture* (Madison: University of Wisconsin Press, 2004), 252–53.

44. Perry, "The Israeli-Palestinian Conflict as a Metaphor," 617.

45. Perry, "The Israeli-Palestinian Conflict as a Metaphor," 616.

46. Perry, "The Israeli-Palestinian Conflict as a Metaphor," 619.

47. Grossman, *The Smile of the Lamb*, 258.

48. Grossman, *The Smile of the Lamb*, 189.

49. Grossman, *The Smile of the Lamb*, 190.

50. Grossman, *The Smile of the Lamb*, 224

51. Grossman, *The Smile of the Lamb*, 274

52. Grossman, *The Smile of the Lamb*, 277.

53. Grossman, *The Smile of the Lamb*, 242

54. Grossman, *The Smile of the Lamb*, 237.

55. Grossman, *The Smile of the Lamb*, 296.

56. Grossman, *The Smile of the Lamb*, 323.

57. Brenner, *Inextricably Bonded*, 267.

58. Barbara McKean Parmenter, *Giving Voice to Stones: Place and Identity in Palestinian Literature* (Austin: University of Texas Press, 1994), 33.

59. Grossman, *The Smile of the Lamb*, 325.

60. Rachel Feldhay Brenner, *Inextricably Bonded: Israeli, Arab, and Jewish Writers Re-Visioning Culture* (Madison: University of Wisconsin Press, 2004), 3.

61. Sahar Khalifeh, quoted in Peter Nazareth, "An Interview with Sahar Khalifeh," *Iowa Review* 11, no. 1 (January 1980): 67–86, at 82, https://doi.org/10.17077/0021-065X.2546

62. Nejd Yaziji, "Exile and Politics of (Self-) Representation: The Narrative of Bounded Space and Action in Sahar Khalifeh's *Wild Thorns*," in *Cross-Addressing: Resistance Literature and Cultural Borders* (Albany: State University of New York Press, 1996), 100.

63. Emile Habiby, quoted in Ehud Ben-Ezer, *Sleepwalkers & Other Stories: The Arab in Hebrew Fiction* (Boulder, CO: Three Continents/Lynne Rienner, 1999), 17.

64. Barbara Harlow, *Resistance Literature* (New York: Methuen, 1987), 176.

Chapter Eight

1. Thomas L. Friedman, *From Beirut to Jerusalem* (London: Macmillan, 1995), 159.

2. Edward Said, "Permission to Narrate," *London Review of Books* 6, no. 3 (1984): 13–17.

3. Rania Khalek, "ABC News Tells Viewers That Scenes of Destruction in Gaza Are in Israel," Electronic Intifada, February 12, 2017, https://electronicintifada.net/blogs/rania-khalek/abc-news-tells-viewers-scenes-destruction-gaza-are-israel

4. Edward Said, *Culture and Imperialism* (New York: Vintage, 1994), 66.

5. Said, *Culture and Imperialism*, 19.

6. John Paul Lederach, *The Moral Imagination: The Art and Soul of Building Peace* (Oxford: Oxford University Press, 2005), 5.

7. Lederach, *The Moral Imagination*, 5.

8. Marcy Jane Knopf-Newman, *The Politics of Teaching Palestine to Americans* (London: Palgrave Macmillan, 2011), 66.

9. Elias Khoury, interviewed in Maya Sela, "A Boycott on Institutions Is a Good Thing for Israelis," *Haaretz*, June 5, 2014, www.haaretz.com/jewish/books/.premium-1.597182

10. Jeff Halper, *An Israeli in Palestine: Resisting Dispossession, Redeeming Israel* (London: Pluto, 2010), chap. 6.

11. Jodie Ruodoren, "In West Bank Settlements, Israeli Jobs Are Double-

Edged Sword," *New York Times*, February 10, 2014, www.nytimes.com/2014/02/11/world/middleeast/palestinians-work-in-west-bank-for-israeli-industry-they-oppose.html?_r=0

12. Ruodoren, ""In West Bank Settlements."

13. Suha Sabbagh, ed., *Palestinian Women of Gaza and the West Bank* (Bloomington: Indiana University Press, 1998), 71.

14. Savyon Liebrecht, "A Room on the Roof," in *Apples from the Desert: Selected Stories*, trans. by Marganit Weinberger-Rotman et al. (New York: Feminist Press at CUNY, 1998), 39–64, 52.

15. Liebrecht, "A Room on the Roof," 44.

16. Liebrecht, "A Room on the Roof," 53–54.

17. Liebrecht, "A Room on the Roof," 54–55.

18. Liebrecht, "A Room on the Roof," 63.

19. Liebrecht, "A Room on the Roof," 63 (emphasis added).

20. Ghareeb Asqalani, "Hunger," *Anthology of Modern Palestinian Literature*, ed. Salma Khadra Jayyusi (New York: Columbia University Press, 1992), 380–88, at 381.

21. Asqalani, "Hunger," 385.

22. Asqalani, "Hunger," 384 (emphasis added in translation).

23. Asqalani, "Hunger," 383.

24. Asqalani, "Hunger," 385.

25. Asqalani, "Hunger," 387.

26. "Miguel de Unamuno," Wikipedia, June 1, 2024, https://en.wikipedia.org/wiki/Miguel_de_Unamuno

27. Marcy Jane Knopf-Newman, *The Politics of Teaching Palestine to Americans: Addressing Pedagogical Strategies* (London: Palgrave Macmillan, 2011), 65–102.

Chapter Nine

1. Zaina Alsous, *A Theory of Birds* (Fayetteville: University of Arkansas Press, 2019), 38.

2. Alsous, *A Theory of Birds*, 5.

3. Alsous, *A Theory of Birds*, 7.

4. Alsous, *A Theory of Birds*, 40.

5. Alsous, *A Theory of Birds*, 13.

6. Alsous, *A Theory of Birds*, 19.

7. Alsous, *A Theory of Birds*, 42.

8. Alsous, *A Theory of Birds*, 54.

Chapter Ten

1. Philip Metres, *Shrapnel Maps* (Port Townsend, WA: Copper Canyon Press, 2020).

2. Wisława Szymborska, *Miracle Fair: Selected Poems of Wisława Szymborska*, trans. Joanna Trzeciak (New York: W. W. Norton, 2001).

3. Simone Weil, *Simone Weil: An Anthology*, trans. Siân Miles (1986; reissue, London: Penguin, 2005), 71.

4. Metres, *Shrapnel Maps*, 133.

5. Donna Haraway, "A Cyborg Manifesto: Science, Technology, and Socialist-Feminism in the Late Twentieth Century," in *Cyborgs and Women: The Reinvention of Nature* (New York: Routledge, 1991), 149–81, at 149.

6. Jason Burke, "'My Wife Thinks I Will Come Home in a Box'—and Three Days Later Gaza Bomb Disposal Expert Was Dead," *Guardian*, August 13, 2014, https://www.theguardian.com/world/2014/aug/13/-sp-gaza-bomb-disposal-expert-bomb-dead

7. Mohammed Omar, "Israeli Jets Destroying Gaza Water and Sewerage Systems: Officials," *Middle East Eye*, February 12, 2015, https://www.middleeasteye.net/news/israeli-jets-destroying-gaza-water-and-sewerage-systems-officials

8. Seamus Heaney, *The Government of the Tongue* (London: Faber, 1988), 107–8.

9. Rami Almeghari, "Israel 'Wipes Out' Gaza Ice Cream Factory That Stored Vital Medicines." Electronic Intifada, August 2, 2014, https://electronicintifada.net/content/israel-wipes-out-gaza-ice-cream-factory-stored-vital-medicines/13683

10. Metres, *Shrapnel Maps*, 136.

11. Metres, *Shrapnel Maps*, 137.

12. Tyler Hicks, "Through Lens, 4 Boys Dead by Gaza Shore," *New York Times*, July 16, 2014, https://www.nytimes.com/2014/07/17/world/middleeast/through-lens-4-boys-dead-by-gaza-shore.html

13. Naomi Zeveloff, "A Year Later, Palestinian Family Mourns 4 Boys Killed on Gaza Beach," *The Forward*, July 14, 2015, https://forward.com/news/311710/one-year-later-the-bakrs-continue-to-mourn/

14. Deema K. Shehabi, *Thirteen Departures from the Moon* (Winston-Salem, NC: Press 53, 2011).

15. Metres, *Shrapnel Maps*, 141.

16. Marcello Di Cintio, *Pay No Heed to the Rockets: Life in Contemporary Palestine* (Berkeley, CA: Counterpoint, 2018), 229–30.

Chapter Eleven

1. Mosab Abu Toha, "Blockade," *Banipal*, Spring 2020, 45.

2. Philip Metres, "Returning to Jaffa (for Nahida Halaby)," section in *Shrapnel Maps* (Port Townsend, WA: Copper Canyon Press, 2020), 106–29.

3. Helit Yeshurun, "'Exile Is So Strong Within Me, I May Bring It to the Land': A Landmark 1996 Interview with Mahmoud Darwish," *Journal of Palestine Studies* 42, no. 1 (September 1, 2012): 46–70, https://www.palestine-studies.org/en/node/162552

4. Yeshurun, "Exile Is So Strong Within Me," 66.

5. Yeshurun, "Exile Is So Strong Within Me," 65.

Chapter Thirteen

1. Philip Metres, "(More) News from Poems: Investigative / Documentary / Social Poetics on the Tenth Anniversary of the Publication of 'From Reznikoff to Public Enemy,'" *Kenyon Review*, April 13, 2018, https://kenyonreview.org/kr-online-issue/2018-marapr/selections/philip-metres-656342/

2. Susan Briante, *Defacing the Monument* (Blacksburg, VA: Noemi Press, 2020).

3. Craig Santos Perez, "Black Lives Matter in the Pacific," *Ethnic Studies Review* 43, no. 3 (2020): 34–38, https://doi.org/10.1525/esr.2020.43.3.34

4. Craig Santos Perez, *from unincorporated territory [saina]* (Richmond, CA: Omnidawn, 2010).

5. Craig Santos Perez, *from unincorporated territory [hacha]* (Richmond, CA: Omnidawn, 2017).

6. Craig Santos Perez, *from unincorporated territory [lukoa]* (Richmond, CA: Omnidawn, 2017).

7. Susan Briante, *Defacing the Monument* (Blacksburg, VA: Noemi Press, 2020).

8. Marlene NourbeSe Philip and Setaey Adamu Boateng, *Zong!* (Middletown, CT: Wesleyan University Press, 2008).

9. James Agee and Walker Evans, *Let Us Now Praise Famous Men* (London: Picador Classics, 1988).

10. Avery Gordon, *Ghostly Matters* (1997; reissue, Minneapolis: University of Minnesota Press, 2008), 6.

11. Philip and Boateng, *Zong!*, 202.

12. Ed Sanders, *Investigative Poetry* (San Francisco: City Lights Books, 1976).

13. Sanders, *Investigative Poetry*, 29.

14. Ghassan Zaqtan, interviewed in Ben Ehrenreich, "The Dead Are Everywhere," *Los Angeles Review of Books*, October 21, 2013, https://lareviewofbooks.org/article/the-dead-are-everywhere/

15. Audre Lorde, "The Master's Tools Will Never Dismantle the Master's House," in *Sister Outsider: Essays and Speeches* (Berkeley, CA: Crossing Press, 2007), 110–14.

16. Audre Lord, "The Uses of Anger," *Women's Studies Quarterly* 25, nos. 1–2 (1997): 278–85, http://www.jstor.org/stable/40005441

17. "Ella's Song," Spotify, track #2 on Sweet Honey in the Rock, *Breaths*, Rounder Records, 1988.

18. Marlene NourbeSe Philip, Facebook, May 30, 2020, Marlene NourbeSe Philip, "Facebook Post," Facebook, June 19, 2020, https://www.facebook.com/share/p/1V8PNohBeWBwtB2E/

19. Beth Cioffoletti, "Secret Grace: A Chosen People," *Louie, louie* (blog), January 17, 2007, https://fatherlouie.blogspot.com/2007/01/

20. "Strange Fruit," Spotify, track #7 on Billie Holiday, *Billie Holiday*, UMG Recordings, 1957.

21. Fannie Lou Hamer, "I'm Sick and Tired of Being Sick and Tired—Dec. 20, 1964," Archives of Women's Political Communication, December 20, 2019, https://awpc.cattcenter.iastate.edu/2019/08/09/im-sick-and-tired-of-being-sick-and-tired-dec-20–1964/

22. Marlene NourbeSe Philip, Facebook, June 19, 2020,https://www.facebook.com/share/p/8BYPFbJx2GKcnHnh/

Chapter Fourteen

1. M. NourbeSe Philip and Setaey Adamu Boateng, *Zong!* (Middletown, CT: Wesleyan University Press, 2008).

2. Philip Metres et al., "Poetics/Documents/Justice: A Conversation Featuring Susan Briante, Philip Metres, M. NourbeSe Philip, and Craig Santos Perez," *Synthesis: An Anglophone Journal of Comparative Literary Studies*, no. 13 (July 19, 2021): 114–29, at 123, https://doi.org/10.12681/syn.27564

3. M. NourbeSe Philip, *She Tries Her Tongue, Her Silence Softly Breaks* (1988; reissue, Middletown, CT: Wesleyan University Press, 2015).

Chapter Fifteen

1. Special thanks to Bennington College and Vermont College of Fine Arts, who hosted early versions of this essay in 2021. I write this essay as a non-Black person in an act of solidarity with the struggle for Black peoples' justice, with the hope that I can inspire writers to see the possibilities of poetry as an engine of social change.

2. June Jordan, *We're On: A June Jordan Reader* (Farmington, ME: Alice James Books, 2017), 341.

3. "Cornel West: Justice Is What Love Looks Like in Public." YouTube video, accessed September 30, 2021, https://www.youtube.com/watch?v=nGqP7S_WO6o&t

4. Thanks to the poets who mentored me (David Wojahn, Yusef Komunyakaa, Catherine Bowman, and Maura Stanton) and fellow writers (especially Simeon

Berry, Rebecca Black, and Anna Meek) who approached my raw work with generosity and vigorous engagement.

5. Philip Metres, *Behind the Lines: War Resistance on the American Homefront, since 1941* (Iowa City: University of Iowa Press, 2007), 6.

6. Denk Smith, "Quarrelling in the Movement: Robert Hayden's Black Arts Era," *Callaloo* 33, no. 2 (Spring 2010): 449–66.

7. Philip Brian Harper, "Nationalism and Social Division in Black Arts Poetry of the 1960s," *Critical Inquiry* 19 (1993): 235–55.

8. Harper, "Nationalism and Social Division in Black Arts Poetry of the 1960s."

9. One touchstone of social justice poetics remains the anticolonial struggle and postcolonial theory. Barbara Harlow's *Resistance Literature* (1987), for example, expanded Palestinian writer and activist Ghassan Kanafani's term into a theorization of the literature of national liberation movements from El Salvador to South Africa.

10. See Evie Shockley's "Shifting the (Im)balance: Race and the Poetry Canon" for an analysis of the problem in poetry criticism. Accessed September 29, 2021, https://bostonreview.net/poetry/shifting-imbalance

11. Harmony Holiday, March 20, 2021, 7:24 a.m. https://twitter.com/Harmony_Holiday/status/1373234091538092037

12. https://www.splitthisrock.org/about-us. Accessed September 27, 2021.

13. https://www.splitthisrock.org/about-us. Accessed September 27, 2021.

14. https://www.splitthisrock.org/poetry-database. Accessed September 27, 2021.

15. https://www.youtube.com/watch?v=8Jzku_jx5DQ. Accessed September 27, 2021.

16. Troy L. Smith, "Samaria Rice Rebukes Tamika Mallory, Others 'Benefitting off the Blood' of Police Brutality Victims," Cleveland.com, March 16, 2021, accessed September 27, 2021, https://www.cleveland.com/news/2021/03/samaria-rice-rebukes-tamika-mallory-others-benefitting-off-the-blood-of-police-brutality-victims.html

17. https://buildingmovement.org/wp-content/uploads/2020/10/Ecosystem-Election-2020.pdf. Accessed September 30, 2021.

18. Adrienne Rich, "The Muralist," in *What Is Found There: Notebooks on Poetry and Politics* (New York: W. W. Norton, 1993), 46–47.

19. Jericho Brown, "Bullet Points," in *The Tradition* (Port Townsend, WA: Copper Canyon Press, 2019). Accessed September 30, 2021, https://www.poetryfoundation.org/poems/152728/bullet-points

20. Toi Derricotte, "Why I Don't Write About George Floyd," Poem-a-Day, July 30, 2020, accessed September 30, 2021, https://poets.org/poem/why-i-dont-write-about-george-floyd

21. Ross Gay, "A Small Needful Fact," accessed September 30, 2021, https://poets.org/poem/small-needful-fact

22. Audre Lorde, "Power," in *The Collected Poems of Audre Lorde* (New York: W.

W. Norton, 1997). Accessed September 30, 2021, https://www.poetryfoundation.org/poems/53918/power-56d233adafeb3

23. Lorde, "Power."

24. Harryette Mullen, "Elliptical," in *Sleeping with the Dictionary* (Berkeley: University of California Press, 2002), accessed September 30, 2021, https://www.poetryfoundation.org/poems/51632/elliptical.

25. Lucille Clifton, "won't you celebrate with me," in *Book of Light*. (Port Townsend, WA: Copper Canyon Press, 1993), accessed September 30, 2021, https://www.poetryfoundation.org/poems/50974/wont-you-celebrate-with-me

26. Maya Angelou, "Still I Rise," in *The Complete Collected Poems of Maya Angelou* (New York: Random House, 1994). https://www.poetryfoundation.org/poems/46446/still-i-rise

27. Danez Smith, from "summer, somewhere," *Poetry Magazine*, January 2016, accessed September 30, 2021,. https://www.poetryfoundation.org/poetrymagazine/poems/58645/from-summer-somewhere

28. Claudia Rankine, "Open Letter on Race and Poetry," accessed September 30, 2021, https://poets.org/text/open-letter-dialogue-race-and-poetry.

29. See, in particular, "Can a Poem Listen? Variations on Being White," by Ailish Hopper, *Boston Review*, April 23, 2015, accessed September 30, 2021, https://bostonreview.net/poetry/npm-2015-ailish-hopper-being-white

Chapter Sixteen

1. Mark Nowak, *Social Poetics* (Minneapolis: Coffee House Press, 2020), 158.

2. Nowak, *Social Poetics*, 181.

3. Nowak, *Social Poetics*, 167.

4. Mark Nowak, *Revenants* (Minneapolis: Coffee House Press, 2000).

5. Mark Nowak, *Shut Up Shut Down* (Minneapolis: Coffee House Press, 2004).

6. Mark Nowak and Ian Teh, *Coal Mountain Elementary* (Minneapolis: Coffee House Press, 2009).

7. Philip Metres and Mark Nowak, "Poetry as Social Practice in the First Person Plural: A Dialogue on Documentary Poetics," *Iowa Journal of Cultural Studies* 12, no. 1 (September 1, 2010): 9–22, at 17, https://doi.org/10.17077/2168–569x.1088.

8. Metres and Nowak, "Poetry as Social Practice," 17.

9. Nowak, *Social Poetics*, 8.

10. Langston Hughes, "My Adventures as a Social Poet," *Langston Hughes Review* 4, no. 1 (1985): 9–15, https://doi.org/http://www.jstor.org/stable/26432666.

11. Hughes, "My Adventures as a Social Poet," 9.

12. Barbara Harlow, *Resistance Literature* (New York: Methuen, 1987), 34.

13. Mary K. DeShazer, *A Poetics of Resistance* (Ann Arbor: University of Michigan Press, 1994), 13.

14. Terri Bush and June Jordan, *The Voice of the Children* (New York: Holt, Rinehart and Winston, 1970).

15. Nowak, *Social Poetics*, 24.

16. Nowak, *Social Poetics*, 63.

17. Nowak, *Social Poetics*, 67.

18. Nowak, *Social Poetics*, 75.

19. Nowak, *Social Poetics*, 161.

20. Nowak, *Social Poetics*, 107.

21. Nowak, *Social Poetics*, 128.

22. Nowak, *Social Poetics*, 129.

23. Nowak, *Social Poetics*, 129.

24. Joseph Bruchac, quoted in Nowak, *Social Poetics*, 47.

Chapter Seventeen

1. Wilfred Owen, *The Collected Poems of Wilfred Owen* (New York: New Directions, 1964), 55.

2. Wilfred Owen, *Collected Poems*, 55.

3. Yoshiko Ikuta, interview with the author, September 2009.

4. Leonard Shelton, interview with the author, September 2009.

Chapter Eighteen

1. Hayden Carruth, *From Snow and Rock, from Chaos: Poems 1965–1972* (New York: New Directions, 1973), 3.

2. Czeslaw Milosz, "Dedication," Poetry Foundation, accessed June 14, 2024, https://www.poetryfoundation.org/poems/49458/dedication-56d22b9082a83.

3. Natalie Diaz and Nathalie Handal, "Map of the Next World," *Guernica*, October 19, 2020, https://www.guernicamag.com/natalie-diaz-and-nathalie-handal-map-of-the-next-world

4. Kathleen Dean Moore, "A Call to Writers," personal website, accessed June 14, 2024, https://riverwalking.com/a-call-to-writers/

5. Amitav Ghosh, "Writing the Unimaginable," *American Scholar*, September 6, 2016, accessed June 14, 2024, https://theamericanscholar.org/writing-the-unimaginable/

Chapter Nineteen

1. Andrei Turkov, ed., *Anton Chekhov and His Times* (Moscow: Progress Publishers, 1990), 291.

2. Richard Berengarten, "War, Shadows, Mirrors," *Paideuma* 47 (2020): 53–99.

3. Charles Simic, *The Unemployed Fortune-Teller: Essays and Memoirs* (Ann Arbor: University of Michigan Press, 1994), 37–38.